At Mesa's Edge

At Mesa's Edge

Cooking and Ranching in Colorado's North Fork Valley

Eugenia Bone

PHOTOGRAPHS BY ARTHUR MEEHAN

HOUGHTON MIFFLIN COMPANY
BOSTON · NEW YORK
2004

For information about permissions to reproduce selections
from this book, write to Permissions, Houghton Mifflin Company,
215 Park Avenue South, New York, New York 10003.

Visit our Web site: www.houghtonmifflinbooks.com.

ISBN-13: 978-0-618-22126-4
ISBN-10: 0-618-22126-3

Library of Congress Cataloging-in-Publication Data
Bone, Eugenia.
At Mesa's edge : cooking and ranching in Colorado's North Fork
Valley / Eugenia Bone ; photographs by Arthur Meehan.
p.   cm.
Includes index.
ISBN 0-618-22126-3
1. Cookery—Colorado.   2. Farm life—Colorado.   I. Title.
TX715.B698 2004   641.5—dc22   2003056896

Book design by Melissa Lotfy

Map by Jacques Chazaud

Printed in the United States of America

QUM 10 9 8 7 6 5 4 3 2 1

Portions of this book were originally published, in slightly different form,
in *Saveur, Gourmet, Food & Wine,* and *Tin House.*

Grateful acknowledgment is made to the following for permission to
reprint previously published material: "Broiled Tomatoes," recipe by Edward Giobbi, from *Italian Family Cooking* (Random House, 1971). Reprinted by permission of Edward Giobbi. "Café Habana's Grilled Corn,"
recipe from *Food & Wine,* September 1999. Reprinted by permission of
Richard Ampudia. "Scrambled Egg Enchiladas," recipe by Joe Gracey,
from *Amazing Afterlife of Zimmerman Fees,* reprinted in *Saveur,* no. 58,
p. 36. Reprinted by permission of Joe Gracey. "Apricot Honey," recipe by
Beulah Martin Fletcher, from *Fruit Fixins of the North Fork* (1972).
Reprinted by permission of Beulah Martin Fletcher. "Pheasants in
Cream" (originally published as "Pheasants or Quail in Cream") and "Elk
Stroganoff" (originally published as "Beef Stroganoff"), recipes from *The
Memphis Cookbook* (Memphis Junior League, 1975). Reprinted by permis-
sion of Suki Carson.

To Kevin

You were right. It's all about living in the moment.

ACKNOWLEDGMENTS

Thanks to my father, Edward Giobbi, for his recipes, insights, and unconditional support, but most of all, for the love of food he inspired in me. No one could have had a more generous mentor. Thanks to my mother, Elinor Giobbi, for a lifetime of encouragement. Thanks to Elise and Arnold Goodman, who thought I could write a book before I did, and to my editor, Rux Martin. I wrote this book for her pleasure.

Thanks to Arthur Meehan, photographer and hipster, whose intuitive response to the West led to such beautiful photographs.

Thanks to Colman Andrews of *Saveur,* who gave me my first food writing gig, and to Margo True, my editor at *Saveur,* who oversaw my coming of age as a writer. Thanks to *Tin House, Gourmet,* and *Food & Wine,* where I had the privilege to develop some of my ideas about canning, hunting, and gathering. Thanks to Thomas Wills, for showing me his witty articles about Hippy LeRoux.

Thanks to the *Delta County Independent,* the *North Fork Merchant Herald,* the *Valley Chronicle,* and the *Daily Sentinel.* I learned much from the many illuminating articles they have published about the region over the years. Thanks to Mamie Ferrier and George Sibley, authors of *Long Horns and Short Tales: A History of the Crawford Country,* a book rich in wisdom and fact. Thanks to the Delta County Cooperative Extension office, for taking countless phone calls and never putting me on hold.

Thanks to the many cookbook authors whose recipes I have used in one form or another, the chefs whose recipes I found in magazines and newspapers, and the friends and family who shared their own marvelous concoctions. I stand in awe.

And finally, thanks to my many friends in the North Fork Valley and its surrounding area—lovers of purple mountains, fresh corn, and living life one day at a time.

CONTENTS

We commonly think that "nothing important ever happens" where we live; but so long as we are there, juggling the trade-offs between making a good living and living a good life, trying to find new combinations to play against the old problems of existence, the most important thing of all occurs on a daily basis: life goes on.

—MAMIE FERRIER AND GEORGE SIBLEY,
Long Horns and Short Tales: A History of the Crawford Country

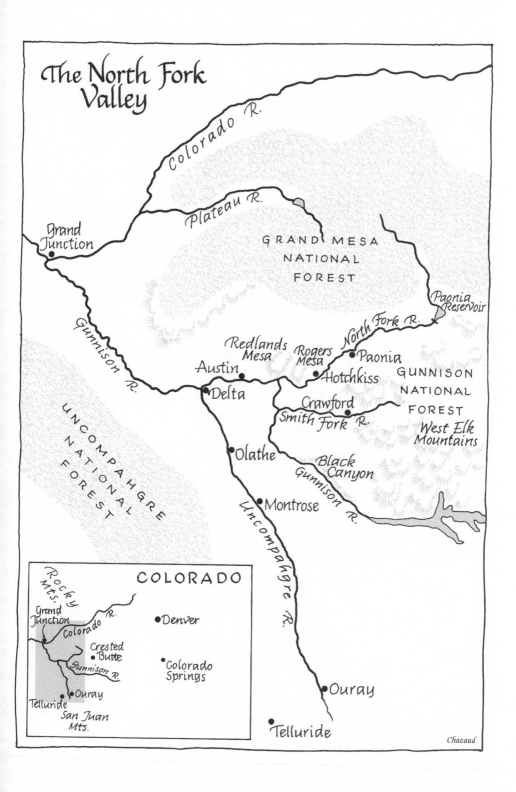

The North Fork Valley

Colorado R.

Grand
Junction

Plateau R.

GRAND MESA
NATIONAL
FOREST

Paonia
Reservoir

Gunnison R.

North Fork R.

Redlands
Mesa

Rogers
Mesa

Paonia

Austin

Hotchkiss

GUNNISON

Delta

NATIONAL

Crawford

FOREST

Smith Fork R.

West Elk
Mountains

UNCOMPAHGRE

NATIONAL

Olathe

Black
Canyon

Gunnison R.

FOREST

Montrose

Uncompahgre R.

COLORADO

Rocky
Mts.

Grand
Junction

Colorado R.

Denver

Crested
Butte

Gunnison R.

Colorado
Springs

Ouray

Ouray

Telluride

San Juan
Mts.

Telluride

Chazaud

PART I

At Mesa's Edge

INTRODUCTION:
THE NORTH FORK VALLEY

I agreed to buy our forty-five-acre ranch sight unseen after my husband, Kevin, came back from a fishing trip to Colorado's North Fork Valley. It had been coming on for a few years: while I was perfectly happy with our life in New York City and the occasional trip abroad, Kevin suffered from a kind of yearning without name, a desire he couldn't articulate, a lack of vigor and contentment that would have been mopey in a lesser man. There was, quite simply, an empty place in him that was not being filled: not by our marriage, not by our children—Carson, a girl, who was seven, and Mo, a boy, who was five—not by his work as an architect and a professor. I signed the mortgage papers the same way I would sign a release for Kevin to have necessary surgery: it had to be done.

The North Fork Valley lies on the western side of the Rocky Mountains due west of Colorado Springs. Its streams drain the Grand Mesa, the Ragged Mountains, and the West Elk mountain range into the Gunnison River. (The Gunnison is a major tributary of the Colorado River.) The valley runs from east to west, with the towns of Delta, Hotchkiss, and Paonia situated in fertile bottomlands 5,000 to 6,300 feet above sea level. Crawford, where our ranch is located, lies on a mesa above the Smith Fork River, another of the Gunnison's feeder streams.

The entire valley is surrounded by public lands. To the southwest is the Gunnison National Forest, which is about the size of Delaware. To the north is the Grand Mesa National Forest, the largest flat-topped mountain in the world. To the southwest is the Uncompahgre (UN-com-pa-GRAY) National Forest, and directly south, Black Canyon of the Gunnison National Park.

It sounded like scenic beauty abounded, but Kevin didn't let me see the place for six months. When we talked on the phone, he alluded to a few problems: exploded toilets, big-rig oil spills, and mounds of rotting carcasses left over from years of poaching. He mentioned the skunks living under the house and the pack rats living in the ceiling. I knew there were plenty of other problems, too, but Kevin didn't share them all with me. He was, in fact, rather evasive on the subject of the ranch's condition. No matter: I was in denial and didn't ask too many questions.

As work on the ranch progressed, I started to worry about this mysterious place I would have to call home. I had never been west of the Rockies, unless you count a short, wild trip to Los Angeles, which I only vaguely remember. I was worried that my children would be run down by mountain lions, mauled by grizzly bears, surprised by rattlers. Was I going to be stranded, miles from hospitals, firehouses, and the Gap? And what would I do for company? What, after all, did I have in common with cattlemen? What was an Italian girl like me going to eat? There was only one way to find out. And so we went west.

1.

THISTLES AND COCKLEBURS

MAY ALONG THE SMITH FORK RIVER is a lovely sight. The mountain lilacs are in bloom, and delicate little wildflowers thrive in spring's just-warm weather before being crowded out by tougher, more heat-resistant plants.

Kevin has to get out of the car to unlock the gate, and we drive down the long driveway—a bumpy, rocky, rutted drive that looks as if it was torn from the mesa with a backhoe (it was). A dozen rabbits dart every which way except, unbelievably, under our tires, and twisted old cedars line the way like short, fossilized tornadoes. And then the view opens up. Our piece of land is long and narrow. It is like a porch step, with the step above to the north and the step below to the south. The house is at the western end of the property, and behind it is a tangle of dead trees and junk piles and snarled, thorny underbrush. In front of the house is a long, long pasture, and looking to the east, I can see the West Elk Mountains' Mendicant Ridge and its distinctive Castle Rock outcropping.

The children scatter, anxious to explore. Kevin puts his arm around my shoulders and gives me an encouraging squeeze. "You're going to love it here," he says, and then he beats a hasty retreat before I can reply.

I don't want to be too critical, but from where I am standing, it looks like we have just made the biggest mistake of our lives. Just north of the house are a collection of slumping outbuildings, various filthy animal pens, and a large, picturesque barn with a thick floor created by a century's worth of cow dung. In front of it all is a muddy, shallow pond filled with ditch-water runoff, algae, and little green frogs.

Tangled brush and dead cottonwood trees stand tippily around the house, just waiting for a good windstorm to topple over and smash in our asphalt roof, which is green and draped with wires, like a low-slung Christmas tree. The immediate yard is bare dirt, and the turnaround in front of the house is big enough for an eighteen-wheeler. The front pastures are nothing but thistles, cockleburs, and dust, surrounded by miles of barbed wire. Wildflowers are blooming everywhere—flowers of such delicate coloration and subtle scent that I can't resist reaching for them—but they nod and fade as soon as they are pulled from the earth.

I look again toward the mountains. It's a glorious, big West, grand-nature view: a recharging view, a humbling view. But to see it, I have to look beyond the 500-gallon propane tank in the foreground. With a sigh, I turn and follow my family into the house.

The cabin is L-shaped, about 1,200 square feet with the bunkhouse, and clad in yellowing aluminum siding. We enter through a breezeway, which separates the main house from the bunkhouse. It is grimy beyond belief, with flimsy walls and marigold vines crawling among old sacks of charcoal, hanging wires, and spiders—everywhere spiders. Its one redeeming feature is a cool floor laid with smooth river stones. I take a quick look in the bunkhouse and spot wasps' nests hanging from the ceiling, old stained mattresses, and bags of discarded clothing before Kevin steers me away.

In the main cabin, the kitchen, once walled up into a couple of cubby-size rooms, is now one room, with a lofty ceiling, freshly refinished cabinets, and a warm red tile floor. Unfortunately, the kitchen window looks onto a closed-in porch made of disparate pieces of plywood and siding. It has some very funky wall-to-wall carpet, which has long lost its color and smells like roadkill. I mark it in my mind for destruction.

The living room once sported numerous false ceilings. Kevin tells me that when they started to pull the ceilings out, pounds and pounds of stale dog kibble that had been stored by the pack rats rained down on the carpenters' heads. Now the ceiling is high and airy, and the back wall features a kooky folk-art fireplace made from stones that look like faces or have fossils in them: geodes, quartz, and granite from the bottom of Black Canyon. On the opposite wall is a bookshelf with a wooden gun rack. Both of the bathrooms are in the process of being redone with no-nonsense blue and white ceramic tile, showers and toilets that use minimal water, and exposed piping, which I like because when there is a problem, it's comforting to know where it is. Under the layers of plasterboard and wallpaper, the carpenters found the twelve-inch-wide sawn pine logs of the original 1880s cabin.

I try to imagine the effort that carving this place out of the wilderness must have entailed. Our ranch was a homestead, granted by Theodore Roosevelt to Elsie Foster in 1902 (and occupied longer than that). There would have been nothing here but scrub and rocks when she took it on. Brushing my fingers along the rough-hewn boards, I feel ashamed of my whininess and decide I need to be on my best behavior. And the truth is, I am impressed by aspects of the place—anyone would be. But the prospect of restoring the ranch seems so overwhelming that I want to turn my back on the whole thing. And, in fact, on that first visit we stay in a hotel.

In the cozy confines of our room, Kevin and I spend hours planning the future of the ranch. The house renovation is due to be completed by next summer, when we plan to return. In the meantime, restoring the pastureland seems key. The Colorado landscape was originally irrigated by ditches put in to water the land that was close to creek bottoms. Over the decades, more elaborate ditches were built as water had to be carried farther and farther. Perversely, Colorado law allows for the sale of water rights independent of the land. Our place came with ten shares of ditch water, enough to irrigate five to ten acres. That's thirty shares short of what the property probably had originally.

The upper pastures on the southern slopes haven't seen water in decades. The lower pastures can be resuscitated, but the ditches need serious cleaning out, and we have enough shares in the local ditch to irrigate only a portion of the land. We hook up with a cattleman neighbor, Clair Hicks—who's had six wives, four ranches, and a chuckwagon—and offer him grazing rights in exchange for opening the ditches and moving the water around. Clair has a Screen Actors Guild card from when he was a wrangler in a John Wayne movie. He has little bitty hips and a cantilevered stomach. When we can't quite figure out how to or-ganize the pasture, we ask his advice. He pauses, all languor and cowboy drama, and finally tells us to keep the maze of barbed wire enclosures—in case we have a sick cow that needs to be sep-arated from the herd, or a pregnant mare. Someone else points out that our barbed wire is worth something to antique dealers and that we should be careful about throwing it away. Honestly, I just want the wire fencing gone. It is rusty and tangled and drapey, like a laundry line with bad intentions. We aren't going to raise cows, and I figure if an antique dealer wants the old wire, he can come and pull out the stakes himself.

Kevin ends up cleaning the ditches by hand. It is muddy work, and difficult, too, because when you plunge your shovel into the wet earth, suction grips it tight. Eventually, Clair, gig-gling behind his bushy mustache, points out that using a ditch shovel, which has a small, short head, would be more effective.

We also put a want ad in the paper asking for water shares.

We get one call, from someone who wants to know if we've had any success, and if so, are we interested in selling any extra shares to them?

Along the northern rim of our property are the remnants of an apple orchard. The scraggly, dry trees haven't produced fruit in years, but many of them are alive. We hire a sweet, paranoid arborist, who impresses us mightily when he lies under the trees (and lies, and lies) studying the configuration of the branches. But he prunes only one before disappearing. We decide the orchard pruning can wait and put in eight young fruit trees next to the house instead. It is a symbolic little kitchen orchard, with two each of apricot, crab apple, plum, and pear.

We buy old mahogany dressers and Shaker-style tables and green wooden chairs that came out of an Elks lodge and are fortified with wire. "Those men," says the tidy woman we bought them from, "they think you can fix anything with a little baling wire." We buy down comforters and thick diner-style dishes; pots and pans and knives and a fax machine. If only we had a few friends, we could have a dinner party—or fax them, anyway.

I'm on the lookout for potential friends, but looks can be deceiving in the valley. You can stand behind the grottiest old farmer in the bank line, and it turns out he is depositing a check for a million dollars. Hunched behind coffee cups at the Go-fer Foods in Hotchkiss are poets and winemakers and engineers. It seems my ability to sum up a person on sight, honed after years of navigating the sidewalks of Manhattan, just isn't going to wash here.

The valley is composed of a fascinating cross section of people. There are lots of folks struggling to survive in Delta County, but others have found their niche. Artisans, such as glass blowers and cheese makers, make a decent living. Many of the original ranch families still live on all or part of their grand spreads, raising cattle, sheep, goats, or elk. People like us, who made their money elsewhere, have come to the valley in search of something they couldn't find anywhere else. There are also retirees. Some are magnificent, like a fellow we call Mr. Clean, age seventy-five. He shows up at our place in a white shirt, pressed jeans, and polished cowboy boots to pull down and haul away a number of large, dead cottonwood trees that would have exhausted a much younger man. Others are small-minded, close-the-door-behind-you types. Middlebrow in every way, they live in a culture of no.

On the last night of our trip, we are invited to a barbecue at Willie and Susan Hillyard's Hidden Creek Ranch on Rogers Mesa. Willie, who is from a longtime ranching family, naps, wrapped in a buffalo hide, in his hammock in winter and has a cell phone not so he can multitask, but so he doesn't have to run to answer it when it rings. Willie and Susan, a laid-back attorney and lover of horses, originally introduced Kevin to the valley.

Over grilled steaks and sweet corn, we meet Kathryn and Michael McCarthy, owners of Sunshine Mesa Ranch, idealists, poets, and mead drinkers; Liz Lilien, originally an East Coaster, who dumped the confines of life in the suburbs and headed west; and Steve and Linda Rubick, both sporting long gray ponytails and living on Fruitland Mesa with a herd of spitting llamas. Linda works in the emergency room at the Delta hospital, and with the specter of rattlesnake bites in the back of my mind, I ask what kinds of injuries she sees. "Well," she answers thoughtfully, "when the cherries come in, we get a lot of people falling out of trees."

We meet Charles and Marilee Gilman, who guide hunters and fishermen and exude boisterous, uninhibited family happiness. We also meet Bob Pennetta, a gentle giant of a Buddhist biker, and his unflappable wife, Candy, who has been known to ride on the back of his Harley in a little black cocktail dress.

Despite the charm of my new acquaintances, and despite the indisputable beauty of the place—from where I am sitting in Willie's yard, I can see the big red sun sink off the blue edge of

Rogers Mesa, just beyond a green field where the Hillyards' colts rear and buck — I am still a very long way from calling the valley home. But then Steve bounds out of the house like a Labrador retriever, with a basket of fried dandelion flowers sprinkled with coarse salt and a couple of Bud longnecks perspiring between his fingers. As I crunch the flowers, which taste as bright and sweet as they look, and watch the lavender colors of night pour across the sky, I think, *Well, maybe everything is going to be okay after all.*

2.

THE LOGIC OF WATER

W**E PLAN TO SPEND** the month of July the following summer at the ranch, and over the course of the next sixty days, I get pretty excited about Crawford. The land becomes greener in my mind, the horses glossier, the sky bluer, the antique stores cheaper, and the cabin worthy of a spread in a Western living magazine. I picture our fields studded with Clair's cows, contentedly wading through knee-high grass.

I am so enamored of my fantasy that I endure the hassle of arranging to take along our cat, Jacques, a large, fluffy hater of human beings. It costs a hundred bucks to vaccinate her for all the things she can get in the mountains. Already annoyed by the expense, I engage in a bitter phone conversation with the airline booker when I learn I have to buy a new animal carrying case and it will cost me fifty dollars for each leg to take her. Each leg?

"Of the trip," she says. "Will there be anything else, Mrs. Bone?" While I write out the umpteenth check, I secretly hope Jacques will get eaten by a coyote this summer.

I am also wary of the eating possibilities. For me, happiness is a great meal, and I intend to make sure we have the necessary provisions. So I pack about twelve pounds of pasta of varying cuts, a half dozen tins of tuna packed in olive oil, bottarga (the smoked roe of a red mullet), a huge brick of Parmesan cheese, a couple of large salamis, a two-pound bag of Arborio rice, dried porcini mushrooms, imported extra-virgin olive oil, pine nuts, and a one-pound can of anchovies packed in salt. Kevin is unfazed by my excess. He just smiles and heaves the inhumanly heavy suitcases into the back of the taxi.

Kevin wants to drive from Denver so we can get a sense of the land. The drive across the mountains is beautiful, especially the stretch along the dancing, furious Crystal Creek, from Carbondale through Redstone, and down into Paonia, but it is 105°F. Mo suddenly becomes ill. We are in the car for five hours with a huge sweating cat whose fur is sticking out of the holes of her airline-sanctioned Sherpa Bag, what seems like a hundred pounds of imported Italian goodies slowly souring in the trunk, and a feverish child.

As we approach the house, we have to swerve around a small group of Rainbow Family people, who have established a gypsy-like settlement in the widest part of the driveway. One girl, a baby on the breast, waves at me as if I have come to pay a social call.

It is July 3, and the entire place is brown. It is like a scene out of *The Grapes of Wrath*. I keep thinking, *I paid for this?* The fellows from Two Guys Construction, whom Kevin has hired to help with the restoration, are still screwing a lopsided door onto the breezeway. Clair's cows have nibbled what grass there was in the front pasture down to a stubble, and there are cowpies everywhere. Then, to my dismay, I see that all but one of the symbolic trees we planted in our kitchen orchard a few months before have been eaten down to stumps. It seems an omen.

I don't say anything more than a cursory hello to the Two Guys, who hold the screen door open for me, even though the bottom hinge isn't attached. I march into the house, Mo in my arms, and put him on a mattress on the floor. I call a local pediatrician an hour away and set up an appointment for the next day. I wash out an old takeout coffee cup and make Mo drink some water. I open a box of sheets to make a bed for him, only to find it riddled with mouse turds. And then I notice that they are every-where—spoor in all the drawers of the furniture, in every pot and pan. For hours I do not notice that the cabin is lofty and cool, the kitchen is well tiled, and the bathrooms are clean and fresh. The Two Guys leave; Kevin gives the Rainbow people's van a jump, and they decamp. Carson, my daughter, does her best to sweep up mouse droppings. Kevin opens a few ditches to send some water down to the nearest field, then hovers around as I watch over my son.

Mo's fever breaks about three hours later with a yell for some-thing to eat and an array of other demands. Within minutes he is scrounging among the luggage, looking for his toys. I retreat to the bedroom, brush the mouse droppings off the bed, lie down, and cry.

But later in the day, we experience the valley's most treasured summer ritual: the summer monsoon rains. Moist air masses originating over the Gulf of Mexico travel north to collide with the warm continental air. As the heat builds during the day, thunderheads form over the high desert and Rocky Mountains. By late afternoon, a curtain of rain sweeps across our ranch, and behind it the clouds separate, and ribbons of sunlight pierce the land. A rainbow appears, framing our view of Mendicant Ridge, glowing and fading in one miraculous moment. Birds start chirping like crazy, and the air cools down. Our first night is chilly enough that we need a down comforter. It is very cozy and very crowded as everyone finds his or her way into our bed: Car-son, Mo, even Jacques, who I think hates us a little less than the coyotes we hear howling in the canyons.

The next day is the Fourth of July parade and Cherry Days festi-val in Paonia, half an hour's drive to the north. Paonia is an or-derly little town surrounded by orchards, some of them among the oldest on the Western Slope. (The first house in town was built by Orion Bone in 1893. To my knowledge, no relation.) It takes some jostling to find a good spot on Grand Avenue to watch the parade.

I always cry at parades. It's embarrassing, and I can't explain it. Usually the marching bands get to me, but at the Paonia parade, I lose it over the fire trucks and emergency service vans, the mountaineering emergency rescue service equipment, and the disaster relief vehicles. It's a relief when they pass and I can enjoy the rest of the parade without hiding my face. Next are the trucks pulling Paonia High School graduates. The classes from the late 1940s tend to be just a few blue-haired ladies in farm dresses and, I imagine, their sweethearts, fifty years married, sitting on hay bales, wilting in the sun. As the classes become younger, they get bigger and friskier. By the time the classes from the 1990s pass by, the crowd is getting drenched with water from their squirt guns. Candy is thrown on the street for the kids to grab, and my children crouch like sprinters waiting for the next peppermint to hit the tarmac. There are farmers on their vintage green John Deeres and lots of people on horseback, dressed as frontiersmen and frontierswomen, shooting ball loaders in the air with a *bang!* and a plume of black smoke. The Shriners are a hit—elderly men in their fezzes driving tiny cars—and there is the occasional tough, wearing mirror aviator sunglasses, a cigarette hanging languorously from his lips, driving his Camaro in the parade for no apparent reason other than to announce that he is here. The cheerleaders and gymnastics team cartwheel up the sweltering avenue, and we follow as they lead us to Town Park, with its ancient cottonwoods and stone-lined ditches running with cold snowmelt.

We get in line to buy barbecue sandwiches (beef in these parts), and then chocolate-covered cherries from a couple of high school girls in cowboy hats and cutoff jeans sitting on a cooler. Craftspeople, such as glass blowers and leather toolers, and real estate agents are stationed in booths under the trees. There are pony rides, along with a Ferris wheel and a couple of the usual greasy carnival rides that colonize fairgrounds across America. It is very crowded—with old and young, hip and hokey, arguing couples and teenagers in love—and there are flags everywhere. The Fourth of July in Paonia makes me feel as American as I've ever felt.

With the celebration behind us, we get to the work at hand. Clair, whose cows have eaten our nascent orchard, explains to us the law of the free range, which technically states that anything that isn't fenced in is legal for his cows to eat. Kevin decides not to challenge him. We are new to the valley and don't want to be party to any disputes. Anyway, there's not a fence that can hold a herd of cows if they want out—or in. I see how they work: they lean, en masse, against the fencing, slowly adding pressure until it inevitably gives, and then they move on, toward the garden, the flowers, the curtains on the kitchen window. In fact, over the next few days, the cows keep getting out of the pasture, and I find them gazing with big wet eyes through my windows, a swarm of flies in tow, chewing on something I've planted and pooping all over the yard. I demand that they leave. A few days later, Clair, his wife, Nola—a pink-cheeked woman ripe and lovely as a peony in bloom—and a few weedy-looking cowboys arrive on horseback and in a big cloud of dust round up the cattle and their flies and herd them away.

Finally, I feel as if I have my own place, or the place to myself anyway, although I definitely have some adapting to do. Water conservation is a new concept. We put a bucket in the shower to catch excess drops, and I begin washing dishes in standing water, although I worry that nothing is getting clean. The children and I are plagued by altitude headaches and dehydration. I've never been at a higher elevation than what you can climb to in an elevator, and so I have trouble grasping the concept of thin air. I keep forgetting to drink water or to bring it in the car and am reminded only when I look in the rearview mirror and see my children lolling on the back seat, panting and weak like over-heated puppies.

It's always about water out West, and Kevin, understanding this, takes over water management as his first priority. I don't help him irrigate. It's not that I can't grasp the notions of gravity and flow. Instead, I resist doing this chore because once I can do it, I will be able to live on the ranch by myself, and I don't want to even consider that kind of commitment. But not Kevin: he loves to put on his rubber boots, grab his shovel and hat, and head out to free the water over different pastures. It is remarkable how grateful the land is, for within a few days of flooding, the grass starts to grow. Every day he moves the water to another area. The children follow him out, ostensibly to help, but really to look for frogs in the ditches and muck up the banks.

We use ditch water from the Clipper Ditch, which runs from east to west on the highest—the northern—segment of our land. Farther south, the large Grand View Ditch passes east to west through our property, but we have no shares in it. To get our water to the southernmost pastures, we have to build a new ditch that will jump over the Grand View. Kevin knows exactly how this can be accomplished, but the actual execution turns out to be a lesson in how the West operates.

Kevin assembles the key players—a backhoe operator and a cement guy—and they walk out into the parched field, kicking clods of dirt with their cowboy boots and saying things like, "Well, water just don't run uphill, Kevin." There is a lot of squinting at the sun and chewing blades of grass. I don't get it: why can't we tell them what we want to do, agree on a price, and get on with it? But Kevin knows Western men prefer to figure out a solution independently. So we wait.

We don't just work on the ranch, although sometimes it feels that way. We discover Delta County's lively auction scene and are reduced to hysterics by a group of elderly cowboys, their big bellies hanging over their big belt buckles, bidding on a box of Christmas tree ornaments, ten cents at a time. Western auctioneers are linguists and humorists at once. They rip through the bidding, throwing out jokes, encouragement, and tall tales. "Now this here elk rack, well, John killed that bull way up on Saddle Mountain, from right here in Hotchkiss, with a rock he threw. Do I have a twenty-dollar bill?" We laugh and bid, and then suddenly the auctioneer yells "Sold!" and we find we have bought a hundred pounds' worth of rusted farm tools. The odd thing about the antique scene here is that everything is deemed valuable if it has any age, even junk. Maybe this is because it was so damn hard to lug everything from back East (and it is still a hassle) that if an object made it over the mountains, it's worth something just by virtue of its existence.

But except for the stray calf weaner or hay saw, we mainly spend our money on local produce. By mid-July the cornucopia comes in: crates of sweet corn from the neighboring township of Olathe (pronounced o-LAY-tha) for five dollars, mounds of vine-ripened tomatoes, all sorts of chile peppers, and heaps of zucchini and string beans fill the markets. The vegetables are so cheap and fresh that I buy way more than I ever would in New York. I just keep pulling over at roadside stands and shoving another load into the back of the car. And then every time Kevin goes to the hardware store, he comes back with a load of produce, too.

There are fresh dried beans, such as red-flecked anasazis and pintos, which are sold in bins marked "new crop." In New York, I buy fresh cranberry beans all winter long, but I hardly ever buy dried beans because I can't tell how old they are. Any rehydrated bean will make you fart, but dried beans under a year old are less likely to do so.

In the kitchen, I try making my usual dinners with tuna and sardines from the delis of New York's Little Italy, but they just don't taste as good as usual. Yet all the raw stuff we are eating is tremendous: tomato and onion salads, apricots sliced into bowls of whipped cream, and delicate salad greens squirted with lemon juice. Before long, I give up on *perciatelli con le sarde* and *caponata alla siciliana* and start making soups: bean soup with shrimp, minestrone with pesto, cold creamy vegetable soups, and hot broths poured over zucchini blossoms or sausage omelets. We eat spicy green chile soup and huge, filling concoctions of bean and corn. Soup is easy to make, but it's also empowering: you leave it on the stove while you do your chores, and when you come back in, sweaty and wondering what to make for lunch, there it is—fuel to tackle the tremendous task of restoring the ranch.

The month goes by fast. The children are in heaven: they spend the entire time running. Even Jacques, who hasn't been killed by a coyote but does have a run-in with a skunk, is purring more and growling less. We are all quite relaxed by August 1, and Kevin begins to hint that maybe the ranch would be a good place to retire. Panic sets in. Retire? I can hardly imagine spending my whole summer here—alone with the kids, away from my family and friends and the summer sample sales—let alone contemplate retiring here. And what about Chinese take-out? *What about that?* Sure, the produce is amazing, but the truth is, our place is a hellhole. I have constant altitude headaches. We know some people, but not well enough to socialize with them. And although the valley is beautiful, is this really where I want to spend the rest of my life? Kevin backs off as soon as my anxiety surfaces, and in the spirit of compromise, I agree to come out with the kids and the cat next summer and see how it goes.

I have no idea what I am in for.

3.

VISITORS

THAT WINTER I begin to think that maybe we have bought ourselves a money pit. We buy a brand-new used car, and we amass more water, bringing our total close to what was probably the original allotment. We contract with the North Fork Nursery, run by Hungarian expatriates Ilona and Gabor, to plant new trees and flowering bushes around the house and to install a small-scale drip irrigation system to care for them. We have the front pasture and future garden area fenced in: nice fencing, with wooden stakes and a wooden crossbar on top, over wire mesh. We get the power lines near the house buried; have the nasty old enclosed porch torn down and replaced with an open one; and have a new, snazzy stove put in. In May Kevin rototills the former garden, in an area behind the house I have not yet ventured into because of the dead things and live things that mingle under the tangled brush.

I am happy he is happy, and I'm rather excited about spending the entire summer with the kids at the ranch. But I am also afraid of being marooned. Kevin must spend the second month of the summer in New York, where he has his architecture practice, returning only at the very end of August. My plans are to take care of two children, with no babysitters or family. Two months of ranch restoration seems a daunting and isolating task, and so I invite lots of guests.

They come in waves, starting a couple of weeks after we arrive, and then peter out a few days after Kevin is to leave. Other folks are supposedly coming later in the summer, but their plans are vague.

Ours are, too. We just show up at the ranch and start working: me inside the house and Kevin outside, cleaning out the clogged ditches and moving the water around. I stand in front of our beautifully rototilled garden holding the trays of plants we have bought and wonder whether they go into the furrows or the mounds. The garden seems like a huge dirty job, and I let Kevin make all the decisions.

I know about the killer farm-stand scene in the area, and I suspect that there are all kinds of enticing growers to be discovered. Indeed, driving from the Montrose (pronounced MONT-rose) airport, I notice acres and acres of zucchini fields—and zucchini fields mean zucchini flowers. So with my copy of *Colorado Farm Fresh* in hand, I start to leave messages on farmers' answering machines.

"Hi, my name is Eugenia Bone, and I'm looking to buy zucchini flowers. I'll pick them myself, and I can assure you I will not damage your plants. Please call me at . . ." No one returns my calls, and I decide to rethink my strategy.

"Hi, this is Gena from Crawford calling. Can you tell me how to get to your farm stand?" Sure enough, I get a call back.

Kathy English has a beautifully tended farm in Olathe. We pull up to her house, me in an orange Denver Broncos cap I bought at the supermarket on the way, and wave at Mr. English as he comes bumping toward us on his tractor. He pulls to a stop but doesn't turn off the motor. I try to explain over the racket that Kathy said we could pick zucchini flowers. Finally, he decides to turn off the tractor, and I tell him I will pick only excess male flowers, which will not harm his plants. (You can tell male and female flowers apart because the female flower is attached to a little seedpod that will eventually grow into a zucchini, and the male flower sticks straight up on its stem.) "Nature is consistent," I say, and with a smile, Mr. English points me toward the zucchini field.

My heart thumps for two reasons: although there are acres of zucchini flowers, in the middle of the field is a large beehive, used to cross-fertilize the plants. This is definitely a problem. I loathe bees. But the flowers beckon: there are so many that when I bend down and look under the plants, I see nothing but orange. Many of the flowers have closed during the heat of the day, and inside I hear the furious buzzing of the trapped bees. Occasionally, a bee manages to wriggle out of its little floral prison, and I jump back and cover my face in horror. Why are they swarming around my head? I hear a buzzing very close to my ear. I swat at it, then *bam!* I feel a sharp sting on my neck. I get up and run, clutching my humming basket, tearing across the field. "Take off your hat!" Kevin yells. And I realize that my hat is the exact same color as the zucchini flowers. I am probably the biggest zucchini blossom the bees have ever seen.

We return to the ranch, and by the time Kevin has shaken the bees out of the flowers and I have drunk a couple of beers, I am sufficiently calm to fry the flowers whole in beer batter and make a cilantro-flavored mayonnaise to dip them in. After that, I feel much better indeed.

We run into Steve Rubick in Hotchkiss early in the summer, and he points us to the truck stand of the Corn Maiden, which is open either on Monday, Wednesday, and Saturday or on Tuesday and Thursday—no one seems to know for sure, or mind much that they don't. The stand is a pickup truck loaded with Olathe sweet corn, which a beautiful woman wearing silver rings—the Maiden—sells by the dozen to a patient line of locals. She also sells thick-skinned Big Jim peppers—just what I am looking for so I can make chiles rellenos.

We hit the Stahl Orchards fruit stand in Paonia, and within two days we have stocked up on cases of yellow Rainier cherries, red Bing cherries, and almost-black sour cherries. We eat them fresh, gluttonously, and find countless pits stuck to the car upholstery all summer long. By the time the apricots come in, so do our guests.

Our entertainment agenda is all the more fun because everything is as new to us as it is to them. We visit the two designated American Viticultural Areas in western Colorado, the Grand Valley around Grand Junction and Palisade and the West Elk region in the North Fork Valley, as well as other, associated regions. There are about twenty-four vineyards altogether, mostly small, family-owned estates. Western Colorado's hot days and cool nights during the growing season, as well as its low rainfall and ample groundwater, make for good grape-growing conditions.

Some of the vineyards in the Grand Valley area suffer from gift-shop-itis, but not all. I love Grande River Vineyards, squashed up against I-70, which makes a delicious wine from fussy Viognier grapes. We drink Plum Creek Cellars' Reserve Cabernet and visit Colorado Cellars, the oldest vineyard in Colorado. It has a kind of Harley-Davidson feel: picture the winemakers wearing studded leather, and you get the idea. On the other side of the Grand Mesa, we drink super Merlot by S. Rhodes Vineyards and fall in love with the Terror Creek Winery, which produces an excellent Chablis-style Chardonnay and a scrumptious Pinot Noir.

Wine drinking is fine and good, but people expect to go hiking when they come to Colorado, and we dutifully take them up one trail or another. Inevitably, the kids get tired and cranky, and Mo tends to flop down on the trail and groan, saying that he can't take another step. But as soon as we are out of sight, he is up and running past us, only to flop down on the trail again just as we walk by. Up on top of the mountains, above the timberline, we sometimes watch the thunderheads, packing rain that evaporates before the drops hit the ground. They are all attitude and no action: weather with intentions only.

We attend the rodeo in Delta, where we sit next to a group of Mennonites—the young men in pressed jeans and white straw cowboy hats, the women in calico dresses and bonnets. They giggle at the rodeo clown's puerile jokes and fervently hold their hats to their hearts while we recite the Pledge of Allegiance. The rodeo features barrel racing; young girls atop big strong horses, ponytails both equine and human flying in the wind; roping; and, of course, bucking broncos with names like Thunder and Tequila Sunrise. When a cowboy is introduced, so is his hometown, and we watch men with names like Dusty Crangle, of Hesperus, Colorado, bounce their way to broken bones and glory. The loudspeaker plays songs with lyrics that promise the USA will come back someday, and when it plays "The Star-Spangled Banner," we all stand up, the men take off their hats, and you can see how many of them have a bald spot.

We ride at Saddle Mountain Ranch and pause to take in views that seem too grand to be in our own backyard. Mo asks our guide, Jim, whose voice and chaps and boots are all made of the same rough stuff, to show him his gun. Jim unloads the Smith & Wesson and hands it over.

"Jim," I say, "really, why do you carry a gun?"

"In case I see a bear," he responds, to Mo's delight.

We visit the north rim of the Black Canyon of the Gunnison, third deepest in the United States (2,772 feet). It is a sheer, dizzying crack in the earth, so deep and narrow that it warps our sense of perspective, and we need to be reminded that the stones at the bottom of the canyon are actually the size of school buses. Dashing among those stones is the Gunnison River, a furious green and white ribbon punctuated by dark holes—home, neighbors have said, to colossal, freakish trout. Some of our guests are drawn to the edge. Others won't get anywhere near the overlook and linger by the car. Everyone is worried that the kids will topple over the edge. Afterward, some friends can't stop describing their awe; a hush falls over the others. There's almost always a snake in the rutted road as we drive out of the park.

We hit some of the local towns outside our vicinity, like Ouray (yer-RAY), a piney-smelling Victorian mining town in the San Juans. Ouray is home to ice cream parlors, rock shops, and hot springs, which are full of kids, grandparents, and hipsters, who wear their dark glasses as they soak in the tepid water and don't move until their hallucinogens wear off. We stay at the Wiesbaden spa and hotel because below the main building is the Vaporcave, which was cherished by the Ute Indians. This large nomadic tribe ranged from Aspen to Utah until first cattle and fruit interests, and then silver prospectors, pushed them into exile and oblivion. The low-ceilinged cave has smooth, wet walls dripping an eternal sheet of hot water into a shallow, 108° to 110° soaking pool. I crawl through the water to a small, partially walled-off space just a few feet in diameter and stick my arm into a hole. It is the bottomless source of the water, a deep, secret, pagan place, as hot and pure as the pit of a warrior's stomach.

Heading farther south into the San Juan Mountains, we visit Telluride, a charming ski resort and Victorian village with lots of developer mansions in the surrounding sheep meadows and cars in the parking lots. But I prefer to go east to Gunnison, where they serve steaks with A1 Steak Sauce and you can buy a stuffed deer or bear if you want. I almost bought a beaver skin once, but it looked too much like a furry bathmat with a peculiar tail. On the way home, just before we cross Kebler Pass, we visit Crested Butte on the cold Slate River, a cheeky ski town that buzzes in the summer with craftspeople, restaurant goers, and good vibes.

In most cases, our guests seem perfectly happy just to tool around the ranch and find what it is they like doing best. Kevin's parents, Roy and Emily, follow the shade under the cottonwoods. Art and Lisa hike. Ross fishes the tiniest mountain creeks and sleeps in his sleeping bag in the driveway. (I'm always afraid of running over him in the morning.) Mark and Mary spend so much time sitting on the porch that we pin RESERVED signs on their chairs. Lisa and Paul get pregnant. Diane shoos kids out of the house and makes lethal cocktails with vodka and zucchini juice. Warren dives into garden and water management.

It takes all day for Kevin and Warren to dig a ditch from the house down to the garden and to dig smaller ditches running between the delicate plants that are just coming in. After hours of labor, they summon us and, sweaty and red-faced, proudly open the little ditch door. A torrent of water comes rushing through. It strips away the fragile cilantro and parsley plants, rips through the baby lettuce beds, and upends the peppers. Water pours into the zucchini and tomato basins and splashes past the eggplants. There is mud everywhere. I look at the destruction, then at the men, incredulous. "How fabulous is that?" Warren asks.

At the end of each set of guests' visit, we take them by the Branding Iron Steak House to have a steak or drink a beer with its proprietor, our neighbor Clair. He chuckles as we take our seats with yet another crowd and says, "Well, that's Colorado for you. Nine months of winter and three months of company."

Pasta is great guest food, and I make it constantly: cut pasta, such as penne, with a raw or room-temperature sauce; thin pasta served with or finished in a hot sauce; egg pasta with a meat or cream sauce; and baked pasta such as cannelloni or lasagna. Often I chop up a few cups of fresh tomatoes and let them macerate in kosher salt for an hour. While the penne is boiling, I grind some blanched, peeled almonds. Then I toss all three ingredients together and garnish the dish with a handful of fresh parsley, basil, or cilantro. I prepare more refined pastas at night while everyone has moved out onto the porch to drink beer and point out the wildlife. If we have trout, I make farfalle with smoked trout and brandy, a dish my father taught me, or spaghettini with flaked poached trout on top. If I'm feeling ambitious, I make cannelloni stuffed with elk meat in a pink sauce, which the kids love because it is so sweet. They eat until their bellies are full and their minds are scrambled. That's when we adults settle down with our wine to watch them dance to country radio, wearing their pajamas and holsters, aiming their six-shooters toward the wagon wheel chandelier.

By the time we are entertaining our last group of guests, I have gone native. I wear a big straw hat, drink beer in the afternoon, and lose track of the date. And then time's up: Kevin returns to New York, the guests leave, and with them goes my new-found Westernness. In a matter of hours, the kids and I find ourselves suddenly, and quite thoroughly, all alone.

4.

VERMIN AND CRITTERS

I AM ALL CONFIDENCE and cheer when I drop Kevin off at the airport, but once we return to the ranch, I feel my confidence slip. What am I *doing* here? It is easy pretending to be a Westerner when I have Kevin around to water the land and make deals with local contractors and shake the bees out of the zucchini flowers, but now it is just me and my own inadequacies. The ranch is so quiet, I can hear the cat lapping meltwater from the empty beer cooler on the porch. Our first night alone, I stay up listening to the growls and howls of creatures as they creep close to the house, waiting for the sound of murderers' tires crunching on our driveway.

But I have a plan: I am going to prettify the ranch, clean it up and have it as neat as a Mennonite farm by the time Kevin returns a month hence. Luckily, I don't have to worry about the big pastures. Kevin has struck a bargain with another local rancher, Dick Hansen, to irrigate the fields while he is gone. In exchange, Dick will take whatever hay he can grow off it. There are many days when Dick is the only person over age eight I speak to, and our conversations seem to consist mainly of weather facts, fence facts, and cow facts.

I try to plant the flowers that grow to gorgeous, gigantic sizes on other people's ranches—cosmos, daylilies, columbine, sand verbena—but it is futile. They always dry out within twenty-four hours. I move stones from all around the house to a sloping area where I intend to put a toolshed. I move thousands of stones by hand, loading them into a wheelbarrow and bumping them over prairie dog burrows across the yard. Sometimes, in the evening, I gaze at my accomplishment: the pile of stones is mounded like a Neolithic cairn. I'm proud of it and humbled when I realize I am just another person in a chain of folks who have cleared this place by hand, one stone at a time. But I also have a nagging feeling that I am building my own tomb.

I hire Dick to move the propane tank out of our view. The project requires pulling a big ditch with a backhoe to bury the fuel line. Of course, the work throws up more rocks of enormous size all over the front lawn, which I proceed to add to my private burial mound. I have one ton of gravel poured in the driveway—not spread, unfortunately, as I neglect to ask for that—and it takes me several dusty days to rake it out. My arms become so suntanned and muscled they begin to resemble prosciutti. When I tell the old farmers down at the Branding Iron about my rock-moving project, they snicker and look to Clair Hicks for his inevitable nugget of wisdom.

"In Colorado," says Clair after taking a thoughtful slug on his Black Velvet whiskey, "rocks grow in fields and disappear in driveways."

At night I listen to the wind roaring through the valley. Sometimes it sounds like traffic, and I wait until it passes by my place. There are constant scuffles outside the bedroom window. Every night Jacques cries to be let outside, and then, hours later, I wake to hisses and screams. I open the door of my bedroom—which leads directly outside—and she runs in, fur on end, ears back, and hides under the couch. After a few nights of this, I discover that Jacques is defending her home turf from a feral cat. I see him one night: he is large but scrawny, and runs like a dog. It feels like a small victory when, driving out of the driveway one morning, we see the feral cat lying dead on the road, having been hit by a car. Over the next two weeks, we observe his carcass swell up, then deflate and become leather, and eventually turn to dust and blow away. There is a lot less howling in the night now, and for a while I get some sleep.

But not for long. A few nights later, Jacques's screeching wakes me up. I open the door to let her in and am hit with a cloud of yeasty skunk scent. Jacques runs under the couch and stinks up the living room. I chase her out, and she runs under my bed and stinks up my bedroom. For the next few nights, she lives in the breezeway while she detoxes. Not long afterward, she is sprayed again.

I have faced down many obnoxious, aggressive New Yorkers in my life, but nothing has prepared me for a *donna a donna* contest with a colossal female skunk.

Most evenings I go down to the garden with the compost from the day and throw it in the corner. I almost always find deep holes under the fence that the skunk uses to raid the compost heap. I see her in the evenings. She turns her butt toward me, and I lob a few stones at her before she takes off in a huff. I pile huge rocks all along the bottom of the fence, but every morning they have been scraped aside again. Sometimes I neglect to take the compost down to the garden. It is on these nights that the skunk comes around the house. Jacques gets territorial, the skunk sprays her, and everything stinks for two days. One night when I forget to take the compost down to the garden, Carson wakes me up and says, drowsily, that Mo is crying. I follow her to the bunkhouse, where Mo is indeed sobbing in his bed.

"I had a nightmare," he whimpers. "A skunk was crawling all over me." I comfort him, saying that skunks can't get in the house and he needn't worry, and then we all return to bed. The next morning, when I rouse the children, I see a tremendous hole torn in the screen door and, at the foot of Mo's bed, a defiant pile of skunk poop.

It is clear the safety of my children depends on the gastronomic satisfaction of this skunk, and I make sure to take down the compost every night thereafter. But one night, after we are all in bed, I realize I have forgotten. In the black blackness, I put on my rubber boots and, in my nightgown, carry the bucket to the garden, where the skunk, damn her to hell, is waiting for her due.

What has happened to me? In just a few months, my life has turned into a yuppie version of *Green Acres*. I have been relegated to the beta female position on the ranch.

The skunk isn't the only varmint I battle. There is a snake living under the door to the basement, and I am too scared to go down because, well, what if it's a rattler? And so for weeks I have no access to my wine. When we hit a dry spell, mice invade the kitchen. I try baiting my traps with all the goodies recommended by the farmers at the Branding Iron — peanut butter, chocolate chips — but succeed only when I coat the traps with expensive balsamic vinegar.

I also have a problem with bugs. First, the maggots. Gabor from the North Fork Nursery says they are breeding in the soft muck of the cottonwoods, which are suffering from a nasty disease called slime flux. I watch him scrape the gooey rotten bark off the trees, revealing all types of insects feeding on my lovely trees: yellow jackets, flies, ants. He shows me how to scrub the wounds with rubbing alcohol, and for the rest of the summer I am scraping or swabbing one tree or another.

My other pest is the box elder beetle. Zillions of these little hard-shelled bugs converge over every crumb, every dead fly. They are supposedly harmless, but mine start to nip. One of the farmers down at the Branding Iron says, "Well, maybe box elder beetles only bite New Yorkers," and they all laugh hysterically into their beers. It is not my imagination, however, that the beetles are copious. They drop from the eves of the porch like hail, bouncing off my shoulders. There are squashed beetles all along the screen door on the south side of the house, where the kids slam through a hundred times a day, squishing the bugs that come to feed on the carcasses of the bugs the kids squished an hour before. I take to using another door.

The kids are having the time of their lives. Usually they are outside, and when they come to the back door to ask me for a glass of water, they rub their noses back and forth across the screen, leaving little streaks of snot. Mostly, they run. Up to the barn in the morning to scare off the young buck that sleeps there at night. Down to the ditches to stomp in the water. Back up to the barn in search of bats. They jump over the clumps of flowering *Lupinus argenteus,* shouting "Lou-penis!" with unreserved glee.

Every morning I drive them to the Hotchkiss pool, where they have swimming lessons. Mo swims with all four limbs doing different things, and he makes a lot of splashes, barely staying afloat. Carson swims like a young porpoise, smooth and limber. When a thunderhead approaches, all the children are ordered out of the pool. We return to the ranch for lunch and a siesta, when the kids read or rest, and then in the afternoon they look for small animals to capture.

"Mom," says Carson, "Mo lost the baby snake in the bunkhouse again." More than once I scold Mo for sticking the heads of grasshoppers through the screen mesh of the door. I find them collared, kicking their strong hind legs furiously until I rescue them. We go to kids' movies at the Egyptian Theater in Delta, and I can hear other parents in the dark, snoring open-mouthed. Afterward, we stop at the C&J Cafe for a sticky bun the size and weight of the Manhattan phone book. There are retired, smoking cowboys in every booth, drinking weak coffee and creaking like old saddles. The kids get riding lessons from a quintessential cowboy: bandy-legged in beat-up Wranglers, leathery face and bright blue eyes, just the right curl in his cowboy hat, arms strong enough to flip over a calf. Quintessential, that is, until he says "Giddyup" in a voice as high as Mo's.

Carson rides with a fearlessness derived from not having images of neck-down paralysis in mind. Mo wears a big black felt cowboy hat, a brown corduroy blazer, straight-legged Wranglers, and black cowboy boots. He carries around a very realistic plastic rifle that Clair gave him, which I have to confiscate when we get in the car, or he'll shoot out the window at sheep and tourists on bicycles. Once, in the general store in town, a cowboy dad asked me how I got my boy to dress like that. He pointed to his own son, who was wearing a basketball outfit with tremendous sneakers, and said, "Mine won't do it." I couldn't help but smile. The boy's shiny shirt read NY KNICKS.

I take them on outings, too. The valley loves a fair, and there are lots of them. At the Carbondale Fair, we listen to a fusion hillbilly band. Young women with fringed shawls tied around crucial parts of their bodies sway and swoop, and old guys with long gray ponytails drink Perrier and smoke clove cigarettes. We visit the rock-climbing wall, buy juice at the juice bar, and pay a lisping girl in batik to draw henna swirls around the calluses on my palms. At one point, the loudspeaker requests the driver of the blue BMW SUV to please move his vehicle so the face makeup truck can pull out.

We attend the Delta County Fair and watch a grandpa judge chickens. He grabs the beautiful hens and cocks from their cages and turns them upside down to inspect their feet, pull on their wings, smooth their feathers, and flick their combs to see how they stand. His hands are varicose and old, but so tender. He strokes each bird before returning it to its cage.

Also on display are rabbits—Siamese-looking ones, white fryers, and floppy-eared specimens with twitching noses. We inspect the pigs, fat and hairless, lying side by side like obese, naked adolescents, and the sheep, which, taken individually, seem quite independent of mind. We sit in the stands next to little boys in cowboy hats and girls in shorts with long brown legs and tight braids.

We sit next to grandmas, too: coifed, wearing pressed checkered blouses, and nibbling on something they have brought in a sandwich bag. I want to strike up a conversation with them; they seem so nice and sensible. But I am too shy, and they don't meet my inquiring looks. Everybody knows everybody else here, but Western-style reserve and courtesy keep neighbors from being overtly interested in one another's business—a holdover, perhaps, from the days when everyone was armed. But I can't wait through a generation's worth of polite distance. I am starving for adult company, and so I invite my reticent neighbors over for dinner with an enthusiasm they must think borders on strangeness.

I cook for Bob and Candy Pennetta, who are vegetarians, and make them *vedura trovata,* a "found vegetable" stew from the garden. We talk about the Buddhist monks who visit the valley and funk music. I entertain the owner of the Black Canyon Guest Ranch, Dennis Gribely, and serve him prosciutto with local cantaloupe, which he eats cowboy style, using his knife and fork thumbs up. I cook poblano peppers stuffed with shredded zucchini and cheese for Steve and Linda Rubick. They reciprocate, and we eat beans at their place on Fruitland Mesa while the kids play with their herd of humming orphan llamas. But otherwise, I am on my own, and slowly going crazy.

At the same time, my eyes are being opened. When you are alone, you notice things. Swallows constantly patrol the ditches—maybe that is why we have so few mosquitoes. The juveniles hang around the remains of their old nest, plump and handsome. I spend some time working on their whistle, and when they answer back, it is exhilarating. I hear woodpeckers first thing in the morning, pecking away at the dead cottonwoods in the grove behind the house. By midday, when I stop to rest, there are bees buzzing and pale yellow butterflies all over the front fields. Only once or twice has it rained the way it can rain in the East. When the thunder booms, it shakes the whole mesa. Driving home from Delta one afternoon, we see the entire perimeter of a storm hanging over Crawford and Paonia. The storm is so defined, it almost seems intelligent. I become interested in the subtle differences in the breeze. One day the wind blows through the live trees with a glorious, big valley sound, all bluster and power; another day it is herby and tight. In the morning, the breeze is long and pillowy; in the evening, it is a gift of minerally coolness. At night, when I pause to look into the deep sky, I gasp at the stars that float in glittering layers so far back in time I feel minuscule, as if I'm not even big enough to exist.

But despite the moments when I quicken to the grandness of the place, I generally feel as if I don't belong. I have no sense of the rhythm of life here. My sunglasses are too cool. I wave too enthusiastically to passing drivers. The stuff I buy at the market is slightly exotic: phyllo dough, mascarpone cheese, imported pasta. Paranoid, I think the overweight ladies in the ten-items-and-under line who buy boxes of frozen dinners look at me as if I am some kind of displaced princess lacking the common touch. I am suddenly afraid of horses.

I'm off on my communication skills as well. I'm too sharp, too formal. You have to strike a particular balance in the West: soft but sure, unassuming but forthright. And in most company, absolutely no randy stories.

If I get up early enough, before the sun has crested the ridge to the east, the ranch feels more like a mountain pasture, and I am happy. But as the sun boils over the treetops, the land becomes a ranch—domesticated but shaggy. It is easy to feel good about the place in the cool morning light, when the shadows throw the curves of the land into relief. But later, when the sun is high, I'm tormented by the dust, the rocks, the relentlessness of nature trying to undo my efforts. I see it all: the thirsty new trees and the struggling flowering bushes, the slowly collapsing barn with sunlight streaming through its warped slats, the old dump behind the garden, and the huge piles of deadwood that can't be burned away because it is so hot and dry. Sometimes I feel like the deer skeleton I found trapped in a thornbush, suspended until its flesh had fallen away. But that is too dramatic, and I feel even more the mewler for thinking it.

Domestic days are easier days. I hang curtains printed with different species of trout (and a nice border of evil little hooks). I freeze corn and can peaches. I can more than a hundred pints of fruit and would can more if I weren't so distracted by the garden, which explodes as soon as all the hungry mouths are gone. I can't pick the zucchini fast enough. Overnight, they grow from the size of cucumbers to that of baseball bats. I go everywhere with enormous zucchini, hoping to meet someone to give them to. "There's only one reason anyone in Delta County ever locks their car doors," says Clair, as I hand him two more monsters. "And that's to keep their neighbors from putting zucchini in 'em."

I make hamburgers and barbecued chicken for the kids, and I eat salads. Lots of salads. Salads with fresh tomatoes and cucumbers and onions and avocado; green beans with mint; roasted poblano peppers stuffed with guacamole; black-eyed pea with chile salads; soft bread salads with olives. I eat steak and potato salads and a local goat cheese combined with herbs rolled up in a big lettuce leaf and chilled. I eat light, get lean, and dry up like a husk. I give up on mascara, jewelry, and hair accessories. But I hunger for it all. I yearn for sushi, high heels, and the *New York Times*. I yearn for Kevin, whom I love enough to be out here in the first place. I carry on through the broiling days, dragging myself from chore to chore like a mule, dreaming of my return to take-out, multiplexes, and lunch dates. I imagine myself on vacation, dressed in swishy silk skirts and drinking Campari and soda in an ancient piazza. But in reality, I move rocks and stay awake at night fuming about the skunk.

And I'm not even halfway through the summer yet.

5.

LOCAL CHARACTERS

As THE SUMMER wears on, I initiate all kinds of time-consuming projects to ensure I am too busy or exhausted to dwell much on my loneliness. I have never been the sort of person to do small handwork—sewing is utterly beyond me—but in an irrational moment, I buy a tattered twenties-era beaded bag and spend the next twenty evenings repairing the minuscule loops of purple beads. Finished, it looks like a shiny eggplant. I try to find someone to sew a lining in the purse and meet with various seamstresses. The most articulate is a lady near Delta who waits for me on her front porch, beside a half-gallon coffee can filled with cigarette butts. She smells very smoky. She probes and prods the bag, and I stand there for quite a while until she finally hands it back to me, saying, "Actually, I just make drapes."

It seems like half of the projects I undertake are duds, doomed to fail. But I keep going, as I don't want to spend too much time wondering what I am doing here. My journal is full of project lists.

1. Lay stone floor in garden shed. (This entails hauling flat stones from all over the property and laying them on top of the huge mound of stones and dirt I have al-

ready piled up, then carting a hundred gallons of sand and brushing it into all the cracks.)

2. Muck out and line ditch in front of cabin with rocks. (I work on this for hours, until Dick Hansen points out that most ranchers prefer to run a few feet of black flexible irrigation tubing in a case like this.)

3. Plant new Russian sage bushes. (Most dry up within the week.)

4. Spread hay where necessary and water (futile lawn reconstitution).

5. Treat fence with linseed oil. (It wraps around ten acres.)

6. Put in well (to water a new kitchen orchard).

I call Bill Kissner Drilling to set up an appointment to dig a well. The secretary, Jeanette, explains that Dennis Harriman will come out and dowse the place first. Dowsing! I'd never seen it done. I hear the phone ringing in the background and offer to sign off so Jeanette can answer it, but she says, "Oh, it does that," and proceeds to tell me her grandmother was a dowser in Nebraska and all her twenty-two grandchildren have the gift, too.

I sort of expected a druid, but Dennis turns out to be a clear-eyed, no-nonsense fellow in construction boots. He looks like a driller, not a sorcerer. He's used to people being hopped up about the mystery of dowsing and offers me a whirl. He gives me what looks like two straightened coat hangers and instructs me to hold them loosely between my thumb and index finger, palms up. I close my eyes and wait to feel the cosmic force, but Dennis says I better open my eyes, or I might fall in a ditch. So, open-eyed, we start walking. Sure enough, the wires begin to swing as I pass over ground water to the north of our house. It feels like a gentle weight pressing the two wires toward each other. I don't feel any pull, just a bump and a swing.

. . .

These are very quiet days. For home entertainment, Carson and her friend from the pool stuff socks in my bras and put on long skirts and do a wiggly dance show. Mo joins in, too. Dressed all in cowboy black, he does his karate chop dance and shoots his toy pistols in the air. I laboriously sew the last of the beads on my beaded bag, tie the knots on the seams of the new silk lining, and slip my hand in. It feels slightly gross, as I imagine the inside of a cow's udder would feel, only cool.

After a while, I get used to being alone. I begin to wander in a slightly bigger circumference, both on our property and in the valley in general. I finally find the nerve to poke around in the barn, despite the piles of hantavirus-laced manure on its way to becoming sedimentary rock, and I discover a dovecote and a couple of old metal wagon wheels. I trade them with a local antique dealer for a long wooden porch bench, and he makes me promise not to throw away anything from the barn without showing him first.

An interesting thing is beginning to happen. I am making my own way. All the stupid projects are getting me out of my own weird vermin-plagued scene and into the landscape. I begin to fall into easy acquaintances.

I become friendly with Ilona, Gabor's wife. I meet her at the pool. She tells me she was on the Senior Olympic swim team and talks nonstop for half an hour about why yellow goggles are superior to clear. And then, without further ado, she turns and dives into the water. I meet an elk rancher who tells me he has a son at Yale and a son in jail. I start to collect hand-embroidered pillowcases. I find beautiful ones at The Ark II, run by Liz Lilien, a freethinker with a tepee in her backyard for guests. I also buy them from an antique store that smells so strongly of cat pee I take a few gulps of air before entering and hold my breath as I sort through the linens. Every time I go in, the proprietress asks if I am a Christian. What can I say? I'm holding my breath. I buy sweet, soft, unpasteurized goat cheese from a beautiful woman who worries about being shut down by the health department, and so I must meet her at a prearranged spot. It feels like buying drugs.

Half the time we drive over the Smith Fork Bridge into Hotchkiss, we have to slow down to avoid a handful of poky goats that are wandering on the road. They belong to Hippy LeRoux, a legendary local who keeps his animals on a little piece of floodplain, or at least tries to. He's skinny and bearded and usually armed. The kids are always on the lookout for him when we drive by. But Hippy is incarcerated now, part of his ongoing enmity with local law enforcement (in this case, something about shooting the marshal's dog). He wears his guns into town, which unnerves some people, but it's legal, and as the writer Thomas Wills says, "Hippy is like the canary in the coal mine. He doesn't have any septic, and still the health department lost its case against him. The day Hippy is run off his land will mark the end of the Old West."

The kids love to pick up the mail from the post office in Crawford because the postmaster always gives them candy. When he hands over my forwarded mail from New York, it's in two piles: important-looking and unimportant-looking. Once, when I was waiting for a package, he made sure someone dropped it by my house on his way home. As time goes on, I feel less vulnerable to bears, saber-toothed tigers, and murderous jail breakouts, because people like R.D., the postmaster, know we are here.

I recognize folks in the stores, but I can't tell whether they recognize me. The ladies in the bank are always cheerful; the Stahl Orchards ladies are always polite. The teenagers who patrol the public pool are always, well, teenagers: lovely, but seemingly from another planet. I stare at their tongue piercings as if I haven't lived within spitting distance of Greenwich Village my entire adult life. But I carry on and act as if I am in my place, even though I'm not. I drive the smooth asphalt roads between the rolling adobes with heavy metal music blaring from the radio. In the privacy of my own vehicle, rock on the open road makes me feel the way it did in college: as if my life is full of potential. When Kevin is around, he drives, but since he has been gone, I have become familiar with the roads and cease to struggle with their odd names, such as 3850 Drive or 24¾ Street. I relax in the knowledge that it is thirty miles to the first stoplight—in any direction. I take on a casual pose at the wheel and lift only my right hand's last four fingers at passing drivers. Incredibly, they wave back. The cool wave, accomplished.

There may not be a lot of goods for sale in the stores, but the personal service makes up for it. I buy clothes for the kids at Farmer Frank's, where even an experienced shopper like me can get talked into a pair of sandals I don't need. When you go in to buy jeans, the salesperson can show you exactly how much they will shrink because the store has freshly washed examples in most sizes. When my car battery dies in Hotchkiss, the fellow from the gas station installs the new one I buy free of charge—in the rain. Bob Pennetta stops by, having recognized my car with the hood up. And I thought I was alone.

I start noticing little eccentricities, and they become dear to me: the church sign that reads IF YOU ARE LOOKING FOR A SIGN FROM GOD, THIS IS IT. Or the answering message on a local bank's machine: "Now you can find out how much money you don't have, right away!" I am reduced to giggles by a helpful Department of Agriculture officer who, when I inform him that there are beavers chewing on one of my trees along the Grand View Ditch, advises me to wrap the tree in chicken wire and put a portable radio at the base of the trunk. "Don't tune it to a Western music station," he warns. "Tune it to a rock station. Beavers hate rock." Since trapping laws went into effect, beavers have proliferated. They wreak havoc on the rivers in Delta County. "I tell you," continues the officer with heat, "if I weren't on coyote control, I'd be over there today."

I spend a lot of time in the evenings, when the kids are parked in front of the TV, sitting on the porch, watching the light change the sculpture of my view. It becomes a Zenlike practice. Watching, watching as the wild animals slowly reveal themselves: a little brown rabbit, a golden eagle gliding silently overhead. Deer come out of the wilder land and pick through the sagebrush. And once, right before daylight is extinguished, I see a lynx. Its muscles ripple under its dun-colored coat, large and powerful and dangerous. Its wide, heavy paws test the edge of the garden fence. Its short tail quivers, and then a hot, hard spray hits the gate. I stay very still and quiet until the lynx finishes sniffing the air and decides to move on.

I am slowly becoming inspired. It is a strange, sneaking-up-on-you kind of inspiration. Not a hit, punch, or blow, but a kind of awakening. I find myself grateful that I have the time, without rushing to feed guests, to sip my morning coffee on the porch and note how cool it is. It's not like the fall or spring coolness that we encounter back East. There's no anticipation of new bulbs or dead leaves. The cool is huge and empty, as on an ocean, beyond seasons. The cool passes over the ranch like a ghost chasing the night. It heads west along the Smith Fork River and continues, running from the morning. The cool is bold and careless and in a hurry. And there is always the sound of the wind, endless, like waves that never crash.

My appreciation for the rural aesthetic grows steadily. I am in awe of the huge, round hay bales that dot the surrounding landscape. They give me the same feeling as the Neolithic rocks and circles in northern Europe. There is almost a logic to their randomness that's just beyond reckoning, and the sight holds me in breathless suspension. I buy eggs from a local rancher and feel as though I'm opening a present every time I lift the top off the carton. The eggs are always different: some small as a bantam's, others big as a duck's; pale green and beige and ivory; white, speckled, and brown; each unique and precious. With them I make zucchini flower omelets and savory pepper tarts, or I poach them over a vegetable stew. I scramble them with shrimp and Tabasco and fry them sunny side up, because their yolks are so high and yellow I can't bear to turn them over.

The eggs are stored in a refrigerator in the rancher's barn. Customers just drop seventy-five cents in an old coffee can and take a dozen. I imagine this system is in place because no one, so far, has dishonored it. The same goes at just about all the businesses. In fact, many times I have tried to pay for gas with a credit card, only to have the very smiley lady at the register glance at her antiquated credit machine with a brief look of panic and suggest that I come back and pay her when I have the cash. "Can I offer some collateral?" I ask incredulously. "Oh, no, no, no. I trust you," she says. I treasure the fact that there are places in the world where the honor system is intact. Indeed, it is a gift to have the opportunity to prove I am an honorable person.

It makes me feel almost Western.

6.

ROUNDUP

T HE ONLY TIMES I've ever been stuck in traffic in Delta County have been when I've encountered a cattle drive. Usually we just sit and wait as the cows moo and surge around us, kicking up dust and trailing flies, their cowboys on horseback smiling, not unpleased, I think, that they've made us wait. Once, a cowgirl with a particularly decisive manner and a pair of Wranglers so tight they'd shock an Italian came round on her painted pony and started smacking the hood of our Jeep, yelling, "Git along, git along." Alarmed, we finally realized that she was, in essence, herding our vehicle, urging us to move at the same pace as the cattle.

I can understand why people pay to go on roundups. They are intermittently tranquil, clamorous, and thrilling and usually take place in splendid surroundings. I'd seen Dick and Susan Hansen moving their cattle over McClure Pass, and it looked very picturesque, so when Dick invited me to ride with them, I said why not?

Dick grew up on a cattle ranch in western Nebraska, and he looks like it. He's tall and weathered and wears a big silver belt buckle with his initials on it. He moved to Crawford in 1983 and set up his cattle operation of two hundred head on fifteen hundred acres, with numerous leases in the surrounding area. He and Susan call their place Tabeguache (TAB-a-watch), which is Ute for "People of the Sunny Side of the Mountain."

I neglect to tell Dick that I haven't ridden in about twenty years. But he must have known, because he hands me the reins of a super-mellow, barrel-shaped creature named Nick: safe for grandmas, small children, and New Yorkers. As soon as I drape my leg over the expanse of Nick's back, however, I know I am in trouble. The long stirrups of the Western saddle don't really allow you to post, so riding at a trot is more about making peace with the bouncing. My brain immediately begins to joggle inside my head. I forgot to wear a bra, and I will say only that I will never do that again. I hardly notice the scenery as we jiggle and jostle up into the West Elks to find the cows. It's beautiful, but I am distracted by the distinct feeling that my saddle is steadily slipping to the left. Then we ride over a ridge, and suddenly the land opens up like a heartbroken lover. Butler Basin is a huge, soft scoop in the earth surrounded by fir-covered mountains and filled with grazing Red Angus cows. We halt in a row, and the cows look up at our silhouettes and moo, then collectively shift away.

Our job is to round up the seventy or so cows that have been grazing here all summer. We see only thirty-five, and so we split into pairs to rustle the strays from under the scrub oaks and up from the creek beds. Susan and I don't find any cows right off, and as we clop along, I forget we are supposed to be looking for them at all. I gaze up at the clouds and let fat Nick grab mouthfuls of grass whenever he wants—and he wants often.

But then Lee, a strawberry blond cowboy who works for Dick, appears, yelling through the aspens, "Come cow, come cow," and pushing ahead a small bovine family unit. We push them along, too, and find another group, and then another, until we join with the larger herd of animals that the rest of our posse has discovered. The pace picks up. We head down the mountain along a wide dirt trail, pressing dozens of bucking, mooing cows along. They run progressively faster as the trail becomes steeper, a roiling mass that splits around trees, with individual cows spinning off and ripping into the underbrush. I kick up my pony and end-run one impudent, terrified calf, urging him back into the pack. I don't know if it is the horse or me, but as the herd begins to gallop and individual cows careen off the main trail, I dash after them, go around, meet them at a right angle, and drive them back onto the trail. I don't even notice the bouncing in the excitement of keeping this fast-moving tangle of animals together. At the bottom of the mountain finally, lunging and snorting, they bolt through a gate into a fenced pasture, abruptly put their noses in the grass, and return to grazing. Atop our sweating and panting horses, we count the cows, but everyone comes up with a different number. The general consensus, however, is *Close enough.*

The original settlers in the Crawford area were of two types: cattlemen and homesteaders. Cattlemen kept herds that were much larger than they could feed during the winter, but as long as there was free grass, they were willing to accept weather-related losses of up to 20 percent of the herd. The winter of 1883–1884 was phenomenally cold, however, and so many horses and cattle died that the nature of cattle ranching in the area changed for good, and stockmen started to act less like barons and more like homesteaders. After years of overgrazing, stockmen stopped putting more cattle on the range than they could feed during the winter, and the hay business began.

There are no industrial-style cattle ventures in the North Fork Valley, only small, mostly grass-fed operations that produce antibiotic-free, quality beef. Sadly, you see very little of the good stuff for sale in the local supermarkets. Most small purveyors just can't compete with cheap, mass-produced beef, even though their product is infinitely better in terms of health, taste, local economic benefits, and the environment. I buy frozen beef from local producers. We throw the T-bones on the fire and slap them with homemade chimichurri sauce. We make dense aromatic stews and spicy ground meat chili and luscious filets with melted blue cheese on top. The meat has flavor and texture. When was the last time your steak tasted like something? I'd rather eat frozen beef or lamb that is grass-finished and drug-free than a fresh steak from an industrial feedlot any day.

The reason fresh free-range beef is hard to find is that it is hard to distribute. Dick tells me that only three packing companies (which slaughter and box meat) control 80 percent of the beef business—and they have their own cattle. When the packers use their own supply, the price that independent ranchers can get for their beef goes down. If packers don't use their own supply, they buy cheap foreign beef, and the same thing happens. The alternative to the big packers is small slaughterhouses, but they have to charge for a minimum volume of beef, and this price is often prohibitively expensive for a person like Dick to pay. Small producers also have problems with storage. Because of their packer problems, they can stay in the loop only if they produce frozen meat. If their frozen inventory gets old, it can't be sold. Even if they have their own freezers, cattlemen still have to transfer their meat to the retailers, most of whom prefer to do business with established distributors who have larger inventories than a small-volume operation like Dick's can provide. And most distributors handle fresh, not frozen, meat. This is essentially the same problem faced by Colorado sheep producers, although their competition is exclusively fresh foreign lamb, not industrialized meat concerns.

The big cattle purveyors implant growth hormones under their cattle's skin. Without growth hormones, it takes Dick forty-five to sixty days longer to finish an animal to sale weight than it does for commercial growers. Although cattlemen like Dick inoculate their cattle against tuberculosis and a few other bovine illnesses, grass-fed cattle don't really need antibiotics. Ninety percent of feedlot cattle are given antibiotics daily because their stomachs are not evolved to eat grain, and when they do, they develop a variety of bacterial infections. But grain is cheaper than grass, the antibiotics are effective, and the consumer is ignorant. "To bring my product to market at a commodity price, we figure it costs us about forty percent more than it does the big producers," Dick says. "Typical small ranches make two percent on their investments." I can't help but ask why he bothers, although I'm grateful he does. "I do it because it's a lifestyle choice," he says. "I love riding horses and watching the sun rise."

I met Eleni Theos Stelter, a terrific chef, at the Leroux Creek Inn one weekend, and she invited us to her family barbecue in Meeker, about two hours northwest of us, in the White River valley. Eleni is ethnic Greek, as was her grandfather who homesteaded a total of twelve thousand magnificent acres along the northwestern Colorado and northeastern Utah border.

The barbecue is held on Eleni's uncle Nick Theos's share of the family land legacy, a sprawling ranch on the edge of the Flat Top Wilderness Area. According to Eleni, their lifestyle has continued virtually unchanged for the past seventy-five years. They still winter their 4,500 ewes in Utah, still trail them back to Meeker for the summer. The Theoses hire Greek, Basque, and Peruvian herders—tough men who spend a week at a time in the high country with the sheep, living out of tidy little wagons parked in groves of aspen trees decorated with decades of graffiti: naive images of churches and madonnas, along with the names and birthdays of the herders' children in countries far away.

Eleni told me that Greeks don't take a person seriously until he or she is sixty, and I think she's right. The old men who slaughter the lambs for the barbecue with stumpy little pocketknives pretty much ignore the younger, stronger men who loiter around, wanting to help. They slit open the lambs' bellies and let the offal roll out and flop into a bucket of water. The sweet parts — the spleen, lungs, kidneys, and sweetbreads — are made into a creepy-looking but luscious sausage called a *koukorètsi*. The carcasses are washed, pieces of leg bone are carved into slender pegs to close the cavities, and the forelegs are tucked into the brisket so they won't burn.

The men dig a shallow pit and fill it with charcoal. They rake the burning coals into glowing banks, then stake and secure the lambs to a rotisserie, where they slowly rotate for four to five hours, dripping sizzling fat onto the hot earth and emitting gorgeous smells. A hundred people show up, mostly Greeks who homesteaded all over the region. Many of them have sold out. It is a sad fact that Western Slope sheep ranchers will never make nearly as much money ranching as their land is worth. Likewise, it is very difficult to start a sheep ranching operation in the area because land values are so high.

One guest, Gerri Lasater, is running about a hundred head of sheep in Bayfield, Colorado. "If you aren't a homesteader, you can't afford enough land to raise the sheep and have to depend on Bureau of Land Management leases," she says, noting the problems involved in grazing on public land that is also used for recreation. As the land disappears into ranchettes and vacation homes, so does the community's connection with the sheep industry. Gerri explains how new residents of Bayfield began complaining when ranchers trailed their sheep through town. But she and a few others got together and turned the trail into the Sheep Trailing and Heritage Days Festival. Soon residents and local merchants began to look forward to the event, and the grumbling stopped. But there is something sad about an agricultural industry that has to turn itself into a theme-park spectacle to get public support.

Finally, the Theoses' lambs are done, and the wafting perfume of crisped skin gathers people from all over the ranch to a huge table, where the old men are carving the meat. Preferred onlookers (eldest first) are handed succulent bits of tenderloin and shoulder. Within fifteen minutes, the lamb pieces are piled into a large stainless steel container, the bones piled into boxes, and the next lamb is hauled from the pit. Every once in a while, I see a cowboy picking through the bone pile, digging around for an overlooked morsel. The meat is so soft it falls into bite-size pieces with only a gentle push of the fork. It is seasoned with salt and pepper only, and through the sweetness of the fat, I can just taste the wild anise that the sheep feed on all summer. This is the ultimate home cooking: no-frills, essential eating that creates a bridge between the eater and the land. And there is nothing more American than a Greek barbecue in western Colorado.

For big farewell-to-the-guests dinners at our ranch, we usually go for a lamb orgy. Sometimes we grill thirty tiny lamb chops — you can tell they are done (and this is ditto for grilling beef steaks) by using the thumb method. Open your palm and press on the flesh between your index finger and thumb. That's what rare feels like when you press on the lamb. Move about one inch south on your palm and press again. That's medium. Now press all the way onto the meatiest part of your thumb muscle. That's well done. I often buy a frozen leg of lamb from one of the local producers and roast it in a slow oven until it is meltingly soft. I serve it with homemade mint jalapeño jelly, fried poblano peppers stuffed with Olathe sweet corn and cheese, and one (or many) of the local Pinot Noirs. For dessert, we always have sour cherry pie with vanilla ice cream. The next morning, we have lamb hash with eggs poached on top and black coffee, and then we send our company on their way, with detailed directions, lots of love and promises to see more of each other in New York, and a couple of lamb sandwiches for the flight home.

7.

RODS AND REELS

T HE GUNNISON RIVER is one of the best places to catch trout in Colorado, and I am eager for fresh fish. But it takes me quite a while to progress beyond a supermarket approach to fishing: I want to get in there, catch a fish for dinner, and get out, preferably without a sunburn or a mosquito bite.

We go out with Joe Lovett, a mindful worrier who teaches me how to fly-fish while he holds the backs of my wiggly children's bathing suits, so they don't slip into the cold water. ("Hypothermia is not something you want to fool around with," he warns, squinting in the sun.) Dehydration is a worse problem, actually. I forget to bring water, and Kevin has brought only beer.

We rent a raft from Leroy Jagodinski, proprietor of the Gunnison River Pleasure Park, which consists of a large bar and outfitter's shop and a few rental cabins on the river's edge. Leroy has the concession to operate his boats from the confluence of the Smith Fork and Gunnison Rivers to Austin Flats, about six miles downriver. Kevin inherited his gear from his father, who used to fish the South Platte in Colorado. Leroy sets me up with a fly rod and flies. He may seem distracted, but ask him what the fish are taking that day, and he will dazzle you with a litany of bug and fly names: Emergent Sparkle Pupa, Chickabou Stone Nymph, Lawson's Yellow Sally. I just nod, take what he tells me I need, and get in the boat.

We motor upriver to where the Smith Fork empties into the Gunnison. It's hard to imagine that this bright, vigorous little stream has carved great canyons; it is so small and tinkling during the summer months. On a little sandy beach waits our raft, a big rubber number with life vests, paddles, and a cooler. Joe pushes us off, and we catch the current in the middle of the river. Having been on commercial boats that take people out to fish for cod, I'm expecting to reel in the fish. But fly-fishing is an entirely different story.

I soon learn that trout are smarter than cod. Joe explains that trout like structure: old logs, stones, and deep pools, and the quieter water off the rapids. He tells me to cast above the fish and let the fly float with the water. He explains the technique of casting over and over: "Use your arm like a hammer. Hesitate at the top. Give it some oomph." I do, and am tied up in the trees overhead and in the visor of my own cap for most of the float. I don't even get a strike.

At the end of the trip, we drag our raft onto a waiting flatbed truck and head back up the road to the Pleasure Park bar. The bar is horseshoe-shaped, and Leroy presides over drinks, conversation, and etiquette, if you can call it that. Polish polka music or a Verdi opera—Leroy's favorites (he's had his own polka radio show for twenty years)—plays in the background. The bar is decorated with years of dusty promotional junk courtesy of every beer, bar snack, and fishing salesman who has come through the valley: mugs, T-shirts, and inflatable fish with beer logos on their bellies that float gently from the ceiling like stranded blimps. I love inspecting the clear plastic bins near the bar, full of tiny colored flies, shiny lures, coils of fluorescent leader, line clips, and suntan lotion—SPF 30, thank you very much. The place smells like cigarettes.

The angler's shop stocks rods and reels and line, boots, pants, shirts, hats, nets, and, oddly, a telephone shaped like a trout: every doodad for the angler and his codependents. Stationed along the bar are jugs filled with beef and deer jerky, little plastic packages of nuts, candy bars, and barbecue-flavored chips. Likewise stationed are the barflies, talking fishing, alimony payments, and favorite ways to cook a steak. Most laughs end in a phlegmy cough, and eventually a jowly, retired fisherman turns toward me, bleary-eyed and smelling of stale Michelob and Jagermeister, and asks if he can buy me something stiffer than my mug of Flat Tire beer. After a morning on the river, the beer makes me lightheaded enough to laugh, like everyone else, at Leroy's remote-control fart machine.

It is too great a scene to give up just because I'm not catching fish, and so I switch to what I know: spin casting. The next time we go out, I have my crappy little rod with me. I keep in mind Joe's lessons about structure. Within an hour of my next float, I catch a sixteen-inch trout with a three-pronged lure. Over time I become quite adept with my rickety rod, and we always come home with a fish or two for supper. But the rod seems unpleasantly noisy on the uncorrupted water, and more than once I catch a young trout on all the barbs. These fish are too small to keep, and I hate tearing up their mouths. Catch-and-release fishing is really a kind of torture, I think. Better to catch (and eat) a few than to brutalize the many. I start to clip the barbs off my barbaric lure. First one, then the other, until only a single tiny hook remains. It's clear there is nothing left to do but try fly-fishing again.

Kevin is thrilled. He buys me a nine-foot rig, because Joe says that's what I need, as I'm young and intense. I do need it—not the footage, necessarily, but the silent, connective act of trying to replicate nature. When the fly pops into the water with the delicacy of a wayward insect, it is rewarding, regardless of whether a trout strikes or not. I feel an intense satisfaction when I know my cast looks like a real bug. But I am a long way from being proficient. One out of twenty casts is good, and then one out of ten good ones attracts a fish. I spend most of my time pulling up my fishing pants, which are man-size, rather than pulling in fish.

Despite my failures, I carry on, because I am overcome by the river's beauty. We fish dark, rocky holes and shallow rapids and grassy banks, while the swallows skim the water, the chukar partridge hop in the red cliffs overhead, and the smell of sage wafts through the air.

We eat the fish the same day we catch them. In Colorado it is illegal to have more than a day's limit of fish in your freezer, which is fine with me. We smoke the smaller trout with juniper branches and woody wild sage, then set them aside to cool. Later we will pick off the flesh and toss it in a salad of boiled potatoes and horseradish, or mash it with sour cream and pipe the paste into zucchini flowers. I stuff the larger fish with mint clippings, lay them in a shallow roaster, and cover them with blanched lettuce leaves. I add about two inches of water mixed with white wine and bake them until their eyes turn white, then serve them with a dollop of lime-flavored mayonnaise. The flesh is the color of lips and cheeks and kisses, and it tastes as sinless as the waters from which it came.

I like to visit the exhibit of stuffed trout and salmon at the Delta Chamber of Commerce Visitor Center almost every time I go to town. The exhibit includes a thirty-pound lake trout caught in Twin Lakes, Colorado, by the undoubtedly spunky Mike Canty, age ten; a king salmon bigger than my son; and a pair of albino trout caught in two different lakes, but together now, finally, for eternity, in their dusty glass box. We ooh and ah over these tremendous specimens, but I never dream of catching such glorious freaks of nature. I'm interested in fishing and hunting for food, not trophies.

I've hunted ducks once a year at a family-owned place in Arkansas for the past decade, but my hunting has always suffered from a lack of shooting practice. Shooting a mallard or teal as it zips overhead is a little like shooting a flying shoe—it isn't big, it isn't slow, and it isn't close. But coming to Colorado and seeing those chukar on the Gunnison's cliffs and hearing the pheasants honk at each other in the fields around our house put the bug in me big-time. I decide to take Casey Stengel's hunter safety course (which is required by the state), get a gun, and start practicing.

I spend four days learning everything the state of Colorado thinks you need to learn about guns, ammunition, gun safety, the Second Amendment, game birds, hypothermia, bear, elk, and other big-game quarry. The class consists of twelve ten-year-old boys and me. I am about six inches taller than any of them, but they make up for their lack of height by constantly raising their eager little hands whenever Casey—a tall, slightly intimidating man with large earlobes—asks a question. "Does anyone know what the effective range of a modified choke is?" Twelve freckled arms shoot straight into the air. I can't help but suspect that these young Coloradans have done some hunting prior to their certification.

We take the course in the basement of the Stengel gun shop on Rogers Mesa. It's furnished with a dumpy old couch and desk chairs. The lighting is fluorescent, and the decor features portraits of Charlton Heston looking slightly deranged as he grips a gnarly weapon and grits his dentures, and bumper stickers with sayings such as GIVE CLINTON TWO TERMS: ONE IN OFFICE AND ONE IN JAIL.

The class makes a big deal about the difference between an automatic weapon and a semiautomatic firearm, but mostly it reiterates the responsibilities of the hunter regarding landowners, clean kills, and poaching. Half of all the animals killed in this country are taken illegally, an appalling statistic. We watch lots of films depicting hypothermia and families that underestimate bad weather and end up freezing to death in the mountains. For a mom, this is scary stuff, but my colleagues just punch one another and pick their noses and never seem to worry about death, bless them. Casey reads us the hunting laws, emphasizing that men with domestic violence convictions can't have a hunting license. He also defines *always* and *never* regarding safety (*always* walk with your safety on; *never* drive with a loaded gun in the car), then digresses into a critique of Clintonian semantics regarding the word *is*. This reference to the Monica Lewinsky scandal is lost on the kids. Casey talks about habitat, how Colorado wants to bring up the blue grouse population so they can be hunted, and how there are more turkeys around today than when the Pilgrims landed. Then we all go home to study for the big test.

I study hard and pass with one error. The boys don't study at all. Most of them get 100 percent.

Certification in hand, I go to Gene Taylor's in Grand Junction, where I hear they won't sell anyone the wrong gun. I pick out a Browning twenty-gauge over and under. It's a light, modest gun and costs a fortune, but I figure it will be the only one I will ever own. When I pass my New York State driver's license across the counter, the salesman starts rolling his eyes and calls over the stock guy, and they both tell me that buying a gun with New York identification is a pain in the rear for all Americans, but especially for them and me. They recommend that I get a Colorado license and start over.

Fine. Except it turns out I have to trade in my New York driver's license, and with it my right to vote for mayor. I go through with it and buy my gun, but on the drive home, I feel as if I'm in exile. Somehow I am being drawn into this Colorado life in a way that I never intended to be. I used to be a tourist. Now I'm a gun-owning Coloradan with a four-wheel-drive vehicle and a cool wave. At least I'm still a Democrat.

My first Colorado hunting experience is with Charlie and Marilee Gilman and a few other guests on a glorious morning in November: cold, clear, wintry. The Gilmans have a beautiful ranch on Redlands Mesa, where they raise chukar and pheasant under huge nets to set free in the fields. There are multiple buildings on the property, a large adobe house for the family, and a smaller bed-and-breakfast called Casa Encantada, with an outdoor bar in the courtyard for guests (paying and nonpaying). The atmosphere is affectionate, rowdy, and, in a raucous kind of way, virtuous.

We walk in a line across a field of hip-high dried and frosted baby's breath. It's like walking through a crackling beige cloud punctuated with saltbush and sage. We kick up pheasants from the underbrush, and with a whir of green-tipped feathers, the drakes lift into the air. Everyone shoots, and it's hard to tell who kills what, but I know I haven't hit one. We stuff the birds into the pouches in the backs of our jackets and pass into hay stubble, where the chukar hide. We have to be very alert because a chukar will stay still until someone practically steps on it, and then it will burst from its cover into the blue, blue sky. Until that erupting moment, it is quiet going. We listen for the sounds of the birds, and the crunching of our boots as we walk through the straw seems loud and coarse. The slightest flutter in the dry ditches makes us pause and listen more closely.

A hunter has to be very silent, so silent that every snapping twig, every soft rustle in the brush becomes perceptible. It is a state of intense focus, of energy without haste. I can almost feel when a bird is in my vicinity before she lifts into the air. I sense her life without experiencing any obvious signs of it. Only in this extreme state of observation can I perceive the invisible connections between wild living things, and it is breathtaking. This is the true character of hunting: a Zenlike state of simultaneous excitement and calm that allows for acute observation of nature.

To clean the birds, we clip off the wings and tail, using garden shears. Then, with a sharp knife, we cut a ring through the skin and feathers at the neck. Holding the bird's head in the left hand, we push down the skin with the right, over the carcass and down to the legs. The feathers are very soft and warm. It's a heart-breaking job, because the birds are so lovely, and yet they are also beautiful when I serve them to the people I love. We snip off the legs, cut off the head high on the neck, cut open the bird from the anus to the bottom of the breastbone, and pull everything out, setting aside the liver. Then we wash the carcass well in cold water.

I freeze my small charity sack of birds, and we eat them over the winter. We stew the chukar in a mess of shallots and white wine, or roast them stuffed with dried fruit that has been soaking in cognac for weeks. We sear the pheasants and then bake them in a sauce of cream, horseradish, and brandy, or we cook the meat in a tangy, plum-flavored ragout and roll it into soft flour tortillas.

Big-game hunters come to the valley for the elk, but I prefer to buy elk from one of the ranches in the area. Elk are big: an average male weighs 750 to 800 pounds. The meat is 92 percent lean and needs to be cooked hot and fast or slow and wet.

Everyone eats elk around here, and soon it becomes my fascination. I try all kinds of Italian classics with it. I make a nearly tomato-less elk Bolognese, as well as elk cannelloni with a pink sauce — as sweet as can be. But the most celebratory of dishes is elk tenderloin with wild mushrooms. The meat is so tender, so true to this place, that there is never enough, even though the tenderloin is as long and thick as a man's arm.

With culinary hunting and fishing (and gathering, for that matter), there comes a responsibility to the natural world. "Any serious delving into wild foods demands adherence to the concepts of sustainability and aesthetics," writes wild food authority Dr. John Kallas. He's right. Still, there are people who see hunting as a sort of plundering of nature. Yet I think the real plunderer of nature is industrialized agriculture, where animals are kept in such close quarters that they have to be pumped with antibiotics to avoid rampant illness. Real perversion is feeding herbivores a mash made from other animal parts that can lead to ghastly diseases such as mad cow. Supermarket chains are equally hideous, because they often sell vegetables that are grown far away, in another country, picked unripe, and transported in vehicles spewing fossil fuels. And really, do animals raised in a cage have less right to live than animals in the wild? And if someone else does the butchering, is it any less of a killing?

Store-bought is no longer synonymous with safe, and the faith Americans put in the corporate culture of agribusiness is betrayed all the time. Ironically, health is one of the reasons we should get back to homegrown and wild foods. Every purchase of local meat and produce is a declaration of support for conscientious land use, family farmers, and regional economics. But there's another incentive: the effort it takes to catch a trout or shoot a pheasant leads to a greater appreciation of and respect for the earth's bounty. This is the true gift of eating from the wild — this and the communion with nature that happens in the field. Let's face it: no one is going to have a spiritual awakening in the meat section of the local supermarket. But in the lacy, frosty fields on top of Redlands Mesa, one can most certainly sense the presence of God.

8.

GARDENS ON THE MESA

I FLINCH when better gardeners ask me questions about our plot. Is our soil high in acid? Low in alkali? What's the pH factor? Hell if I know. We never checked any of that stuff. It seemed evident there had been a garden behind the house once, and that was good enough for us. With a combination of rototilling and many, many wheelbarrows of old chicken manure from the coops Kevin had dismantled before I came into the picture, our garden grew to about twenty-five by forty feet of nice fluffy earth, ready for seeds.

We buy our seeds on our wedding anniversary in early May, over a bottle of champagne, from catalog sources such as the *Cook's Garden* and *Seeds of Change*. Since we get a little drunk, we order way too much. It's easy to have great ambitions at a fancy French restaurant. It's a different story when we are on our hands and knees under the Colorado sun.

I can never remember what seeds we put in, and since the little staked packages promptly disintegrate, I have to wait until they begin to grow. But around the second week of July, everything starts to come in. For herbs, we plant cilantro, sage, flatleaf parsley, rosemary, and mint. We also plant a small amount of tarragon, thyme, and marjoram. And basil, of course, lots of basil. I learn from a cooking show to pile the leaves on top of one another, roll them up like a cigar, and cut them across, width-wise. This makes a thin chiffonade that, when used for a garnish, shows off the taste better than mincing.

I make bulk pestos from cilantro, basil, and arugula. I preserve pesto in two ways—by freezing and by packing it into a jar and covering it with olive oil. The downside of packing pesto with oil is that the pesto will ferment eventually, and quickly if you make it when the leaves are wet. Freezing is a sure bet, but you have to have room in your freezer, and I never do. I don't add any cheese to pesto until I am about to eat it. The cheese can turn rancid in the oil, and I don't like the way it tastes frozen. I sometimes replace pine nuts, which are expensive, with walnuts, almonds, or pecans. The word *pesto* comes from *pestle,* as in mortar and pestle, the hand-grinding system used to make herb purees back in the old days. Although pesto made from pine nuts and basil is the Genoese classic, anything you make in this fashion is a pesto.

Early in the season, the leaf lettuce comes in. It grows in a solid bank of tender greens, too tight for weeds to intrude. The leaves are delicious when dressed and mixed with spaghettini for a light lunch. But if I want head lettuce, I buy it. My favorite is iceberg, which is so nutritionally poor it is not even recommended for turtles, but it's perfect when you're dehydrated. I cut it into wedges and dress it with oil and vinegar that I put in a Ball jar with a couple of tablespoons of crumbled blue cheese and shake with all my might.

We plant climbing beans along the deer fence, and the tendrils wind in and out of the wires. We also plant bush beans. By mid-August there are so many beans that I don't even lift the leaves, for fear I'll find more. We eat lots of them when they are juveniles and the flesh is shiny and wet and crisp. We plant eggplant because there is nothing more delicious than grilled slices dressed with garlic and olive oil, although the leftovers pureed with grilled wild porcini mushrooms, lemon, and salt make a pretty irresistible dip.

We plant too many zucchini plants, because I am greedy for zucchini flowers, but I don't realize our folly until Kevin and all the guests are gone and only the kids and I are left to eat them. I try to pick them when they are about eight inches long, but they seem to double in size overnight. Sometimes I make individual zucchini fritters, and other times I just make a huge skillet of the stuff and serve it like hash browns next to omelets filled with caramelized onions, Monterey Jack cheese, and cilantro. I make chocolate zucchini cake—a surprisingly aerated and moist local favorite. I cook grated zucchini with grated onion, garlic, and tarragon and mix the savory mash into a bowl of hot, buttery penne.

We also plant too many peppers. Just four jalapeño bushes produce hundreds of the fiery things. I make mint jalapeño jelly, but I need only one pepper per pint. I smoke and freeze bags and bags of them, in hopes that my Mexican food–loving friends will like them as gifts. Each year I promise myself: one plant next year. We put in bell, Hungarian, and Italian sweet peppers, which I throw into every stewy dish I make. Most spectacularly, I prepare a pepper condiment from Kathryn McCarthy's recipe and mix it with soft goat cheese, scramble it into eggs, or bake it into corn bread.

I roast a lot of peppers, too, placing them on a cookie sheet and broiling them until the skin blisters, turning them often. Or I put them directly on the gas burner, turning them often to blister the skin all over. (This also works on the grill.) I don't put freshly broiled peppers (red or otherwise) in a paper or plastic bag, since the steam will cook the peppers and they'll be too fragile or slimy to peel. Instead, I peel them as soon as they are cool enough to handle. I remove the seedpods but do not wash the flesh, which would take away the smoky taste. We eat roasted peppers in salads and tarts, stuffed and fried.

We also grow cucumbers. There is nothing more refreshing than a cucumber straight from the garden. I serve them with every meal—cut into wedges, chilled, and salted. I throw them into salads and gazpacho, and I pickle them by the case. Of the green leafy vegetables, we grow collards and Swiss chard. Almost every day, I make a stew with chard, potatoes, garlic, and the wild purslane and dandelion greens that grow between the garden rows.

Tomatoes love our weather, and they ripen red and shiny, firm and juicy, despite my shabby attempts at pruning. I'm too shy to do the job properly, and the plants become unruly tangles. Kevin and some of his buddies from Colorado Springs made tomato plant stakes from twisted, spindly cedar branches. They give the garden a witchy feeling. With the first homegrown tomato of the season, I am transformed into a novice gardener cliché: amazed that it grew, astounded by the taste, proud as a new parent. We eat tomatoes, marveling, with a vengeance: raw in pasta sauces, broiled with slivers of garlic and rosemary leaves, as a base for countless stews and soups. I preserve as many as my energy allows, in pint jars with basil and salt, to be opened, blissfully, in midwinter.

I work in the garden in the very early morning, before the sun gets too hot. The children are usually asleep, and I've had my coffee and planned the day ahead. I walk across the backyard in my rubber boots, hoe in hand, stepping on the tiny white morning glories that blanket the lawn. I follow the shade in the garden, hoeing to aerate the soil. I can see how it loosens things up, creates more of a feather bed than a pile of heavy woolen blankets. One day I hoe up a tidy row of weeds that Kevin has painstakingly transplanted, thinking they were a vegetable. A shame: they were doing so well. When I hoe, I have to lift the skirts of the tomato plants to weed underneath. It's like changing a diaper, and I sympathize with the indignities the plant endures to stay weed-free. Often I hit a rock, and I grunt and moan and try to wedge the thing out. Almost always it turns out to be the size of a small potato.

While hoeing in the cool morning, my mind first empties, then starts to fill with words. It is as if the words come down from the mountains with the meltwater and rush through the little ditches straight into my head. I stay with the tide of articulated feeling, assuring myself that I will not forget a particular metaphor, until the bugs find me and I must go in and scramble eggs or make pancakes for the kids. By the time I leave the meditation of the furrows and am crossing the yard again, my inspiration, like the morning glories, has disappeared with the heat of the day.

When the opportunity arises, I buy a rustic table and chair and place it in the barren part of the garden. I bring my journal with me in the morning and take brief breaks to grubbily write down my thoughts as they come, before they fade away.

There are some beautiful gardens in this valley—rich red soil where the stones have been cleared for more than a hundred years. We see them everywhere: thick orchards, leafy vineyards, tall cornfields. If we allowed ourselves, garden envy would be easy. Kathryn McCarthy's herb garden sits in a circle on top of Sunshine Mesa, with very little between the tops of her plants and the stars. The herbs are huge and bushy, and the delicate leaves burst from woodier stems than my anemic specimens. Likewise, her vegetable garden is of such a fine caliber—such ripeness, such Jurassic hugeness—that I am always overwhelmed. She calls one day and encourages me to come and pick. "I planted too much this year," she admits in her husky, curvy voice, as I suspect she does every year.

After I pick my fill, Kathryn serves boiled sliced potatoes and beets, local goat cheese, raw scallions, and grilled slices of eggplant and zucchini with a Dijon mayonnaise. We wrap our choices in beet leaves; there is no bread. We drink Michael McCarthy's grassy homemade mead, chilled and slightly effervescent, and sit in a backhoe-dug kiva on the edge of the mesa. Once when I visited, there was a full moon, and the kiva filled up with spirits. It was very creepy and lovely.

I suppose my favorite garden is Mrs. Burritt's, atop Redlands

Mesa, which rises out of the adobe lands. I follow a switchback road up, up, up, wondering how a farm could exist in such an arid, rocky environment; up, up, up, until we reach the mesa top and the wide farm. It is green and lush, with fields filled with tidy rows of corn, green beans, cantaloupes, cucumbers, potatoes, carrots, and tomatoes. We park near a huge barn with a sign that reads BURRITT PRODUCE. PLEASE HONK. We do.

Out of the house comes Ann Burritt, an elfin woman with callused hands and a sun-browned face, short hair and nifty blue eyes. She looks to be in her fifties, but she's twenty years older. Mrs. Burritt is very polite, in that courteous and careful Western way. She leads me into the barn, and I am met by the most amazing smell: cantaloupes ripened on the vine. They are so sweet you can smell them over the gasoline in the tractor parked nearby. "Oh, my cantaloupes have been in the paper," Mrs. Burritt says mildly. I buy half a dozen, each the size of a softball. I also buy lemon cucumbers. On the long, dusty ride home, during which we get lost because Mrs. Burritt suggested a shortcut, we eat a bag of the cucumbers, brushing the dirt off on our jeans and consuming all but the little dried stems at the end.

The truth is, once you have become accustomed to a vine-ripened cantaloupe or a summer tomato, it's a drag to eat the tasteless junk shipped from elsewhere in the world. But if you choose to eat seasonally, you can usually do pretty well using local producers. Who needs Tuscany or Provence when most of us have it all in our own backyards?

The best-tasting foods come straight from the wild, and nature's wild gardens are the greatest of all. But you have to hike to find them, and that's not something I have ever really cared to do. Kevin is a hiker: his first Christmas gift to me was a sleeping bag. I've always had a hard time separating the act of looking where I am going from the act of looking where I am stepping—a qualitative difference. But then I met Peggy Tomaske, a massage therapist who taught me that hiking in Colorado can be synonymous with mushrooming.

Mushrooming, for me, has always involved a certain kind of conjuring, not unlike the experience of hunting and fishing. That is, if I want a trout, a pheasant, or a chanterelle badly enough (and I've applied a little common sense), I can focus with extra intensity. By focusing, I have a chance to succeed. And the magic is that once you see one mushroom, you see dozens. Like an optical illusion, the mushrooms are always there, just not visible until you are in sync with nature.

In the dark, piney woods of the nearby Uncompahgre Plateau, I follow Peggy about, wishing to find a mushroom she can identify for me. And she wishes, too, because we are new friends, and the granting of our wishes would be a positive omen. It is early August, almost too early in the season to find anything, and as we tromp along, I feel, rather pettily, the undertow of disappointment—that without mushrooms, our newfound kinship will lose momentum. But Peggy can conjure, too. With a cry of delight, she finds one perfect porcini mushroom (*Boletus edulis*), fat-stemmed and fat-headed, with a shiny brown cap and no gills. We continue—giddy, instantly bonded—and suddenly there are mushrooms everywhere. She points out chanterelles (*Cantharellus cibarius*) and delicious milky caps (*Lactarius deliciosus*). We find about two pounds of chanterelles that day, and once home we sauté them in butter and roll up the slick, fleshy nubbins in delicate crepes with *queso anejo,* a crumbly Mexican cheese.

At the end of the summer, after Kevin returns, I reluctantly agree to a hike up Bald Mountain. We have guests, and guests expect to climb mountains in Colorado. Kevin, as always, is way ahead of me. I trudge up the trail in a grumpy fog—Douglas firs to my left and right; so what?—and almost bump into him. He is standing astride a mushroom with a cap as big as a salad plate. It is a king boletus, a great prize. No one in our party is as adept at finding these mushrooms as Kevin, who has used the initial magic. After gathering as many as I can carry, I return down the trail to wait by the car, poring over each individual in the hoard, while the rest of our party hike to the summit they have come to scale.

Once home we cut cross sections of the stems to see if any are wormy, then sample each cap to make sure it is sweet (a sour boletus will spoil the entire batch). We cook some of the sliced caps with farfalle, chicken broth, and lemon zest, then throw all of the stems in a robust oxtail and hominy soup. I sauté what's left of the caps until they release their liquid, or blanch them in boiling water, then pack two cups at a time in freezer bags. During the winter, I just dump the frozen mushrooms directly into stews and sauces.

Kevin's desire has finally been fulfilled: now I enthusiastically hike with him. But while he forges ahead, his long strides covering the miles, his head held high, breathing in the view, I walk in small circles, head down, and check the foot of every tree.

Despite the valley's allure, I am still in a state of denial about the ranch. I force myself to load one more wheelbarrow full of rocks because I can't get beyond my idea of a verdant, tidy ranch. Every day I struggle with the evidence that I am failing in the fight against dumpiness: the young cottonwoods have oozed to death, the little pond is so thick with green muck it looks like linoleum, wasps have moved into the woodpile, my cosmos are as good as dead, and the curtain rods aren't long enough and fall off the windows every time the wind blows through the house. A neighbor has voiced a long-held opinion that I am a member of the Puerto Rican Mafia, and a local blowhard has decided to take me on as evil incarnate: the summer resident. But most disheartening of all, the skunk, my nemesis, has had babies and comes waddling fluffily around the house one night to show them off, settling for good that she is the true alpha female on the place.

In late August, about a week before Kevin is due to return, something happens. I finish weeding the garden in the early morning and release the dams to flood it with water. I stand, leaning on my hoe, watching. And then I start to hear an unusual sound: a sucking noise, like a dry sponge, slowly expanding. I realize I am listening to the water percolating into the earth, quenching her thirst. In that moment, I stop fighting the ranch. I suddenly understand that the land needs to be fed, and, ironically, that is the very thing I love to do. At the same time, I comprehend something else: that although I can pinpoint the morning when I started loving the ranch, I think that maybe I really started loving it long before.

9.

BEARING FRUIT

OUR PLACE is still a little shabby, but if it were too tidy, it would look uptight. I look at my shriveled flowers now and think *yucca*. I'm still moving rocks, but I stop when I begin feeling like a draft animal. I brave the snake that lives under the cellar door and start popping open the good bottles of wine, even though it's just me and it takes only one glass before I'm nodding out at the table, oblivious to the whizzing suction-cup arrows my shrieking children shoot from behind the couch.

Conserving water has become second nature, and the pots of herbs and flowers on the porch grow thick and bright with the constant dousing of gray water from my sink. I nap, which I never do in New York unless I get the flu or a rejection letter. I get into tacky books that describe his stiff rod and her deep well and stop working as hard. I mean, I am working as hard, but somehow it doesn't feel like it. I even get over the skunk. After all, she's gotta live *somewhere*.

It is in this frame of mind that I finally break the ice with the Stahl Orchards ladies, who, in their cool cordiality and in my lonely and isolated dementia, have come to signify the impossibility of my ever really understanding the West.

Delta County is Colorado's primary fruit-producing region.

I've heard it called the Napa Valley of the West, the Banana Belt of the West, and the Garden Spot of Colorado. With its warm days, cool nights, clear ground water, and 255-day growing season, it's easy to see why. The North Fork Valley has been in the fruit business for over a century. As early as 1893, North Fork apples were winning medals at the world's fair. Many orchards are organic or are making the transition to organic. In great part family-owned, these orchards manage to stay in business by planting new strains of fruit trees that are more compact and bear more fruit per acre, using wind machines to forestall late-spring frosts, and packaging their own fruit.

But few have been continuously owned by the same family. One exception is Stahl Orchards, founded in 1924 by Louis Stahl on ten acres near Paonia. Today it's a thriving business of one hundred acres, producing cherries, apricots, peaches, plums, apples, and pears. Louis's grandson Arvin is in charge, and as he told the *Delta County Independent* in 1999, "Unless it's proven that it works and it is cost effective, I'll stick to the old ways."

When I first visit the Stahl Orchards fruit stand—a large, cool shed full of perfectly sweet, ripe Bing, Rainier, and sour cherries—I know this is a relationship that is going to last. Right off I introduce myself, but the ladies in their aprons—tending the cash register, lovely and reticent as birds—don't tell me theirs. I watch other farmwomen enter and buy their fruit and the ladies say a simple, "Good morning, Grace," but for me, nothing. Am I too obviously Western purchased at Bloomingdale's? I crave that no-nonsense camaraderie, but it isn't mine to have. I ask how they prepare their cherries, and they say, "Well, you know, in pies mainly." I buy a copy of *Fruit Fixins of the North Fork*—a dignified little spiral-bound volume of local fruit recipes—for guidance.

I love the biographical details about the book's contributors, such as this one regarding Jill Stradley VanDenBerg, whose Cherry Chiffon Pie is in the book: "Jill's descent from Valley pioneers is especially notable, because one member, the hermit Reuben Dove, is a locally historic personage. Her grandmother (Dove) lived for awhile in the Hammond (Edwards) house." Or this one about Dorothy M. Sellars, author of *Apple Pan Dowdy,* "whose grandparents came from Germany to the North Fork in 1889. Her father came from Wales, and she taught Spanish."

The book is most helpful in preparing me for the variety of fruit to come. It is from *Fruit Fixins* that I learn to make fruit honeys—ground fruit cooked with sugar—which I use to replace the applesauce in applesauce cakes, drizzle into coffee cakes, and puddle under spicy poached pears or crispy ricotta fritters flavored with brandy. Dried local fruits go into baklavas or soak in brandy until they are swollen and fuzzy as drowned kittens, then stuffed into chukar or quail and roasted. Cherries, well, cherries I pit by the crate, spattering so much juice that I start to see through rose-colored glasses. They find their way into everything, and on top of everything else, but the best desserts are rich brownies studded with halved Bing cherries and, as the Stahl ladies would say, "pies mainly."

I freeze most of the stone fruits—peaches, apricots, and plums—and the cantaloupes. I cube the flesh, mix it with sugar and lemon juice, and freeze it for a couple of hours, then remove it from the freezer and let it get soft enough to scoop into bowls with big dollops of whipped cream and a garnish of fresh mint.

We all love peaches in wine. My parents always served this dessert during the summer. My mother would put a bowl of peaches floating in cold water on the table next to a pile of paring knives, and everyone would peel for themselves, dropping the wet fragments into their wineglasses. Wonderful peaches are available in the North Fork Valley and Palisade, on the other side of the Grand Mesa. Miles of bright orchards produce peaches so excruciatingly good, so powerfully sweet and fresh, that before you know it, you are on the verge of weeping and singing at once.

I return to the Stahl Orchards fruit stand time and time again and report my fruit failures and successes to the Stahl ladies.

They nod politely, take my money, and send me on my way. There is one lady whom I especially admire. She seems feminine and sensible, the kind of woman who can comfort a child and tell him to pull himself together at the same time. As the summer draws to an end and I become more comfortable in my jeans, I grow bold enough to approach her and say, "I'm sorry, but I don't think I've ever asked you your name."

"Fiona," she says, and smiles. "Good morning, Eugenia."

When I pick Kevin up at the airport, I feel like a different person. He is thrilled with my accomplishments: the garden is well cared for, the lawns are mowed, and the propane tank is out of view. The house is filled with the good smells of ongoing projects: canning, marinating, smoking. Bunches of herbs decorate the table in lieu of flowers. The curtains, however tipsy, keep out the midday sun, and thanks to a chatty exterminator, the only box elder beetles to be seen are the squished remains that still line the screen doors. The toolshed is rickety and silly-looking, perched precariously on its huge mound of stones, but inside the hoses are rolled and the tools are wiped and put away. The driveway has fresh gravel and is lined with railroad ties that I have dragged from disparate parts of the ranch. Lots of junk has found its way into the giddy hands of our local antique dealer. There are benches on the porch, covered with old Indian rugs, and a pitcher of homemade lemonade is in the fridge. The one lone tree that survived Clair's cows, a crab apple, has miraculously produced a bushel of glowing red fruit that waits for canning in a wire basket by the door.

The minute he gets home, Kevin is filled with the loose gracefulness of the place. His professional seriousness gives way to loopy grins. His lace-up business shoes go into the closet, not to be worn again until fall. He can't wait to put on his rubber irrigation boots and tromp out into the upper pasture to move around the water. As he strides through the tall grass, he looks tall and fine as a good tree.

We replace the little orchard that Clair's cows have demolished with another—this one irrigated with the water the dowser found and surrounded by a large fence: two apricot trees, two pear trees, two apple trees, two cherry trees, and two peach trees. Gabor from the North Fork Nursery shows up to help. He seems scattered, until he focuses on one particular tree, and then the flood of his knowledge pours out. He explains how we must train the branches up, because if they are too low, grasshoppers will crawl on them. He teaches us how to tie one of the branches onto a stick to act as the main upward shoot; once it is established, we can cut all the lower branches off. From the porch, the little trees look like rows of children in a kindergarten pen. Although they are so vulnerable and young and I imagine frustrated deer circling them at night, I know they are safe.

We follow a now-familiar pattern of ranch work and ranch cooking and ranch resting, which pretty much means admiring the view and observing the weather. One early evening, a dark and threatening storm gives way to a golden luminescence and a double rainbow that bathes our fields in an eerie, iridescent glow, shimmering and saturated. The children are enchanted and dance in the strange light, as if it were a plaything. The atmosphere is so charged and clear I feel as if I don't need my glasses to see. As we watch the kids cavorting, I tell Kevin about my morning in the garden when I heard the earth drinking.

"That's why I love this place," he says, eyes on the hills. "Because here you can live in the moment. It's only when you live in the moment that you can experience something like that." I don't say anything, because there is nothing to say. But now I understand how the ranch has fulfilled him, and I admire the fact that he was able to recognize it right away, when he first came to fish with Willie two years before. Now, oddly, I am fulfilled, too.

The truth has been underfoot all along: the miracle of living in the moment is that time passes slower, life seems to last longer, and death, because it is daily observable in nature, is not quite as frightening a prospect as it was before. Within minutes, the sky turns purple—deep purple to the east, lavender to the west—and then the electricity stutters and the lights go out.

We light candles and the oil lanterns we originally bought as a hoot (Western life and all that), and we snuggle into bed early, plunged into darkness and peace.

10.

AT MESA'S EDGE

I CAN TELL Kevin is back because in the morning, while I am shuffling around the kitchen making coffee, I can hear him on the side porch, whistling to the birds. We go about our separate projects as the time nears for heading back to New York: he in the fields with his irrigation shovel, me in the kitchen with bushels of fruit to can.

There used to be a culture of canning throughout this country, but a combination of health-related fears, decreasing time, and the cheapness of store-bought canned fruits and vegetables have had a serious impact on home canning. Not so in Delta County. By mid-July the canning sections in the local hardware stores are full of every canning gizmo and gadget you can imagine. Everyone seems to have a bushel of fruit in the back of his or her truck. In New York, a jar of home-canned preserves is a novelty. In the valley, another family's jellies are a burden: just one more jar to find a place for in the cellar.

In July I can cherries: yellow Rainiers with basil or mint, which I roll up in crepes or dump beside pork chops; red Bings and the leftover cherry-flavored syrup, which we mix with soda water and pour over ice for the kids; and sour Montmorencies. We pack the small and wrinkled sour cherries into quart jars—

enough for one pie. By mid-month the apricots come in, so ripe they practically fall into halves. I can them with brandy or puree them into a honey to pour over pancakes in the morning and ice cream at night.

The old fruit trees on our property don't produce much fruit, as they suffer from a variety of ills and years of neglect, but one little apricot tree manages to flourish along our driveway. It is full of fruit the size of eyeballs. I drive by slowly so the kids can rip the apricots from the branches through the car windows, then eat them in the back seat, grimacing at their tartness. I can a few pints of them as well, writing "ranch apricots" proudly on the labels.

The plums arrive in August. There are big red Santa Rosa plums, purple prune plums, Black Friar plums, and, most exquisite of all, red blood plums—intense, sweet, and tangy. What we don't gorge on at the table, I can as purees, jams, and jellies. Peaches and nectarines come in, too. Halved and canned in syrup, they'll nourish us all winter long, as we eat them with cottage cheese and freshly ground black pepper. I also send some to my grandmother in Memphis, who, at nearly one hundred, won't open her eyes but will open her mouth for their clean, tender taste.

Everything I feel confident canning, I do: tomatillos, red tomatoes, green tomatoes (for the Italian fish stew we make in the winter), pickles of all sorts, and jalapeño mint jelly. A batch of that jelly suffers from too much green food coloring and looks like something I imagine you'd find in a nuclear spill, but it tastes cool and snappy nonetheless. I also make jelly from the crab apples on our lone tree, flavoring them with spearmint. My brother, Cham, who comes for a visit, announces that it tastes like candy canes. The jars are beautiful resting on the kitchen counter, and at night I hear the lids pop as the cooling air inside creates a vacuum.

. . .

I have always loved county fairs, and the Delta County Fair, held at the Hotchkiss fairgrounds, is as good as it gets. All the towns compete in a variety of classes: livestock (llama, swine, goat, poultry, rabbit, cattle, sheep), horticulture (fruit), agriculture (grasses, hay), produce (including largest and oddest), pantry (canned, frozen, dried, and baked goods; soap, candy, and honey), needlework (sewing, knitting, crocheting, embroidery, afghans, and quilts — beautiful quilts that hang on rods, to be fingered by expert grandmas), crafts (such as pottery and doll-making), art, and flowers. There is a vegetable sculpture competition for kids, a dog obedience show (which is rather chaotic), a horse show, a demolition derby, and a rodeo.

With some trepidation, I enter my Candy Cane Jelly among the sixty or so other beautiful, glistening jars of preserves. The next day, when we return to see how the jelly has fared, there are lots of blue ribbons — the Crawford booth has done very well — but my jar is not to be found. And then a petite lady with a gray perm hands me my jar, hidden behind a tremendous multicolored ribbon. "Well, now, you're just going to have to give us the recipe," she says. My kids puff up with pride, but I feel a rush of gratitude: it is the first time I've ever won anything.

We leave for New York when the pears come in. Most of the canned and frozen goods are shipped back to the city, and we scramble to sort through the kids' stuff and pack our clothes and sheets and towels into big plastic tubs so the mice can't get at them. Projects are hastily completed, arrangements are made to keep the fields irrigated, and meals entail fewer and fewer ingredients as I try to use up all the perishables. I can feel the slightest hint of coolness in the air, and I wonder what it is like here in the winter. Is it lovely? What do the West Elks look like covered with snow? But there is no time for regrets. School — and all the rest of colorful, stimulating New York life — is around the corner.

. . .

In the fall of 2001, we are back in the city only a week when everything changes: we run to gather the children from their schools while buildings collapse and people with loved ones in those buildings crumple on the sidewalk. Hordes of men and shoeless women covered in white ash walk like living dead up my street and every other northbound street in the neighborhood, passing by in silence and horror. We stay up all night, fearful that the fires will spread from the nearby disaster site. My children cringe when they hear a fighter jet overhead and ask, "Is that a good plane or a bad plane?" A few days later, I become sick with something in my throat and head. We don't open the windows because the burning smell is so strong. It makes the kids' eyes red and their throats sting. I have to excuse myself at odd times — during dinner, while on the phone — when I feel the weeping coming on. Our friends call us frequently, and when Kathryn and Michael McCarthy suggest that we spend Thanksgiving in the valley, it seems like a very good idea.

The land is golden and brown and army green, and the gnarly cottonwoods are black silhouettes against the pastures. A dusting of snow, like confectioners' sugar, covers the adobe hills, and bigger snows fill the West Elk gullies. The Gunnison, Smith Fork, and North Fork Rivers are running green, cold, and clear. The ponies and llamas are very fuzzy. Smoke rises from chimneys; the air is cool and the sun low. For the first time, we see the cliffs of the Smith Fork canyon through the bare cottonwoods behind our cabin. The garden is dormant, with rotting squash on the vines and some bushy rosemary still holding on. The deer have come down, and there is a herd of twenty in the upper pasture. A hundred elk graze in the stubby hay fields above the McCarthys' place, where we eat Thanksgiving dinner. They look like a piece of moving geography.

It is a grieving Thanksgiving. The McCarthys care for us tenderly, like sick children. They make a huge wild turkey and mashed potatoes with green chiles and garlic. They serve home-made mead flavored with wild raspberries. There are pickles on the table and hot rolls wrapped in cloth napkins. While everyone digests on the couch, I clean the turkey meat off the bone and bust up the carcass for soup. I feel some release of tension as I smash away, but in truth I am just as fragile and sob all over the bones. In my journal, I summarize the weekend: two recipes, one breakdown, much beauty.

One of the amazing things about the Western Slope is that within a day, you can go from alpine snow to red rock desert. During the children's spring break, we travel to Powderhorn on the Grand Mesa, about an hour from our house. It's a low-key family ski resort situated at 9,800 feet. The views are of eons of sedimentary layering and river carving. The employees are young and pierced; there are lots of oddly shaved goatee and mustache combinations. Indeed, the boys look like snowboard-ing Pans. Lift passes are cheap, lines are short, the snow is corny, and the sun is hot. Some kids ski in shorts and T-shirts. It's a col-legiate scene, and yet fifteen minutes down the slope, in the town of Mesa, you can buy bait at the general store, where a sign reads BARETTA RIFLE, $2,600; SCOPE, $49.50; ONE CLEAR SHOT, PRICE-LESS over a photo of Osama Bin Laden's face.

Mo looks like a grinning punk demon going down the slopes in a fearless snowplow, arms wide and a huge gap-toothed grin on his face. Carson disappears into the trees, barreling along, knees in her armpits. I'm not so bold and prefer to ride the lift, scoping for future mushroom hunting grounds. We stay at a slope-side condo because everyone is too tired to drive home at night. We eat lentil soup made with our own frozen wild mush-rooms, and toast with home-canned jam. As the days warm up, the snow cover diminishes. Bald patches appear on the moun-tains, the trees drip, and the icicles that were growing under the roof fall and stab the breasts of the aging snowdrifts below.

We move on. A few hours farther west, following the Colorado River from Grand Junction, we enter Utah. We scamper among the sculptural rocks at Arches National Park and take in the breeze and view of eternity in Canyonlands National Park. The streams and rivers that drain the West Elks, and pass by our land and through our community, have helped cut these eternal formations. I think, looking at the vast landscape, that no one can blow up the canyons, or stop the little Smith Fork from contributing to this great natural endeavor. The carving will go on forever—as a valley resident wrote nearly one hundred years ago, "as long as the sun shines and the water runs downhill."

It is summer again, and I am back at the ranch. Our view of the West Elks changes every few minutes. Sometimes it is murky and lavender, other times towering and dark green. In the morning, the hills are pale blue silhouettes; at dusk they are golden. Rainbows are common marvels.

I have much to be grateful for, and I am. I have come to love this place, for its restorative powers, its beauty, and what it has taught me about living. And so I put down my pen to rest and to gaze, from right here, at this rough table in my garden, facing the mountains.

PART II

The Recipes

APPETIZERS

Goat Cheese with Hot Peppers

Makes 1 cup

There are numerous goat cheese makers in the valley. I've bought a gently soft cheese from a lady in Crawford, an aged crumbly cheese from a fellow in Stevens Gulch, and a mild feta made by a gifted twelve-year-old girl. I've made this recipe with all three, although soft goat cheese makes for a creamier spread. I serve this tangy appetizer on the porch with crackers, baby carrots and radishes from the garden, and cold beer, to occupy friends who are used to the splendid views and the golds and purples of sunset.

You can use store-bought hot green peppers packed in oil in this recipe. Just add a pinch of oregano and ½ teaspoon of minced garlic to approximate the taste of Kathryn's peppers.

1 cup fresh goat cheese, softened
2 tablespoons Kathryn's Hot Peppers packed in oil (page 300) or store-bought hot green peppers in oil
2 tablespoons minced fresh tarragon
2 tablespoons minced fresh chives
Salt

Combine all the ingredients except the salt in a small bowl. Add salt to taste and serve.

Stuffed Eggs with Chile

Serves 4

I must confess to egg greed. I can't just buy one dozen, not when they are so fresh and so variable in their color and size. Nor can I resist the taste of a truly fresh egg, or its high, orange yolk and runny white. People in the North Fork Valley don't eat eggs with pale yellow yolks and gluey whites. It's a shame anyone does.

There is no more delightful appetizer than a cool stuffed egg, and no more effective way to move along a carton. The downside is, eggs are filling and rich, and people eat more of them than they mean to (especially if your children are passing the plate). So I use ricotta cheese rather than mayonnaise to soften the yolks, which makes for a lighter stuffing and adds a delicate flavor.

4 large hard-boiled eggs, peeled
1/2 medium-hot chile pepper, such as poblano or Anaheim, charred and peeled (see note)
2 tablespoons ricotta cheese
1/2 teaspoon hot mustard
1 tablespoon white vinegar
Salt and freshly ground black pepper to taste
Chili powder for garnish (optional)

Slice the eggs in half lengthwise and gently remove the yolks. Place the yolks in a small bowl. Mince the chile pepper and add it to the yolks. Add the remaining ingredients, except the chili powder, and mash with a fork until the mixture is soft and smooth. Spoon the mixture back into the yolk cavities. Serve the eggs garnished with a sprinkling of chili powder, if you like.

Note: To char the peppers, place them on a gas burner or under the broiler and turn them until they blister all over. Remove them from the heat, and as soon as they are cool enough to handle, slide off the skin. Cut the peppers in half lengthwise and remove the seedpods and veins. Don't rinse the peppers, or they will lose their smoky taste.

Eggplant and
Porcini Mushroom Dip

Makes 2 cups

E ggplants and mushrooms come into season at about the same time in the valley. Over the past few years, our eggplants have tended to be dusty, runty embarrassments, stunted early on by the depraved vermin that raid my garden at night. As a result, we buy them from Mrs. Burritt, who farms outside Hotchkiss. There is no produce like Burritt produce: her big, glossy specimens grow within sight of the San Juan and West Elk Mountains and God. And porcini mushrooms are always available if we get enough rain. The children scream "Boletus!" when they find one, and proudly plop their trophies, plump as hamsters, into my basket.

We often grill eggplant and mushrooms to accompany a main course, and I usually make this dip with the leftovers. It's similar to baba ghanoush, and so smoky, rich, and lewdly earthy that there are plenty of times I've grilled the vegetables just to make this recipe. I like to serve this dip with a mound of tortilla chips.

4 thick slices grilled eggplant (about
   1 inch thick), warm or at room
   temperature
4 thick slices grilled porcini
   (boletus) mushrooms (about
   1 inch thick), warm or at room
   temperature
4 garlic cloves
$\frac{1}{2}$ cup olive oil
$\frac{1}{4}$ cup fresh lemon juice
   Salt and freshly ground black pepper
1 tablespoon finely chopped fresh
   cilantro for garnish
   Truffle oil for garnish (optional)

Place the eggplant, mushrooms, garlic, olive oil, and lemon juice in a food processor or blender. Process until the ingredients are blended, but not to a smooth paste (a few little chunks are good).

Transfer the dip to a serving bowl and add salt and pepper to taste. Garnish the dip with the cilantro and a drizzle of truffle oil, if you like. Serve warm or at room temperature.

Refried Bean Crostini

Serves 4

We eat a lot of beans in Colorado. We can buy dried beans from the most current crop, rather than hoping the bags in the grocery store have been grown sometime during our lifetime. These are usually pintos, and this recipe is so savory that when I first made it, my family couldn't stop dipping into the pan prior to dinner. Hence the crostini idea. I started by giving the kids a little on a thin piece of toasted bread. Now I serve it Tuscan style, to keep the children out of my hair and my company's margaritas from catching up with them too soon.

1 cup dried pinto beans, soaked overnight and drained

2 strips bacon

1 teaspoon salt

2 tablespoons olive oil

1/2 cup minced onion

1 tablespoon minced garlic

1/2 cup seeded and minced green bell pepper

1/2 teaspoon minced jalapeño pepper, or more to taste

12 thick slices French or Italian bread (about 1 1/2 inches thick)

3 tablespoons grated Monterey Jack cheese (use the large holes of the grater)

3 tablespoons minced fresh cilantro

Place the beans, bacon, and salt in a medium pot. Cover the beans with about 2 inches water and cook at a low boil over medium-low heat for 1 hour, or until the beans are tender. Be sure to check the water periodically. If it is below the level of the beans, add more water.

Meanwhile, heat the olive oil in a skillet over medium heat. Add the onion and garlic and cook until the onion is translucent, about

5 minutes. Add the green pepper and jalapeño and continue cooking until the pepper is soft. Drain the beans. Add the cooked beans and mash them into the vegetable mixture with a fork until they are quite smooth. Add salt to taste.

The beans are ready when they begin to pull away from the sides of the pan. Toast the bread lightly. Spread the pinto beans on top of each slice. Decorate half of the crostini with the Jack cheese and half with the cilantro. Serve promptly, since the refried beans don't look as nice once they cool.

Smoked Trout Crostini

Serves 8

O n any given day, we usually don't catch our limit of trout. I'm happy if between the two of us, we get two fish, one for dinner right away and the other for my husband, Kevin, to smoke. He packs the smoker with cedar chips and apple wood from the countless dead or dying apple trees on the northern edge of our property. (He often chucks a couple of poblano or jalapeño peppers in there, too.) After the fish is smoked, it is allowed to rest, usually overnight.

This pâté is very fresh-tasting, not fishy and strong like store-bought versions. If you can't find whole smoked trout, use vacuum-packed smoked trout fillets. The whole smoked trout meat will mix to a smoother paste than the fillets. You can also make this recipe with other smoked fish, such as salmon, shad, or whitefish.

Avoid horseradish sauce, which I think has a sour taste. Go for the spiciness of freshly grated horseradish or horseradish preserved in vinegar. You could use wasabi, too, but add it in small quantities, tasting all along.

$3/4$ pound smoked trout, flaked (about 2 cups)

$1/2$ cup plus 2 tablespoons sour cream

$1/4$ cup minced fresh dill

1 teaspoon fresh horseradish or prepared white horseradish

Juice of $1/2$ lime (about 1 table-spoon)

Dash of Tabasco sauce

Dash of Worcestershire sauce

Salt and freshly ground black pepper

$1/2$ cup chopped walnuts (optional)

$1/2$ cup chopped scallions

16 slices French or Italian bread, lightly toasted

In a small bowl, combine the trout, sour cream, dill, horseradish, lime juice, Tabasco, Worcestershire, and salt and pepper to taste. Mix well, mashing the trout with the back of the spoon. When the mixture is quite smooth, add the nuts (if using) and scallions and mix well. Smear the mixture on the toasted bread and serve.

Fried Zucchini Flowers with Cilantro Mayonnaise

Serves 4

I've written this recipe for four, assuming that the reader will be serving it to adults and that they'll eat modestly. But the truth is, in the valley, people don't eat modestly, and it's rare to set a table for just adults. Kids, dogs, houseguests, relatives—they all seem to find their way to the table. So when I'm planning to serve these dainty flowers, with their delicately dry, just-salty crunch and their tender, floral taste, I make a ton of them. We serve them in baskets with a bowl of mayonnaise for dipping, although they are wonderful with just a squirt of lemon juice and a sprinkling of salt.

You can also make this dish with dandelion flowers. Be sure to pick them when they first bloom, in early spring.

> 16 zucchini flowers
> 2 cups lager beer or one 12-ounce bottle
> 1½ cups all-purpose flour
> 2 teaspoons baking powder
> Salt
> Vegetable oil for frying (corn, safflower, or other oil—<u>not</u> olive oil)
> Cilantro Mayonnaise (recipe follows)

Check the insides of the zucchini flowers for insects and shake them out. Brush any dirt off the flowers, but do not wash them, or they won't be crisp when you fry them.

Combine the beer, flour, baking powder, and a pinch of salt in a medium bowl and refrigerate for 1 hour (a little more or less is okay).

Heat ¾ inch vegetable oil in a large nonstick skillet over high heat. The oil must be very hot. You can test it by throwing a dash of flour into the oil. If the flour pops, the oil is ready for frying. Dunk the flowers in the batter and place them gently in the hot oil. Don't put in too many flowers at once, or they will bring down the temperature of the oil. They also mustn't touch each other, or they will stick together. Do not flip the flowers over until the lower edges have turned golden brown, about 2 minutes. If you are using a cast-iron skillet and the flowers stick, let them cook for 30 seconds more. Turn the flowers over with tongs and fry for 1 minute, then remove them from the skillet and drain them on paper towels. Do not add more battered flowers until you are sure the oil has come up in temperature again.

Serve immediately with the mayonnaise on the side.

Cilantro Mayonnaise

Makes ¾ cup

T ry to use a very fresh egg for this recipe. As a rule, I don't feed raw egg recipes to small children and immune-suppressed friends.

 1 large egg yolk
 1 scant teaspoon Dijon mustard
 ¾ cup vegetable oil (<u>not</u> olive oil)
 3 tablespoons minced fresh cilantro
 ½ teaspoon fresh lemon juice
   Salt and freshly ground black pepper

Place the egg yolk and mustard in a small bowl. Using a whisk, beat the egg yolk by hand for a few seconds, then start pouring in the oil in a thin stream, beating all the while. The mayonnaise should start to thicken right away. If you dump in the oil all at once, the mayonnaise won't thicken. The more oil you add, the milder the mayonnaise will be, so you can adjust this recipe to your taste. When you've used all the oil you wish, stir in the cilantro, lemon juice, and salt and pepper to taste and serve. You can make the mayonnaise up to 4 hours ahead. Just add about 1 teaspoon of water to stabilize it and refrigerate.

Hubbard Creek Company
Pesto Torta

Serves 12

Hubbard Creek Company is a commercial pesto manufacturer located in Paonia. More accurately, the company is really Eleni Theos Stelter, who makes pestos, whole-grain mustards, caramel sauce, and other goodies in her kitchen. Eleni's torta is a valley favorite. It's so rich and savory, it verges on pornographic. Like a terrine, the dish is made of frozen layers of ricotta cheese and two kinds of pesto. Defrost it in the refrigerator for about 12 hours before serving. Eleni flips it over onto a platter and serves it with crackers. I like it with thin pieces of bread, too.

CREAMY LAYER

- 1 8-ounce package cream cheese, softened
- 4 tablespoons (½ stick) unsalted butter, softened
- ½ cup (4 ounces) whole-milk ricotta cheese

BASIL PESTO

- ¾ cup almonds
- 1½ tablespoons chopped garlic
- 3 cups fresh basil leaves
- ¾ cup olive oil
- ¾ cup grated Parmesan cheese
- ¼ teaspoon sea salt

SUN-DRIED TOMATO PESTO

- ½ cup almonds
- 2 tablespoons chopped garlic
- 2 cups chopped sun-dried tomatoes
- 1⅓ cups olive oil, or more if needed
- ¾ cup grated Parmesan cheese
- ½ teaspoon sea salt

To make the creamy layer: Using an electric mixer, beat the cream cheese until smooth. Add the butter and beat until smooth. Add the ricotta and mix until smooth. Set aside.

To make the basil pesto: In a food processor, pulse together the almonds and garlic until they are chunky. Add the basil and begin to drizzle the olive oil slowly into the processor. Check the consistency of the pesto after adding ½ cup of the olive oil: it should be thick and chunky, not a smooth paste. If it is thick but spreadable, stop. If not, continue to add oil. Add the Parmesan cheese and sea salt. Process until the ingredients are just mixed. Set aside 1 cup for the sun-dried tomato pesto. Set aside the remainder for assembling the torta.

To make the sun-dried tomato pesto: In a food processor, pulse together the almonds and garlic until they are chunky. Add the sun-dried tomatoes. Pour in ½ cup of the olive oil. Process for 1 to 2 minutes, then begin drizzling the remaining oil into the pesto: it should be thick and chunky, not a smooth paste. Add the Parmesan cheese and sea salt. Process until the ingredients are just mixed. Add the 1 cup reserved basil pesto and pulse briefly until well mixed. Set aside.

To assemble: Prepare a mold—a small brioche pan, an elongated flowerpot, or an ordinary cake pan. The mold should be at least 3 inches deep.

Line the mold with cheesecloth or plastic wrap, with some hanging over the edges. Beginning with the creamy layer, put one third in the bottom of the mold. Place the mold in the freezer until the layer has hardened, about 30 minutes. Layer the basil pesto over the cream. Again, let the mold sit in the freezer until the basil layer is hard to the touch. Put another one third of the creamy layer into the mold and freeze. Add the sun-dried tomato pesto and freeze again. Finish off the torta with the remaining creamy layer.

Fold the overlapping cheesecloth or plastic over the top layer. Wrap the mold with plastic wrap and refrigerate or freeze it. (Freezing each layer ensures that the pestos won't bleed into the creamy layer.)

About 12 hours before you plan to serve, transfer the torta to the refrigerator. When you are ready to serve, unwrap the torta and place it upside down on a dish. Lift off the mold and pull off the plastic or cheesecloth. You can freeze the torta, well wrapped, for up to 1 month.

Zucchini Flowers Stuffed with Smoked Trout

Serves 8

I had imagined this dish for a while. I'd made the trout pâté many times, but stuffing it into those paper-thin blossoms seemed daunting. I ended up trying it for a memorable lunch with Yvon and Joanna Gros, owners of the Leroux Creek Inn and staunch epicures. We ate these delicious zucchini flowers as a first course. The trout pâté was soft and rich, balancing the crispiness of the fritters. Afterward, we ate a poached trout salad with potatoes and mint, and drank champagne the Groses brought. We spent half the day at the table, dawdling over fresh peaches, and got up only when the wine ran out.

I've made piping cones with wax paper, and they work, or you can use a soft plastic pastry piping cone. It's easier to stuff flowers that are young and stiff.

30 zucchini flowers
3 cups lager beer
2 cups all-purpose flour
3 teaspoons baking powder
Salt
³/₄ pound smoked trout, flaked (about 2 cups)
¹/₂ cup sour cream
Dash of Worcestershire sauce
Dash of Tabasco sauce
Vegetable oil for frying (corn, safflower, or other oil — not olive oil)
Lime wedges or Lime-Flavored Mayonnaise (recipe follows)

Check the insides of the zucchini flowers for insects and shake them out. Brush any dirt off the flowers, but do not wash them, or they won't be crisp when you fry them.

Combine the beer, flour, baking powder, and a pinch of salt in a medium bowl and refrigerate for 1 hour (a little more or less is okay).

To make the filling, combine the trout, sour cream, Worcestershire, and Tabasco in a small bowl and mash them together until the mixture is quite smooth. Use a soft plastic pastry cone, or roll two layers of wax paper into a cone and cut a small hole in the tip. Spoon a couple of tablespoons of the trout mixture into the wide end of the cone and press the mixture down toward the tip by twisting the top. With one hand, gently open the petals of a zucchini flower; with the other hand, pipe the trout inside. You will need about 1 tablespoon of the trout mixture per flower. Repeat this process with the remaining flowers.

Heat ¾ inch vegetable oil in a large nonstick skillet over high heat. The oil must be very hot. You can test it by throwing a dash of flour into the oil. If the flour pops, the oil is ready for frying. Dunk the flowers in the batter and place them gently in the hot oil. Don't put too many flowers in at once, or they will bring down the temperature of the oil. They also mustn't touch each other, or they will stick together. Do not flip the flowers over until the lower edges have turned golden brown, about 2 minutes. If you are using a cast-iron skillet and the flowers stick, let them cook for 30 seconds more. Turn the flowers over with tongs and fry for 1 minute, then remove them from the skillet and drain them on paper towels. Sprinkle the fried flowers with salt. Do not add more battered flowers to the oil until you are sure it has come up in temperature again.

Serve immediately with lime wedges or Lime-Flavored Mayonnaise.

Lime-Flavored Mayonnaise

Makes ¾ cup

Use only very fresh eggs when making homemade mayonnaise. You can substitute a gourmet mayonnaise such as Delouis Fils; just add the lime zest and juice.

    1 large egg yolk
    1 scant teaspoon Dijon mustard
    ¾ cup vegetable oil (<u>not</u> olive oil)
    1 tablespoon fresh lime juice
    ½ teaspoon grated lime zest
    ½ teaspoon fresh lemon juice
       Salt and freshly ground black pepper

Place the egg yolk and mustard in a small metal bowl. Beat the egg yolk by hand for a few seconds, then start pouring in the oil in a thin stream, beating all the while. If you dump the oil in all at once, the mayonnaise won't thicken. The mayonnaise should start thickening right away. The more oil you add, the milder the mayonnaise will be. When you've used all the oil you desire, add the lime juice, lime zest, and lemon juice. Season with salt and pepper to taste and serve. You can make the mayonnaise up to 4 hours ahead. Add about 1 teaspoon water to stabilize it and refrigerate.

SOUPS

Cold Zucchini Soup

Serves 4

I always start the zucchini season picking the smart little ones, but inevitably, as the summer rolls on and the bounty comes in, the zucchini get larger and larger, until I am stuck harvesting colossal monsters. That's when I start making cold zucchini soup, which uses lots of zucchini (although if you use big zucchini, you must remove the seeds). This soup is cool and creamy. We often eat it with garlicky toast and a fresh tomato and onion salad.

I use a mild powdered chile in this recipe. You can use any kind you like.

1/4 cup olive oil

2 medium onions, coarsely chopped

2 medium zucchini, grated on the large holes of the grater

Salt

2 cups low-sodium or homemade chicken broth

Vegetable oil for frying (corn, safflower, or other oil—<u>not</u> olive oil)

2 tortillas, cut into strips

1 cup light cream

Mild powdered chile to taste

Heat the olive oil in a large nonstick skillet over medium heat. Add the onions and cook until they are translucent, about 5 minutes. Add the zucchini and 1 teaspoon salt and continue cooking until all the zucchini water cooks out, about 20 minutes.

Place the zucchini mixture in a food processor and puree. You should have about 3 cups. Transfer the zucchini puree to a saucepan and add the broth. Bring the soup to a boil over medium heat, then turn off the heat and let cool.

Heat ½ inch vegetable oil in a small nonstick skillet over high heat. Test the oil by throwing a dash of flour into the oil. If the flour pops, the oil is ready for frying. Drop the tortilla strips into the oil and fry until they are golden and crisp, about 2 minutes. Remove the strips with a slotted spoon and drain on paper towels.

When the soup is cool, add the cream and salt to taste. Serve each portion with a sprinkling of chile, dividing the fried tortilla strips evenly among the dishes.

Green Chile Soup

Serves 4

During the summer months, when the green chile peppers are in and the roaster at the Big B fruit stand near Austin is working overtime, we make big pots of green chile base from this recipe—basically, the vegetables without the broth, hominy, or garnishes. I freeze numerous containers of this base for the winter. Kevin and I eat green chile soup whenever we feel a cold coming on.

We usually serve this soup with an array of condiments—lime, avocado, crispy fried tortilla strips, grated Monterey Jack cheese—all of which make it into a substantial meal. We also prepare this dish with leftover roast pork. Just add 2 cups of chopped meat to the vegetables after they have softened. You can add a couple of cups of chopped tomatoes, too, and simmer the whole thing together before adding the broth and, if you like, the other ingredients.

10 mild chile peppers, such as Anaheim, charred (see note, page III), peeled, seeded, and chopped

2 large onions, chopped

1 medium tomato, chopped

2 garlic cloves, chopped

1 cup water, or more if needed

1 teaspoon salt

1 quart low-sodium or homemade chicken broth

1 cup cooked hominy or one 8-ounce can, drained

Vegetable oil for frying (corn, safflower, or other oil—<u>not</u> olive oil)

About 40 tortilla strips for garnish (stale tortillas are best, since they will absorb less oil)

1/4 cup chopped avocado for garnish

1/4 cup chopped fresh cilantro for garnish

Place the chile peppers, onions, tomato, and garlic in a food processor and pulse until coarsely ground. Place the vegetables in a heavy-bottomed pot or kettle. Add the water and cook at a low boil over medium heat for 1 hour, or until the mixture is reduced by about a third. Stir the soup often so it doesn't stick. If the liquid cooks out in less than an hour, add another cup of water. Add the salt.

Combine the vegetable mixture and chicken broth in a saucepan and bring to a low boil over medium heat. Add the hominy and adjust the seasoning.

Heat ½ inch vegetable oil in a small nonstick skillet over high heat. You can test the oil by throwing a dash of flour into the oil. If the flour pops, the oil is ready for frying. Drop the tortilla strips into the oil and fry until they are golden and crisp, about 2 minutes. Remove the strips with a slotted spoon and drain on paper towels.

Pour the soup into deep bowls and garnish with tortilla strips, avocado, and cilantro. Serve immediately.

Sweet Pea Soup

Serves 4

One of the luxuries of living in the country is that I can give a bag of peas to the kids and send them outside to shell them. Their help certainly encourages me to make this simple and pure soup when the first spring peas come in. Don't substitute frozen peas for fresh. Although you can use frozen peas in many stewy recipes, they just won't work here.

4 cups fresh peas
I quart low-sodium or homemade chicken broth
Salt and freshly ground black pepper
I cup sour cream
4 small slices Italian or French bread
1/4 cup minced fresh mint for garnish

Place the peas in a saucepan and cover with water. Bring the water to a boil and cook the peas for about 12 minutes, or until they are tender (if they are very big, the cooking will take a little longer). Drain the peas and place them in a food processor or blender.

Warm the broth in a large pot. Remove 1 cup of the broth and pour it into the food processor with the peas. Puree the peas until they are smooth, about 25 seconds. (For a more luxurious soup, press the pea puree through a sieve.)

Add the puree to the pot, season with salt and pepper to taste, and simmer for 10 minutes. Transfer the soup to a tureen and stir in the sour cream. There may be some clumps; it's okay. Just keep stirring until they all melt.

Toast the bread. Transfer the soup to bowls. Right before serving, place 1 piece of toasted bread into the soup and garnish with 1 tablespoon of the mint. You can also cut the toast up into little cubes if you like. Either way, if you put the toast in the soup, serve it right away, because the toast will get soggy.

Sunshine Mesa Ranch Sorrel Soup

Serves 2

Sorrel is a perennial herb with a slightly sour, intensely lemony taste. When cooked, like spinach, it reduces from a huge volume to a little bit of wet vegetable. Our friends Kathryn and Michael McCarthy have been eating this piquant soup for years. Now we do, too. We serve it cool at lunch and warm at dinner, often studded with croutons.

4 tablespoons (½ stick) butter
3 small leeks, cut into big chunks and washed well
1 medium white or red potato, cut into big cubes
3 garlic cloves
1½ cups low-sodium or homemade chicken broth
12 cups chopped sorrel (about 1 pound)
Salt and freshly ground black pepper
1 cup light cream
Pinch of ground nutmeg (optional)

Melt the butter in a large heavy-bottomed pot over medium heat. Add the leeks, potato, and garlic. Reduce the heat to low, cover the pot, and cook, stirring frequently, for 15 minutes, or until the potatoes are al dente. Add the chicken broth, turn up the heat, and bring the soup to a boil. Wash the sorrel and add it wet to the soup. Cover and cook for 5 minutes. The sorrel will turn a greenish brown color. (It's not pretty, but it's okay.) Add salt and pepper to taste. (Kathryn likes ½ teaspoon salt and 12 grinds of the pepper mill.)

Transfer the soup to a food processor or blender and puree. You should have about 4 cups. Return the puree to the pot, swirl in the cream, and add the nutmeg, if using. Serve hot or cold.

Vegetable Soup with Pesto

Serves 4

This is the ultimate garden soup. Since I grow or have on hand almost all of the ingredients, I end up making it, or variations of it, many times during the summer. It is green and ambrosial, wonderful served at room temperature with a loaf of good bread, a piece of cheese, and a glass of white wine. The recipe, which is adapted from a Genoese-style minestrone my dad makes, is extremely flexible. You can keep that pot going indefinitely by just throwing in another day's worth of fresh vegetables.

1 cup dried navy beans, soaked overnight and drained

2 cups green beans, broken into 2-inch pieces

2 cups chopped cabbage, preferably savoy

1 large carrot, sliced

1 celery stalk, chopped

2 mild chile peppers, charred (see note, page 111), peeled, seeded, and chopped

1 cup chopped sorrel (optional)

Salt

3 quarts water

1 medium zucchini, chopped

1 cup fresh or good-quality frozen corn kernels

1 large white or red potato, diced

1 cup fresh basil leaves

1/2 cup fresh parsley leaves

1 tablespoon pine nuts

2 tablespoons olive oil

Grated Parmesan cheese for garnish

Place the navy beans, green beans, cabbage, carrot, celery, chile peppers, sorrel (if using), 1 teaspoon salt, and water in a large soup pot. Bring to a boil over medium heat. Reduce the heat to medium-low, cover the pot, and simmer the soup for 1 hour. Add the zucchini, corn, and potato and continue to cook at a low boil for 1 hour more.

To make the pesto, combine the basil, parsley, pine nuts, olive oil, and ¼ teaspoon salt in a food processor or blender. Puree until coarsely ground, scraping down the sides of the bowl with a spatula as needed.

Swirl the pesto into the soup during the last 15 minutes of cooking. Garnish with Parmesan cheese and serve.

Marilee's Tortilla Soup

Serves 4

Marilee Gilman makes this delicious tortilla soup with pheasant broth from her own pheasants, but chicken broth will do, as long as it is strong and, preferably, homemade. Now about the hot sauce: Marilee makes her own, and it is intense, but any hot sauce will do.

Other garnishes also suit this soup, such as sliced radishes, chopped scallions, cooked pheasant or chicken, chopped fresh tomatoes, or boiled corn.

2 tablespoons olive oil

1 medium onion, chopped

4–6 garlic cloves, minced

2 tablespoons all-purpose flour

1 quart warm pheasant broth or low-sodium or homemade chicken broth

Salt

1 medium tomato, peeled, seeded, and pureed, or ½ cup canned tomato puree (I like Pomi brand strained tomatoes)

1–4 tablespoons Marilee's Hot Sauce (recipe follows) or store-bought, depending on your taste

½ cup vegetable oil (corn, safflower, or other oil—not olive oil)

About 40 tortilla strips (stale tortillas are best, since they will absorb less oil)

¼ cup chopped fresh cilantro for garnish

¼ cup chopped avocado for garnish

¼ cup grated Monterey Jack cheese (use the large holes of the grater) for garnish

1 lime, cut into 4 wedges

Heat the olive oil in a soup pot over medium heat. Add the onion and garlic and sauté until they soften, about 5 minutes. Add the flour and stir to coat the vegetables. Continue cooking, stirring all the while to prevent scorching, for 3 to 5 minutes, or until the flour begins to brown. Add the broth, 1 cup at a time, stirring as you pour it in. Season with salt to taste. Turn the heat down to medium-low and allow the soup to simmer for a few minutes. Add the pureed tomato and hot sauce. Stir to combine well and continue cooking for 20 to 30 minutes.

Meanwhile, heat the vegetable oil in a small skillet over high heat until it is very hot. You can test if the oil is ready by placing 1 tortilla strip in the oil. If it bubbles violently, place all the tortilla strips in the oil. Fry them until they are golden brown, a couple of minutes. Use a slotted spoon to transfer the strips to paper towels to drain.

To assemble the dish, divide the soup among four bowls. Garnish each bowl with one fourth of the tortilla strips and 1 tablespoon each of the cilantro, avocado, and cheese. Serve with a lime wedge.

Marilee's Hot Sauce

Makes 1 pint

Marilee Gilman's hot sauce is never the same from one year to the next. This recipe is adapted from one called Santa Familia Monastery Hot Sauce.

- 1 cup habanero peppers (about 15 peppers), stems and seeds removed
- 1/2 cup jalapeño peppers (about 4 peppers), stems and seeds removed
- 1 1/2 cups white vinegar (white wine vinegar is okay, too)
- 2/3 cup water
- 1 medium carrot, sliced
- 1 medium onion, sliced
- 1 large garlic clove, chopped

Bring a large pot of water to a boil over medium-high heat. Add the habanero and jalapeño peppers. Boil the peppers until they are soft, about 10 minutes, then drain.

Bring the vinegar and water to a boil in a separate pot. Add the carrot, onion, and garlic and boil until the carrot is soft, about 15 minutes. Drain the carrot mixture.

Place the peppers and carrot mixture in a blender or food processor and puree to a smooth paste. The sauce will keep in the refrigerator for months.

Wild Mushroom Soup

Serves 4

I love this rich, musky soup—crave it, even—and make it frequently in the winter with our frozen wild mushrooms. We also use our own dried porcini mushrooms for this recipe. To dry them, we slice the mushrooms and bake them on a cookie sheet in a 200°F oven for about 3 hours. This recipe is adapted from *The Cuisine of Normandy* by Marie-Blanche de Broglie. I like to add a dollop of mascarpone on top of each serving, but you can use sour cream or crème fraîche as well.

   2 tablespoons olive oil
   I cup minced onion
   I pound wild mushrooms, sliced
     Salt and freshly ground black pepper
  1/3 cup Marsala or other sweet wine
   I tablespoon all-purpose flour
   3 cups low-sodium or homemade
     chicken broth
   2 sprigs fresh thyme
   4 tablespoons mascarpone cheese or
     sour cream or crème fraîche
     Chopped fresh thyme for garnish

Heat the olive oil in a heavy soup pot over medium heat. Add the onion and cook until it is soft, about 3 minutes. Add the mushrooms and sauté until they give up their liquid, 10 to 15 minutes. Add salt and pepper to taste, then add the wine, cover, and bring to a boil. Remove the cover and allow the wine to cook out, 3 to 5 minutes. Stir the flour into the mixture. Add the chicken broth and thyme sprigs. Bring to a boil, then reduce the heat and simmer for 20 minutes.

Using a slotted spoon, remove about half of the mushrooms and grind them in a food processor. Return the ground mushrooms to the soup and stir to combine. Adjust the seasonings.

To serve, stir 1 tablespoon mascarpone into each bowl of soup and garnish with chopped thyme.

Bean, Corn, and Chile Soup

Serves 4 to 6

W e eat this tasty, robust soup when the Olathe sweet corn comes in, around the beginning of August. The chile peppers start to show up at the same time. Often I head down to Caja's Veggies, a fruit stand outside Delta, and buy dense ears of sugary corn, fished from a vat big enough to hold a classroom of children. Then I drive on to the Big B fruit stand near Austin and buy a case of chiles, which they roast right in the parking lot.

- 3 tablespoons olive oil
- 1 large onion, coarsely chopped
- 3 garlic cloves, chopped
- 4 large tomatoes, chopped (2 cups)
- 2 tablespoons chopped fresh basil
- 2 tablespoons chopped fresh cilantro
- 3 cups dried pinto beans, soaked overnight and drained
- 3 small carrots, diced
- 1 celery stalk, with leaves, chopped
- 1 mild chile pepper, such as Anaheim, charred (see note, page 111), peeled, seeded, and chopped
- 1 bay leaf
- 2½ quarts water
- 2 cups fresh corn kernels (6 ears) or good-quality frozen corn
- Salt
- Sour cream for garnish (optional)

Heat the olive oil in a large saucepan over medium heat. Add the onion and garlic and sauté until the onion is translucent, about 5 minutes. Add the tomatoes, basil, and cilantro and cook at a low boil for about 15 minutes, or until the tomatoes break down (or, as my dad likes to say, they make a little sauce).

Place the beans, carrots, celery, chile pepper, and bay leaf in a large soup pot. Add the water and the tomato mixture. Bring to a boil over medium heat, then lower the heat so that the soup remains at a low boil. Partially cover and cook for 2 ½ hours, or until the beans are tender. Do not lose the boil. Add the corn and salt to taste. Cook the soup for 10 minutes more, or until the corn is cooked. Adjust the seasoning. Garnish with sour cream, if you like.

Bean Soup with Cooking Greens

Serves 4 to 6

This is a great way to approach bean soup, especially if you have a garden. Every morning I collect whatever green leafy stuff seems collectible—Swiss chard, beet tops, kale—and bring them up to the house for the day's eating. If I have a bean soup going, often I'll chop up the greens and throw them in to make this dish. The greens add a slightly bitter, iron-y taste to the sweet bean soup, making it a more sophisticated dish. If there is any left over, I just use it as a base for the next batch.

4   strips thick-cut bacon, chopped
1   medium onion, chopped
1   bay leaf
4   cups chopped mixed cooking
      greens (such as kale, chard,
      escarole, collards—the more
      variety, the better)
2   cups dried pinto beans, soaked
      overnight and drained, or 4 cups
      fresh cranberry beans, shelled
1   large tomato, chopped, or 1 cup
      canned plum tomatoes
      (without puree)
2   tablespoons chopped fresh parsley
2   tablespoons chopped fresh basil
2   quarts water
      Salt
      Grated Parmesan cheese

Put the bacon in a large soup pot and cook over medium heat until the fat melts and the meat begins to crisp, about 4 minutes. Add the onion and bay leaf and cook, stirring often, for about 5 minutes, or until the onion is translucent. Add the remaining ingredients, except the cheese, cover the pot, and boil over medium heat for 1½ hours. You don't want to boil the beans hard, but you must keep a boil going.

Partially uncover the pot and continue to maintain a low boil for 1 hour more, or until the beans and greens are tender. (Fresh beans will cook a little faster.) You can mash some of the beans with a potato masher if you would like the soup to be a little thicker. Adjust the seasoning and serve with Parmesan cheese.

Bean Soup with Shrimp

Serves 4

Bean soup has always been a ranch staple. The kids have never rejected it, the adults love it, and the pot can bubble away on the stove without any oversight. Still, bean soup is a rustic dish, so I was particularly pleased with this elegant recipe. Of Tuscan origin, it's a smooth, mellow bean puree bobbing with sweet, fat shrimp. We use frozen shrimp, which are perfectly adequate when cooked in this manner. But if you have access to fresh, that's all the better.

¼ cup olive oil
1 large onion, chopped
2 garlic cloves
2 medium tomatoes, chopped
2 tablespoons chopped fresh basil
2 tablespoons chopped fresh parsley
1 cup dried pinto beans, soaked
    overnight and drained
1 small hard cheese rind, scraped
    clean (optional)
1 small hot chile pepper (optional)
1 teaspoon dried oregano
2 small bay leaves
Salt
1 quart water, or more if needed
20 fresh or frozen shrimp, peeled and
    deveined
Extra-virgin olive oil for garnish

Heat the olive oil over medium heat in a large soup pot. Add the onion and garlic and sauté for 3 to 4 minutes, or until they begin to take on color. Add the tomatoes, basil, and parsley and cook for about 10 minutes, or until the tomatoes boil and their liquid begins to evaporate. Add the beans, cheese rind (if using), chile pepper (if using), oregano, bay leaves, salt to taste, and water. Bring to a boil, then lower the heat to medium-low and cover the pot. Be sure the soup never loses a low boil and the beans are always covered with liquid. If the liquid gets low, add another cup of water. Cook the soup for 2 hours, or until the beans are tender.

Remove the bay leaves and pepper. Puree three quarters of the soup in a food processor or blender. Return the soup to the pot and turn the heat up to medium. Once a low boil has started again, throw in the shrimp. Fresh shrimp will take 3 to 5 minutes to cook; frozen shrimp will take 10 minutes. Serve the soup immediately, garnished with a drizzle of extra-virgin olive oil.

Beef Soup with Sausage Omelet

Serves 4

This dish takes advantage of two things we have a lot of in the North Fork Valley: beef and eggs. It is quite elegant: light, because of the clear broth, but sturdy because of that nice hot omelet inside. I've served it as a first course at dinner parties as well as a main course with a salad or vegetable afterward.

An omelet in a soup may seem odd, but it's common in Gascon duck soup. Likewise, the Mexicans drop omelets into green chile soup, and the Italians put in *crespelle,* a kind of crepe.

4 tablespoons olive oil

1/2 cup chopped pancetta or bacon (about 1/4 pound)

1 cup chopped onion

1 cup chopped carrot

1 cup chopped celery

1 tablespoon minced garlic

1 1/2 quarts store-bought or homemade beef broth (homemade is best)

Salt

4 large eggs

2 sweet pork sausages, casings removed (about 1/2 pound)

1/2 cup chopped fresh parsley

Freshly ground black pepper

Heat 2 tablespoons of the olive oil in a large soup pot over medium heat. Add the pancetta and cook for 3 minutes, or until the fat begins to melt. Add the onion, carrot, celery, and garlic and sauté until they are tender, about 6 minutes. Add the broth, bring to a boil, and reduce the heat to low. Simmer the soup for 15 minutes. Add salt to taste.

Meanwhile, combine the eggs, sausage meat, and parsley in a medium bowl. Add salt and pepper to taste.

Heat the remaining 2 tablespoons olive oil in a medium nonstick skillet. Add the egg mixture and cook over medium heat for 6 minutes, or until the edge of the omelet looks dry and when you lift the edge with your spatula, you can see it is browning underneath. Slide the omelet onto a plate. Hold the skillet upside down over the omelet and flip both plate and skillet so that the omelet falls back into the skillet, cooked side up. Cook the omelet for 3 to 4 minutes. With a sharp knife, cut the omelet into quarters and slide it into the soup.

Continue simmering the soup for 15 minutes more, then serve.

Oxtail Soup
with Porcini Mushrooms

Serves 4

The idea to add porcini mushrooms came from an oxtail soup with chanterelles that I had at a terrific little French joint called Soupçon in Crested Butte. The restaurant is housed in an old-time cabin, with low ceilings and thick walls, and it smells like cognac-warmed gravy when you close the door behind you. I have found hundreds of wild mushrooms in the mountains just west of Crested Butte. The place is blessed. This recipe is adapted from an old *Joy of Cooking* (1956).

1½ pounds oxtails

1 medium onion, sliced

5 tablespoons butter

2½ quarts water, or more if needed

1 teaspoon salt

4 black peppercorns

¼ cup chopped fresh parsley

¼ cup chopped celery

1 mild chile pepper, such as Anaheim, charred (see note, page 111), peeled, seeded, and chopped

¼ cup chopped carrot

¼ cup chopped tomato

1 bay leaf

1 tablespoon chopped fresh marjoram or 1 teaspoon dried

1 tablespoon all-purpose flour

2 cups chopped porcini (boletus) mushrooms

1 cup cooked hominy or one 8-ounce can, drained

¼ cup dry red wine

Place the oxtails, onion, and 2 tablespoons of the butter in a deep soup pot and brown the meat over medium heat, about 10 minutes. Add the water, salt, and peppercorns. Cover the pot and simmer over low heat for 4 hours. Skim off the scum while it is boiling.

Add the parsley, celery, chile pepper, carrot, tomato, bay leaf, and marjoram and continue simmering the soup over medium-low heat for 30 minutes more. If the soup is reduced to less than 6 cups of broth, add another 2 cups of water.

Strain the soup, refrigerate, and skim off the fat. Reheat the broth. Make a roux by melting 2 tablespoons of the butter in a small saucepan over medium heat. Add the flour and stir until the mixture is creamy and begins to turn yellow. Add about 1/4 cup of the broth and cook, stirring, until the roux is dissolved. Add the roux to the soup pot.

Heat the remaining 1 tablespoon butter in a medium skillet over medium heat. Add the mushrooms and sauté until their liquid cooks out, about 15 minutes. Add the mushrooms, hominy, and wine to the soup. Heat through and serve.

Game Bird Broth
with Cilantro Crespelle

Serves 4

I've shot chukar and pheasants (shot *at* them, anyway), but since I
am not usually in the valley during hunting season, I have to get
my birds elsewhere. Luckily, Charles and Marilee Gilman, who have a
glorious spread on Redlands Mesa, keep me supplied with birds from
their cavernous freezer.

I love this elegant soup because it is so dressy and savory. I often
end up making the broth with leftover roasted game bird carcasses,
which are better than raw carcasses because the bones have more flavor. If you use raw carcasses, you should brown the bones in a 400°F
oven first, then dump them into the soup pot with any drippings that
may have accumulated in the roasting pan. You can also make this
with a combination of duck and chicken.

> 4 small roasted bird carcasses, such
>   as quail or chukar, or 2 pheasant
>   carcasses
> 1 large onion, peeled
> 2½ quarts water
>   Salt
> 4 large eggs
> 2 tablespoons milk
> ½ cup grated Parmesan cheese
> 2 tablespoons chopped fresh
>   cilantro
> 1 tablespoon all-purpose flour
>   Freshly ground black pepper
> 2 tablespoons butter
> 1 lime, cut into 4 wedges

Place the bird carcasses, onion, and water in a soup pot. Cover the
pot and bring to a boil over medium-high heat. Cook the soup, covered, for 2 hours. Skim off the scum while it is boiling. Add salt to

taste, remove the cover, and continue boiling the soup until it is re-duced by nearly one half, about 40 minutes. Adjust the seasoning and set the soup aside. You probably won't have to remove any fat (game birds are lean, and these have been roasted), but if some rises to the surface, skim it off.

In a small bowl, whisk together the eggs, milk, cheese, cilantro, flour, and salt and pepper to taste. Heat a small nonstick skillet over medium heat. Rub the inside of the skillet with the butter and pour in about ¼ cup of the egg mixture. Swirl the mixture to cover the bottom of the pan and cook for 3 minutes, or until the bottom of the *crespelle* begins to brown and little holes begin to appear on top, as in a crepe. Do not flip the *crespelle;* slide it out of the pan and onto a plate. Roll the *crespelle* up and place it in the bottom of a soup bowl. Continue doing this until all of the egg mixture is used up. Place 2 *crespelle* in the bottom of each soup bowl. Pour 1½ cups of the broth over the top and serve each bowl with a lime wedge.

All-Purpose Chicken Broth

Make 2 quarts

For weeks one summer, my neighbor Linda Rubick was sporting terrible bruises on her legs from a vicious rooster that lived in her barn. I once told her that my dad always said the best soup was made from an old rooster. It must have stuck, because one morning she called me and said the rooster had gone too far, and she asked for this recipe.

I make chicken broth almost every weekend. Not only does it improve my cooking to use fresh broth, but the recipe is ridiculously easy, and after a while, you start saving all kinds of stuff to throw in, like the bony parts of other birds, celery leaves, and old cheese rinds. I don't freeze the broth, but reboil it every 3 days, which kills any bacteria that may have formed.

1	whole chicken or 3 chicken backs with gizzards and wingtips
3/4	pound beef bones
2	carrots, halved
1	onion, peeled and stuck with 4 whole cloves
1	turnip
1	parsnip
1	celery stalk, halved
1	bay leaf
6–10	black peppercorns
	Salt to taste

Put everything in a big soup pot and add water to cover. Bring to a boil over high heat. Reduce the heat to medium, cover the pot, and gently boil the soup for 2 hours. Skim off the scum while it is boiling. Remove the cover and continue cooking for 30 minutes more, or until the broth is reduced by one half.

Strain the broth and pick over the chicken to reserve the meat for another use. Adjust the seasonings and refrigerate the broth for a couple of hours. The fat will rise to the top and harden. Remove the fat. Transfer the broth to quart jars and refrigerate. The broth may be refrigerated for up to 3 days (see headnote) or frozen for up to 1 month.

All-Purpose Beef Broth

Makes 2 quarts

I almost always have beef broth in the fridge. Bones are plentiful and cheap in the North Fork Valley (this is cow country, after all), and many dishes I prepare call for beef broth.

The trick to making broth is to be loose: throw things in. Once I chucked leftover osso buco into the pot, and the gravy added a wonderful taste. Use other root vegetables, such as parsnips and turnips, or the tops of carrots and fennel. You'll be straining everything off in the end anyway.

3 beef shanks (about 3 pounds)
1 large onion, peeled and stuck with
    5 whole cloves
3 celery stalks, cut into 4-inch
    lengths
3 carrots, cut into 4-inch lengths
1/2 cup chopped fresh parsley
20 black peppercorns
4 quarts water
Salt to taste

Put all the ingredients in a large soup pot and bring to a boil over high heat. Reduce the heat to medium, cover the pot, and gently boil the soup for 2 hours. Skim off the scum while it is boiling. Remove the cover and continue cooking the soup for 30 minutes more, or until reduced by one half.

Adjust the seasonings and strain the liquid. Refrigerate the broth for a couple of hours. The fat will rise to the top and harden. Remove the fat. Transfer the broth to quart jars and refrigerate. The broth may be refrigerated for up to 3 days, or more if brought to a boil every third day, or frozen for up to 1 month.

Note: If you want clear broth, pass it through a double layer of cheesecloth. Alternatively, preboil the bones, drain them, and make the soup as directed.

VEGETABLES

Peas with Mint Butter

Serves 4

One summer I planted a modest mint plant next to the porch door. Within two years, the mint had spread into a bank three feet tall and six feet long, covering up every other living thing and sucking all the moisture out of our domestic tube irrigation system. But I'm not complaining. Supposedly, flies hate mint, and I hate flies. Plus, I use the herb constantly — in bouquets on the table, in iced tea, in jellies and jams, and in this butter.

You can make the mint butter ahead of time. Just push the mixture into a small crock and refrigerate it for about an hour. It will actually stay tasty for quite a few days if you keep it covered with plastic wrap. I also use it on top of grilled lamb chops.

$\frac{1}{2}$ **pound pearl onions (about I cup)**

I **pound fresh peas, shelled (about 2 cups)**

Salt

2 **tablespoons unsalted butter, softened**

2 **tablespoons minced fresh mint**

Peel the onions by rubbing two of them together in your hand. The friction will cause the skin to come off.

In a small saucepan, boil the peas and onions in salted water over medium heat until they are tender, about 12 minutes. Drain and return them to the saucepan.

Combine the butter and mint in a small bowl. Spoon the mint butter into the peas and onions and toss them over medium heat until the butter melts. Add salt to taste and serve immediately. The butter can be made up to 3 days ahead and refrigerated in a small crock covered with plastic wrap.

Green Bean and Mint Salad

Serves 4

A bean ready for the table should be crisp and snap in two easily, and the bean inside should be embryonic. Haricots verts, the skinny little beans you find in the market, work very well in this salad, which requires minimum cooking, but any young, fresh bean (of any color) is wonderful. This salad gets better if it sits for a while—I usually make it about an hour before eating and serve it as a second course after soup or pasta, or next to a main dish.

> 1 pound green beans, broken into
>   2-inch pieces
> ³/₄ cup coarsely chopped fresh mint
> 1 tablespoon minced garlic
> 2 tablespoons extra-virgin olive oil
> 1 tablespoon fresh lemon juice
>   Salt and freshly ground black pepper

Bring a large pot of water to a boil over high heat. Add the beans and boil them until they are bright green and tender but still snappy, about 5 minutes. Drain the beans and run them under cold water to stop the cooking.

Toss the beans in a big serving bowl with ½ cup of the mint and the remaining ingredients. When ready to serve, toss in the remaining ¼ cup mint so that you have some perky-looking herbs on the plate.

Broiled Tomatoes

Serves 4

When the tomatoes come in, they really come in, and we eat them with every meal: sliced with chopped basil and extra-virgin olive oil, rubbed into slices of bread, in pasta sauce raw and cooked, and in salads of all types. But I think one of the most unusual ways we eat them is broiled, the way my father's family in Italy prepares them. The tomatoes produce a savory golden syrup flavored by the garlic and rosemary, which we drizzle on top of the cooked fruit. This recipe is so easy that I often prepare it as a side dish, even for breakfast.

2 **large tomatoes**
2 **garlic cloves, cut into slivers**
2 **tablespoons fresh rosemary leaves**
    or 2 teaspoons dried
2 **tablespoons olive oil**
    Salt and freshly ground black pepper

Set the rack in the top third of the oven. Preheat the broiler.

Cut the tomatoes in half crosswise. Arrange the halves to fit snugly on a broiler pan. Shove a few slivers of garlic and one quarter of the rosemary leaves into the cut side of each tomato. Sprinkle the tomatoes with the olive oil and season them with salt and pepper to taste.

Broil the tomatoes for 12 to 15 minutes, or until the edges begin to brown. Remove the tomatoes from the oven and let them cool to room temperature on the pan. You can discard the garlic slivers or leave them in. Serve the tomatoes with the rendered juices spooned over the top.

Fennel and Red Pepper Salad

Serves 4

I enjoy putting out foods that have a lot of color, and I remember how this salad looked the first time I served it, as a second course following a bowl of bean soup: red and white salad, blue napkins, green chairs, and yellow sunflowers.

2 large red bell peppers
1 bulb fennel, cored and thinly sliced
   (about 4 cups)
¼ cup olive oil
   Juice of ½ lemon (1½ table-
      spoons)
   Salt and freshly ground black
      pepper to taste

Char the peppers by placing them on top of a gas burner or under the broiler. Turn the peppers so that they blister all over, then remove them from the heat. As soon as they are cool enough to handle, peel off the burned skin. Slice off the stems and tops and pull out the seedpods and veins. Avoid washing the peppers, or you will wash away the smoky taste. Allow the peppers to cool, then cut them into slivers.

Combine the peppers and the remaining ingredients in a bowl. This dish can be made 1 to 2 hours in advance and served at room temperature.

Avocado Salad

Serves 4

Weeat a lot of avocados on the ranch in the summer—in salads like this one, in most of the Mexican-inspired dishes I make, and as a cooling condiment in a variety of spicy dishes. I prepare this salad in the late morning and let it sit in its juices until everyone is ready to eat. The lime juice keeps the avocado from browning. It's also nice to serve this with fried tortilla strips on top.

4 avocados, cut into bite-size pieces
1 Vidalia or other sweet onion, thinly sliced
2 medium cucumbers, thinly sliced
24 cherry tomatoes, halved
2 tablespoons chopped fresh cilantro
Juice of 2 limes (about 1/4 cup)
1/2 cup extra-virgin olive oil
Salt and freshly ground black pepper to taste

Combine all the ingredients in a large salad bowl and let sit for 30 minutes or so before serving.

Asparagus Vinaigrette

Serves 4

Yvon and Joanna Gros run the Leroux Creek Inn in Hotchkiss. I love the shortcuts Yvon has created in his kitchen. This is his vinaigrette, and it is so simple, quick, and pleasing that I make it every day the asparagus is in, with both asparagus we buy and the wild spears that grow in our ditches.

1 pound asparagus, trimmed
½ cup olive oil
1 tablespoon white vinegar
1 teaspoon Dijon mustard
   Salt and freshly ground white pepper
2 large hard-boiled eggs, finely
      chopped
1 tablespoon capers

Steam the asparagus over medium heat for about 15 minutes if the spears are fat (less if you use pencil-thin asparagus), or until tender. Allow them to cool to room temperature.

In the meantime, whisk the olive oil, vinegar, mustard, and salt and pepper to taste in a small bowl. Add the eggs and capers and mix them in gently.

Lay the asparagus spears on a platter, pour the vinaigrette over them, and serve.

Zucchini Fritters

Serves 4

This is a ranch favorite, and one of the few ways I can get zucchini into my kids. We usually serve these fritters on a platter, with bowls of sour cream and tomatillo sauce on the table, and let everyone help themselves. The fritters go very well with grilled beef or elk steaks or lamb chops. Plus, if they've been fried hot and dry enough, they'll hold together for quite some time, so you don't have to worry about frying them at the last minute. Be careful, though: if you forget to salt the grated zucchini before allowing it to drain, the fritters may come out too wet. I've also made this as zucchini hash browns (but not always intentionally).

4 cups grated zucchini (2 medium zucchini; use the large holes of the grater)

Salt

6 tablespoons vegetable oil (corn, safflower, or other oil—**not** olive oil)

2 cups grated onion (2 medium onions; use the large holes of the grater)

1 large egg, lightly beaten

2 tablespoons all-purpose flour

Freshly ground black pepper

Sour cream for garnish

Put the zucchini in a colander, add about a teaspoon of salt, and let it drain for at least 1 hour. Press out any additional water by wrapping the zucchini in cheesecloth and squeezing.

Heat 2 tablespoons of the oil in a medium nonstick skillet over medium heat. Add the onion and sauté until it is translucent, about 5 minutes. In a large bowl, combine the zucchini, onion, egg, and flour.

Heat the remaining 4 tablespoons oil in the same nonstick skillet over medium heat. Gently form the zucchini mixture into 8 patties about ½ inch thick. Working in batches, fry the patties in the hot oil until they are browned and crisp, 2 to 3 minutes per side. Don't flip them over too early; wait until the edges start to turn brown. Drain the fritters on paper towels and season them with salt and pepper to taste while they are still hot. Garnish with sour cream and serve.

Café Habana's Grilled Corn

Serves 4

We make this luxurious dish with our excellent Olathe sweet corn. Grilled corn is a popular Mexican street food. The recipe is adapted to accommodate the sweeter taste of American corn, as opposed to the saltier taste of Mexican corn.

If you can't find *chile piquin,* a good-quality Mexican chile powder, you can always make your own by combining 2 teaspoons paprika, 1 teaspoon cayenne pepper, and 1 teaspoon salt. Likewise, you can replace *cotija,* a Mexican grating cheese, with Pecorino Romano.

My friend Richard Ampudia, who owns Café Habana in New York, came up with this recipe.

> 8 ears fresh corn
> 6 tablespoons crème fraîche or sour cream
> 6 tablespoons mayonnaise
> ¾ cup grated cotija or Pecorino Romano cheese
> ¼ cup chile piquin (Mexican chile powder), or to taste
> 2 limes, cut into wedges

Preheat the grill, or preheat the oven to 500°F.

Remove the husks and silk from the corn. Bring a large pot of water to a boil and add the corn. Cook it for 3 minutes, or until it is tender but still crisp. Drain the corn.

Place the corn directly on the grill and cook it for 10 to 12 minutes, turning it often and being careful not to let it burn, or it will taste bitter. Alternatively, you can place the corn on a baking sheet and bake it for 10 to 15 minutes, turning it often. Remove the corn from the grill or oven and insert a skewer or two corn holders in each ear.

In a medium bowl, combine the crème fraîche and mayonnaise. With a flat spatula or the back of a spoon, lightly coat the corn with the mixture. Make sure you coat all of the corn, so that the other ingredients will stick. Sprinkle the cheese freely over the corn, then sprinkle the chile powder over it. Serve with the lime wedges.

Warm Mushroom Watercress Salad

Serves 4

Wild watercress grows in the ditches at the ranch all summer long. I put it in this substantial salad, which is good for a luncheon or second course. I've added thin slices of grilled pork sausage to this dish as well. You can get pumpkin seed, pistachio, or walnut oil at most gourmet or health food stores.

2 tablespoons olive oil
3/4 pound wild mushrooms, chopped
1/4 teaspoon soy sauce
1/4 teaspoon sugar
1/4 teaspoon salt
Freshly ground black pepper
2 bunches watercress (4 cups)
1 tablespoon fresh lemon juice
1 tablespoon pumpkin seed,
   pistachio, or walnut oil
2 tablespoons pumpkin seeds,
   pistachios, or broken walnuts
   (depending on the oil you use)

Heat the olive oil in a large skillet over medium heat. Add the mushrooms and sauté until they give up their liquid, about 10 minutes. Add the soy sauce, sugar, salt, and pepper to taste.

Meanwhile, wash the watercress and cut it into 3-inch-long pieces, discarding the stems. In a salad bowl, toss the watercress with the lemon juice and nut oil of your choice. Add the hot mushrooms (the greens will wilt from the heat—it's okay). Add the nuts, toss gently, and serve immediately.

Summer Vegetable Mélange

Serves 4

This is perfect ranch food: hearty, filling, and fresh from the garden. I combine a variety of vegetables in different ways, depending on what's survived the rampaging skunks from the night before. None of the ones listed below is set in stone. Purslane and dandelion are probably growing in your yard, but you can replace them with any leafy vegetable, such as chicory, kale, mustard greens, or broccoli raab. This dish is derived from one that my dad's Italian relatives make, called *vedura trovata,* meaning "found vegetables." The traditional recipe calls for edible weeds.

I love to eat this mélange at room temperature, with a drizzle of extra-virgin olive oil on top. (My sister likes a sprinkling of grated Parmesan cheese.) But don't let it sit around in an iron skillet, or it will take on a metallic taste. Transfer the vegetables to a bowl until you are ready to reheat them (which you can do in the skillet). You can also add orecchiette or linguine, broken in half and cooked until al dente, just before serving, to make this dish into a main course.

> 2 cups chopped Swiss chard (2-inch pieces)
>
> 2 cups chopped young dandelion greens (2-inch pieces)
>
> 2 cups chopped purslane (2-inch pieces)
>
> 2 cups chopped beet greens (2-inch pieces)
>
> 2 medium white or red potatoes (I pound)
>
> 6 tablespoons olive oil
>
> I medium onion, sliced
>
> 4–6 large garlic cloves, minced
>
> I small dried hot chile pepper, or hot pepper flakes to taste
>
> I sprig fresh rosemary
>
> Salt
>
> Extra-virgin olive oil for garnish

Bring a large pot of water to a boil over high heat. Blanch the Swiss chard, dandelion greens, purslane, and beet greens in the boiling water. Remove the greens and drain them in a colander, but do not discard the water yet.

Put the potatoes in the large pot of water and boil them until they are al dente, about 10 minutes. Transfer the potatoes to a bowl of cold water to cool. Reserve the cooking water. Peel and slice the potatoes.

Heat the olive oil in a large skillet over medium heat. Add the onion, garlic, chile pepper, and rosemary and cook until the onion is translucent, about 5 minutes. Add the greens and potatoes. Cook for several minutes, until the vegetables are hot, then add ½ cup of the cooking water. Turn the heat down to medium-low and cook the vegetables, stirring them periodically to keep them from sticking, for about 15 minutes. Add more cooking water, ½ cup at a time, if the skillet seems dry. After about 10 minutes, mash the potatoes into the vegetables with a fork. Cook the vegetables for 15 minutes more, or until they become soft and thoroughly combined. Remove the rosemary, season with salt to taste, and garnish each serving with a little extra-virgin olive oil.

Fried Zucchini Flowers Stuffed with Refried Beans

Serves 4

Once you figure out that zucchini flowers can be filled (the French have been doing it for ages—they insert lobster mousse), any soft, pliable stuff becomes game. These flowers are a tidy, whimsical way to serve refried beans. They are best used as a side dish.

16 zucchini flowers
1¼ cups lager beer
1 cup all-purpose flour
1 teaspoon baking powder
Salt
½ cup dried pinto beans, soaked overnight and drained
1 bay leaf
1 tablespoon olive oil
2 large garlic cloves, minced
1 tablespoon charred (see note, page 111), peeled, seeded, and chopped mild green chile pepper or canned chopped green chiles
Vegetable oil for frying (corn, safflower, or other oil—<u>not</u> olive oil)
Tabasco sauce for garnish

Check the insides of the zucchini flowers for insects and shake them out. Brush any dirt off the flowers, but do not wash them, or they won't be crisp when you fry them.

Combine the beer, flour, baking powder, and a pinch of salt in a medium bowl and refrigerate for about 1 hour.

Place the beans and bay leaf in a medium pot and cover with water. Bring to a boil, cover, and cook over medium heat for 2 hours, or until the beans are tender. Drain the beans, but save a cup or two of the bean broth, and discard the bay leaf. Place the beans in a blender or food processor with about ¼ cup of the bean broth and process the beans into a smooth puree. If the beans seem sticky, add a little more bean broth to smooth them out.

Heat the olive oil in a medium nonstick skillet over medium heat. Add the garlic and chile pepper and sauté until the garlic softens, about 4 minutes. Add the bean puree and salt to taste. Cook for 3 minutes, or until the beans pull away from the sides of the pan.

To fill the flowers, use a soft plastic pastry cone, or roll two layers of wax paper into a cone and cut a small hole in the tip. Spoon a couple of tablespoons of the refried beans into the wide end of the cone and press the beans down toward the tip by twisting the top. With one hand, gently open the petals of a zucchini flower; with the other hand, pipe the beans inside. You will probably need about 1 tablespoon of the beans per flower. Repeat this process with the remaining flowers. If the refried bean mixture begins to dry out, add a little bean broth to keep it smooth.

Heat ¾ inch vegetable oil in a large nonstick skillet over high heat. The oil must be very hot. You can test it by throwing a dash of flour into the oil. If the flour pops, the oil is ready for frying. Dunk the flowers in the batter and place them gently in the hot oil. Don't put too many flowers in at once, or they will bring down the temperature of the oil. They also mustn't touch each other, or they will stick together. Do not flip the flowers over until the lower edges have turned golden brown, about 2 minutes. If you are using a cast-iron skillet and the flowers stick, let them cook for 30 seconds more. Turn the flowers over with tongs and fry for 1 minute, then remove them from the skillet and drain them on paper towels. Garnish the flowers with a dash of Tabasco and serve immediately.

Chiles Stuffed with Corn and Jack Cheese

Serves 8

The trick to stuffing and frying a pepper is the pepper. It should be shiny and tight; an old, soft pepper will not hold its shape after charring. You can make this dish with thick-fleshed Anaheims or mild-flavored poblano peppers.

I can never make enough of these peppers. I've seen my mother-in-law, Emily Bone, squirrel away a couple in the refrigerator to be warmed up for breakfast. Indeed, they are excellent next to scrambled eggs and hot sauce in the morning, but we usually have a couple of them each for dinner, along with Avocado Salad (page 158) and a cold beer.

1¼ cups lager beer
1 cup all-purpose flour
1 teaspoon baking powder
   Salt
8 Anaheim or poblano peppers
2 tablespoons olive oil
1 medium onion, minced
2 large garlic cloves, minced
2 cups fresh corn kernels (6 ears) or good-quality frozen corn
   Freshly ground black pepper
1 cup grated Monterey Jack cheese (use the large holes of the grater)
   Vegetable oil for frying (corn, safflower, or other oil—<u>not</u> olive oil)
   Sour cream and lime wedges

Preheat the broiler.

Make the batter by combining the beer, flour, baking powder, and a pinch of salt in a medium bowl. The batter should be the consistency of runny yogurt. Refrigerate for at least 1 hour.

Place the peppers on a baking sheet and broil them until the skin blisters, about 2 minutes. Turn the peppers often so that they char all over. Remove the peppers from the oven, and as soon as they are cool enough to handle, slip off the skin. For Anaheims, make an incision the length of the chile and remove the stems and seeds. For poblanos, remove the seedpods by cutting around the stems and pulling out the pods whole. Gently pull out the veins. Set the peppers aside.

To make the stuffing, heat the olive oil in a large skillet over medium heat. Sauté the onion and garlic until they are translucent, about 5 minutes. Add the corn and salt and pepper to taste and continue cooking until the corn is tender, about 3 minutes. Allow the corn mixture to cool, then add the cheese.

To assemble the dish, stuff the corn filling into the peppers. Sometimes the peppers tear, but it's okay. When you fry them, they will hold together. Close the tops of the peppers with toothpicks.

Heat 1½ inches vegetable oil in a large nonstick skillet over medium heat until hot. Carefully dip the peppers in the batter and place them in the oil. Fry the peppers until they are golden brown on both sides, about 2 minutes per side. Drain them on paper towels. Serve immediately with sour cream and lime wedges.

Note: On rare occasions, the batter does not stick to the peppers, but instead slides off. If this happens to you, roll the stuffed peppers in a little flour first. This gives the batter something to latch on to.

Poblanos Stuffed with Grated Zucchini

Serves 4

Once I mastered the stuffed pepper technique, I went kind of crazy. I trolled my garden daily for vegetables to stuff inside. I tried beans (too heavy), mixed leafy greens (kind of mucky), and rice with tomato sauce (not bad). But my favorite was this recipe. The zucchini stuffing is super-sweet and lovely in its crunchy, salty crust. I usually make the sauce for company. When I'm serving it just to the family, I tend to prepare it as a side dish or a vegetarian dinner, garnished with limes and dollops of sour cream.

1¼	cups lager beer
1	cup all-purpose flour
1	teaspoon baking powder
	Salt
6	tablespoons olive oil
2½	cups chopped onion
1	large zucchini, grated on the large holes of the grater (3 cups)
1	cup grated Monterey Jack cheese (use the large holes of the grater)
½	pound zucchini or squash flowers (about 24), coarsely chopped
2	tablespoons chopped fresh parsley
	Pinch of saffron, soaked in 2 tablespoons warm water for 5 minutes
1¾	cups low-sodium or homemade chicken broth
8	large poblano peppers
	Vegetable oil for frying (corn, safflower, or other oil—**not** olive oil)
	Freshly ground black pepper

Make the batter by combining the beer, flour, baking powder, and a pinch of salt in a medium bowl. The batter should be the consistency of runny yogurt. Refrigerate for at least 1 hour.

Heat 4 tablespoons of the olive oil in a medium nonstick skillet over medium heat. Add 2 cups of the onion and cook until it is translucent, about 5 minutes. Add the zucchini and a pinch of salt and cook, stirring frequently, until all the zucchini water has cooked out and the zucchini is soft, about 10 minutes. Turn off the heat and add the cheese. Set aside.

Heat the remaining 2 tablespoons olive oil in a medium nonstick skillet over medium heat. Add the remaining ½ cup onion and sauté until it is translucent, about 5 minutes. Add the zucchini flowers, parsley, and saffron mixture and sauté for 1 minute. Add ¾ cup of the chicken broth and cook until the flowers are soft, about 4 minutes. Puree the mixture in a blender and return it to the skillet. Add salt to taste. Set aside.

Preheat the broiler.

Place the peppers on a baking sheet and broil them until the skin blisters, about 2 minutes. Turn the peppers often so that they char all over. Remove the peppers from the oven, and as soon as they are cool enough to handle, slip off the skin. Remove the seedpods by cutting around the stems and pulling out the pods whole. Gently pull out the veins. Stuff the peppers with the zucchini mixture and close them with toothpicks.

Heat 1½ inches vegetable oil in a large skillet over medium heat until it is hot. Dip the peppers in the batter and place them in the oil. Fry the peppers until they are golden, about 1 minute per side. Drain them on paper towels.

Add the remaining 1 cup broth to the sauce and bring to a boil. Add pepper to taste. Serve the peppers right away, on top of the sauce.

Poblanos Stuffed with Guacamole

Serves 4

One morning at the ranch, Kevin asked me to make him a stuffed chile pepper dish without frying it. This is the recipe I came up with. These peppers can look kind of messy if you've mauled them during the charring process (I often do), but they are absolutely refreshing and quite filling. I've served them many times as a second-course salad at lunch, one per person.

4 poblano peppers
4 tablespoons chopped onion
3 tablespoons chopped fresh
   cilantro
$\frac{1}{2}$ teaspoon chopped jalapeño pepper
$\frac{1}{2}$ teaspoon salt
2 avocados, chopped
1 medium tomato, chopped
Juice of 1 lime (2 tablespoons)
Sour cream for garnish (optional)

Preheat the broiler.

Place the peppers on a baking sheet and broil them until they are blistered all over. Remove the peppers from the oven, and as soon as they are cool enough to handle, slip off the skin. Carefully remove the seedpods by cutting around the stems with a paring knife and removing the pods whole. Pull out the veins and scoop out any loose seeds with your fingers.

Make the guacamole. Combine 1 tablespoon of the onion, 1 tablespoon of the cilantro, the jalapeño, and salt in a mortar or small food processor and puree. In a bowl, combine the puree and the remaining ingredients, except the sour cream, with a fork, pressing the avocado into a mash. Divide the guacamole into four portions and scoop it into the peppers. Garnish each pepper with a dollop of sour cream, if you like, and serve.

Whole Porcini in Parchment

Serves 4

Once we get our baskets of porcini mushrooms home from the West Elk Mountains, we usually spend about an hour poring over each specimen. Those that aren't beautiful get sliced up promptly and sautéed, to be used in future dishes. Perfect porcini, however, are too gorgeous to cut, and so we make this recipe. It also works very well with portobello caps, or any thick mushroom, whole or cut in half.

8   medium porcini (boletus)
     mushrooms
2   tablespoons chopped fresh basil
2   tablespoons chopped fresh parsley
¼   cup olive oil
     Salt and freshly ground black pepper

Place the rack in the middle of the oven. Preheat the oven to 500°F.

If the tube layer of each porcini—the equivalent of the gills—is discolored, spongy, or yellowing, cut it out with a paring knife and trim any dirt off the stem.

Place a large piece of parchment paper (about 2 feet long) on a baking sheet. Place the mushrooms and herbs in the center. Drizzle them with the oil and add salt and pepper to taste. Fold over the parchment and crimp the edges. Place the parchment envelope in the oven and cook the mushrooms for 20 minutes. Remove them from the oven and check for doneness with a fork. Remove the mushrooms from the parchment and serve. If, after you open the parchment, the mushrooms are watery, just leave the parchment open and continue cooking for about 5 minutes to dry them out a bit.

Yvon's Vegetable Terrine

Serves 8

Yvon Gros conducted a pâté and terrine class at the Leroux Creek
Inn one summer, as part of a recreational cooking class series.
Although all the classes started out serious, they inevitably became
noisy social gatherings with great food and wine. I woke up the morning after the terrine class with this recipe and a terrific hangover.

This sumptuous but light terrine is very easy to make and open to
countless variations—whatever vegetable you have can be cooked
(grilled, roasted, boiled) and layered in. Though quite beautiful, it is
not hardy and after about an hour, it starts to soften up. I serve a slab
of it on a plate as a first course, or I serve it for lunch, with a salad. The
terrine must be refrigerated for 12 hours before serving.

3 small eggplants (about 2 pounds
  total), sliced into $1/2$-inch-thick
  rounds
Salt
6 small zucchini (about 2 pounds
  total), sliced lengthwise $1/2$ inch
  thick
4 small red bell peppers
$1^{1}/2$ pounds ricotta cheese
5 large garlic cloves, minced
Freshly ground black pepper
1 cup fresh basil leaves
2 tablespoons blanched almonds
1 tablespoon olive oil
1 tablespoon water

Preheat the broiler. Lightly oil a baking sheet.

Place the eggplant slices on the prepared baking sheet without
overlapping them. Sprinkle the slices with salt, then let them rest for
about 15 minutes. Broil the eggplant slices until they have browned,
about 4 minutes, then turn them over with a spatula and broil them
for another 3 or 4 minutes. Remove the slices and set aside.

Place the zucchini slices on the baking sheet and broil them until they are browned, about 3 minutes per side. Set aside.

Place the peppers on the baking sheet and broil them until the skin blisters, about 2 minutes. Turn the peppers often so that they char all over. Remove the peppers from the oven, and as soon as they are cool enough to handle, slip off the skin. Remove the seedpods and pull out the veins. Slice the peppers into 2-inch-wide strips. (You also can grill the vegetables.)

Combine the ricotta, 2 tablespoons of the garlic, and black pepper to taste in a medium bowl. Set aside.

Make the pesto by combining the basil, almonds, remaining ½ tablespoon garlic, the olive oil, and water in a blender or food processor and blend to a coarse puree. Add salt to taste.

To make the terrine, line a loaf pan (7½ x 3¾ inches) with plastic wrap. Drape one long sheet lengthwise and another sheet widthwise across the pan. Since you're going to be flipping the terrine over, make sure the bottom layer is pretty. Lay the zucchini slices neatly in the bottom of the pan. Top with a layer of the ricotta mixture, about ½ inch thick. Lay the eggplant slices on top of the mixture. Add a layer of pesto and another ½-inch-thick layer of the ricotta mixture. Top with a layer of red pepper strips and another layer of the ricotta mixture. Continue building up these layers until you have used up all the ingredients.

Fold the plastic wrap over the loaf pan. Cut a small piece of cardboard or fold a few pieces of newspaper to create a flat surface and lay it on top of the plastic wrap. Place weights such as canned goods or bricks on top of the cardboard and place the loaf pan in the refrigerator. Refrigerate the terrine for 12 hours or overnight.

Remove the weights and the cardboard and open the plastic wrap. Place a plate on top of the terrine and flip it over. Gently remove the plastic wrap. Slice the terrine and serve.

Italian Rice and Beans

Serves 4

Rice and beans is a ranch staple, in demand during the lunch hour, after we have all worn ourselves out in the garden, irrigating the pastures, or fixing one aspect or another of the ranch infrastructure. I like New Orleans red beans and rice, but I prefer this Italianized version, which is tomato-sweet and garlicky. We eat it in pasta bowls, with warm corn tortillas and an arugula salad.

1 cup dried pinto beans, soaked overnight and drained
1 bay leaf
2 strips bacon, chopped
1 small onion, chopped
1 small carrot, chopped
1 mild chile pepper, charred (see note, page 111), peeled, seeded, and chopped (optional)
3 large garlic cloves, chopped
2 medium tomatoes or 1½ cups whole canned plum tomatoes, chopped
½ teaspoon dried oregano
Salt and freshly ground black pepper
½ cup rice
1½ cups store-bought or homemade beef broth
Grated Parmesan cheese

Place the beans and bay leaf in a medium pot and add water to cover. Bring to a boil over medium heat and boil the beans until they are tender, about 2 hours.

Cook the bacon in a large skillet over medium heat until the fat is rendered, about 5 minutes. Add the onion, carrot, chile pepper (if using), and garlic and cook until the onion wilts, about 5 minutes.

Add the tomatoes, oregano, and salt and pepper to taste. Cover and cook over medium-low heat for 15 minutes, or until the carrot is tender.

Place the rice in a small saucepan. Add the beef broth and bring to a boil. Cover the pan, lower the heat to a simmer, and cook for 15 to 20 minutes, or until the rice is tender and has absorbed all of the broth.

Stir the beans and rice into the sauce. Cook for a few minutes, until they are heated through. Adjust the seasoning. Serve the rice and beans with a sprinkling of Parmesan cheese on each portion.

Chile Potatoes

Serves 4

One year we spent Thanksgiving with Michael and Kathryn McCarthy, our friends who live on Sunshine Mesa. It was a wonderful weekend of pheasant hunting, drinking Michael's home-made mead, reading by the wood-burning stove, and cooking. Kathryn prepared a huge wild turkey with herbs, broccoli with melted cheese, and a big buttery bowl of these chile mashed potatoes. My children went wild for them, and we have been making this dish ever since.

 4 large red potatoes
 3 tablespoons butter
 ½ cup heavy cream
 4 garlic cloves, minced
 2 medium-hot green chile peppers,
     charred (see note, page III),
     peeled, seeded, and chopped
     (I cup), or ¼ cup canned
     chopped green chiles
 I tablespoon salt

Cook the potatoes in a large pot of boiling water for 40 minutes, or until they are soft. Drain and peel the potatoes.

Place the potatoes in a mixing bowl and mash them by hand or press them through a ricer. (Do not put them in a food processor, or they will get starchy.) Add the butter and cream and whisk until the potatoes are light and smooth. Mix in the remaining ingredients and serve.

Note: You can use a hotter or milder chile, depending on your taste.

PASTA

Rigatoni Salad

Serves 6 as a first course, 4 as a main course

I make this dish at the ranch because almost all the ingredients are readily available in my garden, and because it is such a crowd pleaser. I often take it to potluck dinners, as it holds up well on a picnic table. I loathe what is commonly called pasta salad and is actually a Russian dish: cold, slimy with mayonnaise, and flecked with nasty little black olives cured in lye. In this recipe, pasta is tossed with tomato wedges and gently boiled vegetables and flavored with pesto and tuna. My father made versions of it throughout my childhood.

Salt
1/2 pound rigatoni
3 medium creamer or red potatoes, cut into small cubes
1 cup green beans, broken into 2-inch pieces
1 small head broccoli, broken into florets; stems peeled and cut into bite-size pieces (about 3 cups)
6 tablespoons olive oil
1 cup fresh basil leaves
1/2 cup fresh parsley leaves
2 tablespoons pine nuts
2 tablespoons grated Parmesan cheese
1 garlic clove
2 tablespoons water
1 cup chopped scallions
1 8-ounce can tuna packed in olive oil, drained
3 medium tomatoes, cut into wedges
Freshly ground black pepper

Bring a large pot of salted water to a boil. Add the pasta and potatoes. Boil for 5 minutes, then add the green beans. Continue boiling for 5 minutes more, then add the broccoli. Continue boiling for about 3 minutes more, or until the broccoli is tender. (The pasta usually takes 12 minutes to cook at sea level, but since the water temperature goes down slightly when the vegetables are added, it takes a couple of minutes longer to cook. The best thing to do is just take little nibbles to see how everything is doing.) Drain the pasta and vegetables and place them in a large serving bowl. Drizzle with 4 tablespoons of the olive oil and set aside.

Make the pesto by placing the basil, parsley, pine nuts, cheese, garlic, remaining 2 tablespoons oil, and water in a food processor or blender. Pulse the pesto until it is the consistency of heavy cream. Add salt to taste.

Right before serving, toss the pesto with the pasta and vegetables. Add the scallions and tuna and toss again. Add the tomatoes last and toss very gently (you don't want them to get smashed). Add salt and pepper to taste and serve.

Ranch Carbonara

Serves 6 as a first course, 4 as a main course

I like to serve this dish as a first course, in lieu of a potato or other starch, before we eat grilled steaks and salad. It's definitely hearty, but not heavy, as this recipe doesn't call for cream.

12 strips bacon (about ½ pound), chopped
2 large onions, finely chopped
  Salt
1 pound spaghettini or spaghetti
4 tablespoons olive oil, or to taste
3 large egg yolks
2 tablespoons water
1½ cups finely chopped fresh parsley
1 cup grated Parmesan cheese
  Freshly ground black pepper

Fry the bacon in a large nonstick skillet over medium-low heat for 20 minutes, or until the fat melts. Don't be tempted to cook the bacon fast, or it will get too crispy. Add the onions and cook until they are soft, about 10 minutes.

Bring a large pot of salted water to a boil and add the pasta. Cook the pasta until it is al dente, about 12 minutes. Drain the pasta, transfer it to a serving bowl, and toss it with 2 tablespoons of the olive oil.

Beat the egg yolks and water together and add the mixture to the pasta. Toss well. The yolks will cook in the heat from the pasta. Add the bacon mixture to the pasta and toss well. Add the parsley and cheese and toss well.

This is not a saucy dish, so I often add 2 more tablespoons olive oil just before serving to make the pasta shine. Add salt and pepper to taste (this dish likes lots of black pepper) and serve.

Farfalle with Ricotta

Serves 6 as a first course, 4 as a main course

This dish requires as good a ricotta as you can find. If possible, buy ricotta made exclusively from the whey of the milk: no whole or skim milk added. Luckily, this is beginning to show up in markets more and more, and I was pleasantly surprised to discover it in my local supermarket. If you can buy ricotta made from the whey of sheep's milk, you have it made. Hand-packed ricotta is better than processed ricotta.

> 2 cups fresh basil leaves
> 2 cups ricotta cheese
> 6 medium garlic cloves, minced
> Salt and freshly ground black pepper
> 1 pound farfalle or other flat pasta
> 1 cup pasta cooking water
> Extra-virgin olive oil for garnish
> 20 cherry tomatoes, halved, for garnish

Pile the basil leaves on top of each other, as if you were stacking plates. Make a few small piles rather than one large one. Roll the pile up from end to end and cut thin slices of the roll crosswise. When you let go of the roll, you will have a nice pile of basil cut julienne style. Continue doing this until you have cut up all the basil leaves.

Place the basil, ricotta, garlic, and salt and pepper to taste in a large serving bowl and gently combine.

Bring a large pot of salted water to a boil over medium-high heat and add the pasta. Cook the pasta until it is al dente, about 12 minutes. Drain, but reserve 1 cup of the cooking water. Dump the pasta into the serving bowl over the basil mixture and mix gently. Add a little of the cooking water to keep the dish moist, if necessary. Do not add so much that the sauce becomes wet and creamy. Drizzle the olive oil over the top and garnish with the tomatoes. Serve immediately.

Macaroni with Cheese

Serves 6 as a first course, 4 as a main course

This dish is my version of the mac and cheese that you see at every potluck dinner out West. It is not baked, but soft and loose, with the sauce resembling a classic Italian Gorgonzola sauce.

Onion grass is an onion-scented weed grass that grows wild in our yard. You can use chives, which taste about the same.

3 tablespoons olive oil

1 large onion, minced

1 celery stalk, minced

1/3 pound wild mushrooms, minced

3/4 pound Gruyère cheese, grated on the large holes of the grater (3 cups)

3/4 pound Monterey Jack cheese, grated on the large holes of the grater (3 cups)

3/4 pound Parmesan cheese, grated (3 cups)

8 tablespoons (1 stick) butter

1 cup heavy cream

2 tablespoons dry white wine, or more if needed

Salt

1 pound ziti or other small-cut pasta

Freshly ground black pepper

GARNISH OPTIONS

2 tablespoons ground black truffles in oil (I like La Rustichella Black Truffle Pâté)

2 tablespoons minced fresh onion grass or chives

1/2 cup fresh peas, boiled until tender

In a small skillet, heat 2 tablespoons of the olive oil over medium heat. Add the onion and celery and sauté until they are soft, about 5 minutes. Scrape the vegetables into the bottom of a serving bowl. In the same pan, heat the remaining 1 tablespoon olive oil over medium heat. Add the mushrooms and cook until they release their liquid, about 10 minutes. Set aside.

In a heavy-bottomed saucepan, melt the cheeses and butter over low heat, stirring constantly, about 5 minutes. Add the cream and wine and stir. The cheese sauce may look curdled. It's okay; just keep stirring, and it will smooth out. Cook for about 5 minutes, or until the sauce is smooth and the butter is fully incorporated. The sauce will be a little thicker than heavy cream. If it is too thick, add more wine, 1 tablespoon at a time, until you get a creamlike consistency. (When you add the pasta, the sauce will cool down and become thicker.)

Meanwhile, bring a large pot of salted water to a boil and add the pasta. Cook the pasta until it is al dente, about 12 minutes. Drain the pasta and pour it on top of the celery and onion. Add the cheese sauce and mushrooms and mix well. Add salt and pepper to taste. Serve right away with the garnish of your choice. This dish is best eaten piping hot.

Pasta with Beet Sauce

Serves 6 as a first course, 4 as a main course

Beets are an indicator of soil health, and there are lots of beets in the North Fork Valley. This pink dish is particularly flavorful and splendid to look at. It's a real surprise on the plate. My dad had it in Rome, and we figured it out in Colorado, using Sunshine Mesa Ranch's fresh garden beets.

6	strips bacon, chopped
4–5	beets, quartered and thinly sliced (4 cups), with greens (if you can get them), washed
2	tablespoons olive oil
	Salt and freshly ground black pepper
1	large onion, coarsely chopped
1	tablespoon chopped garlic
3	tablespoons chopped fresh parsley
2	tablespoons chopped fresh basil
1½	cups warm low-sodium or home-made chicken broth
1	pound farfalle or other flat pasta
1½	cups grated Parmesan cheese (use the large holes of the grater)

Sauté the bacon in a medium skillet over medium heat for 5 minutes, or until the bacon is crisp. Remove the bacon with a slotted spoon and drain on paper towels. You should have about 1½ cups.

Cook the beet greens, if using, in boiling water just until the water returns to a boil. Drain and chop coarsely.

Heat the olive oil in a large nonstick skillet over medium heat. Add the beets and salt and pepper to taste and sauté for 10 minutes. Add the chopped beet greens, onion, garlic, parsley, and basil and continue cooking for 5 minutes more. Add ¾ cup of the chicken broth and cook for 5 minutes, then add the remaining ¾ cup broth and cook for 5 minutes more.

Bring a large pot of salted water to a boil and add the pasta. Cook the pasta until it is al dente, about 12 minutes. Drain the pasta and place it in a serving bowl. Toss in the beets. The pasta will become a deep pink color. Sprinkle the pasta with the Parmesan cheese and bacon and serve immediately.

Fettuccine with Wild Mushrooms

Serves 6 as a first course, 4 as a main course

My brother, Cham Giobbi, and his wife, Laine, were with us when we first discovered there were porcini mushrooms growing in the West Elk Mountains. Cham made this delicious fettuccine that same night.

1/4 cup olive oil

1 large onion, finely chopped

2 garlic cloves, minced

1 pound mixed wild mushrooms, cut into chunks and slices

1/4 teaspoon soy sauce

1/4 teaspoon sugar

1/4 teaspoon salt

1 pound fettuccine

1 1/4 cups warm low-sodium or home-made chicken broth

3 tablespoons butter

2 teaspoons grated lemon zest

1 tablespoon fresh lemon juice

1 1/2 cups grated Parmesan cheese

3 tablespoons finely chopped fresh lemon basil or regular basil

Heat the oil in a large nonstick skillet over medium heat. Add the onion and garlic and cook until the onion is translucent, about 5 minutes. Add the mushrooms and cook until their liquid cooks out, about 15 minutes. Add the soy sauce, sugar, and salt and continue cooking for 2 minutes more. Set aside.

Bring a large pot of salted water to a boil. Add the pasta and cook until it is almost al dente, about 10 minutes. Drain the pasta and add it to the mushrooms. Add the chicken broth, butter, lemon zest, and lemon juice. Toss over medium heat until the pasta is saturated by the broth, about 5 minutes. Sprinkle the pasta with the cheese and basil and serve immediately.

Penne with Grated Zucchini
and Tarragon

Serves 6 as a first course, 4 as a main course

I make this dish to deal with the abundance of zucchini in the garden and guests in the cabin. The zucchini is meltingly tender, and the flavor of tarragon is strong and appealing. You can get away with using an older, bigger zucchini as long as you remove the seeds before grating.

$\frac{1}{4}$ cup olive oil

2 medium onions, finely chopped

4 large garlic cloves, minced

2 medium zucchini, grated on the large holes of the grater

2 tablespoons finely chopped fresh tarragon

Salt

1 pound penne or other small-cut pasta

2 tablespoons butter

Freshly ground black pepper

$\frac{1}{4}$ cup grated Parmesan cheese for garnish

Heat the olive oil in a large skillet over medium heat. Add the onions and garlic and sauté until the onions are translucent, about 5 minutes. Add the zucchini and cook until it releases its water and the water evaporates, about 10 minutes. Add the tarragon.

Bring a large pot of salted water to a boil and add the pasta. Cook the pasta until it is al dente, about 12 minutes. Drain the pasta and combine it and the zucchini mixture in a serving bowl. Toss in the butter and salt and pepper to taste. Garnish each serving with Parmesan cheese and serve immediately.

Spaghettini with Anchovies

Serves 6 as a first course, 4 as a main course

I eat a lot of fish when I'm not at the ranch, and sometimes during the summer, I miss it. This recipe gives me a hit of the sea without having to search for fresh seafood. It's derived from a dish my father makes.

If possible, use anchovies that have been cured in salt. They are milder than anchovy filets in oil and not at all greasy.

6   tablespoons olive oil
1   large poblano pepper, charred
    (see note, page 111), peeled,
    seeded, and minced
1   medium onion, minced
2   cups minced mixed fresh herbs
    (any combination of parsley,
    dill, basil, and/or cilantro)
4   large garlic cloves, minced
1½ quarts fish broth made from fish
    bouillon (I like Knorr)
1   cup dry white wine
2   whole anchovies, preferably
    packed in salt
1   pound spaghettini or thin linguine,
    broken in half
    Salt and freshly ground black pepper
1   cup grated Parmesan cheese for
    garnish

Heat 3 tablespoons of the olive oil in a heavy-bottomed soup pot over medium heat. Add the pepper, onion, 1 cup of the herbs, and half of the garlic. Sauté until the vegetables are soft, about 5 minutes. Add the fish broth and wine. Turn up the heat and boil for 6 minutes, or until you can smell the vegetables and herbs in the steam. Strain off the vegetables and herbs and discard them. Return the broth to the soup pot.

Meanwhile, if you are using anchovies packed in salt, soak them in water for 5 minutes, or until the flesh is soft. Remove them from the water and, with a sharp knife, slice down the back of each fish. With your fingers, gently pull the meat off the bones. If you are using anchovy fillets in oil, rinse off the oil. Finely chop the anchovy fillets.

Heat the remaining 3 tablespoons olive oil in a small saucepan over medium heat. Add the remaining 1 cup herbs, the remaining garlic, and the chopped anchovies. Turn up the heat and sauté until the garlic and herbs are soft and the anchovy has just about disintegrated, about 4 minutes. Turn off the heat and set aside.

Bring the strained broth to a boil and throw in the pasta. Cook the pasta until it is al dente, about 7 minutes. The pasta will absorb most, if not all, of the broth by the time it is done. Turn off the heat. Add the anchovy mixture to the pasta and toss well. Add salt and pepper to taste. Garnish with the Parmesan cheese and serve immediately.

Pasta with Tomatoes and Almonds

Serves 6 as a first course, 4 as a main course

I always make this dish for big parties in the summer because much of it can be prepared ahead of time and it appeals to all kinds of palates, from young Mo Bone to old Clair Hicks. It is basically a primavera recipe, but I think the tomatoes are more tomatoey if they are macerated before they are pureed.

4 large tomatoes, peeled, seeded,
  and coarsely chopped
Kosher salt
1/3 pound whole almonds with skins
  (1 1/4 cups)
1 pound penne or other small-cut
  pasta
Freshly ground black pepper
Extra-virgin olive oil for garnish

Place the tomatoes and 1 tablespoon kosher salt in a nonreactive bowl and let the tomatoes rest for 1 hour.

Meanwhile, blanch the almonds in boiling water and drain them. When the almonds are cool enough to handle, pinch off the skins. Grind the almonds in a food processor or blender until they are the consistency of coarse bread crumbs.

Bring a large pot of salted water to a boil and add the pasta. Cook the pasta until it is al dente, about 12 minutes. Drain the pasta and combine it with the tomatoes and almonds in a serving bowl. Add pepper to taste, garnish with the olive oil, and serve immediately.

Note: You can use packaged blanched almonds in this recipe.

Farfalle with Smoked Trout

Serves 6 as a first course, 4 as a main course

I make this dish when Kevin smokes a trout. It's extremely sweet and fancy, too. If you want, you can hit each serving with a thimble more of brandy.

4 tablespoons (½ stick) butter
6 shallots, minced
Salt
1 pound farfalle or other flat pasta
4 medium tomatoes, peeled, seeded, and pureed, or 2 cups canned tomato puree (I like Pomi brand strained tomatoes)
1 cup heavy or light cream
¾ pound smoked trout, flaked (about 2 cups)
3 tablespoons brandy
Freshly ground black pepper

Melt the butter in a large skillet over medium heat. Add the shallots and sauté until they are tender, about 4 minutes.

Bring a large pot of salted water to a boil and add the pasta.

Meanwhile, add the pureed tomatoes and salt to taste to the shallots. Cook at a low bubbling boil for about 15 minutes.

Boil the pasta until it is al dente, about 12 minutes. Drain the pasta.

Add the cream to the tomato mixture and reduce the heat to low. The sauce may curdle; it's okay. Do not let the sauce come to a boil after you have added the cream, just keep it very hot. Add the trout and let it heat through in the sauce. Add the pasta and stir well, letting the pasta cook in the sauce for another 2 to 3 minutes. This will break the cream's curdle. Add the brandy and salt and pepper to taste. Toss the pasta in the sauce for 1 minute more, then serve immediately.

Egg Pasta with Elk Bolognese

Serves 6 as a first course, 4 as a main course

Because elk is very lean, it's not the best meat to substitute for hamburger. However, it's perfect for Bolognese sauce, which does not benefit from excess fat. I prefer Bolognese sauce with hardly any tomato, so don't be surprised by this decidedly rich brown sauce, which is made with just a little tomato paste.

Avoid mass-market fresh pasta, since it will often cook up to a gluey mess.

- 3 tablespoons olive oil
- 1 medium onion, chopped
- 2 large garlic cloves, chopped
- 1 pound ground elk
- 1½ cups dry white wine
- 2 tablespoons chopped fresh basil
- 2 tablespoons chopped fresh parsley
- 1 tablespoon chopped fresh oregano or 1 teaspoon dried
- 2–3 tablespoons tomato paste
- 6 cups warm store-bought or home-made beef broth, or more if needed
- Salt and freshly ground black pepper
- 1 pound imported Italian egg noodles or good-quality pappardelle or ziti
- Grated Parmesan cheese for garnish

Heat the olive oil in a large nonstick skillet over medium-low heat. Add the onion and garlic and cook until the onion is translucent, about 5 minutes. Add the ground elk and sauté until it is browned, about 10 minutes. Add the wine and herbs and continue cooking until the wine cooks out, about 10 minutes. Add the tomato paste and 4 cups of the beef broth and stir well. Cover the skillet and simmer the sauce over low heat for 1 hour, or until the broth evaporates. Add the remaining 2 cups broth, 1 cup at a time, as the sauce continues to cook and dry out, 1 to 1½ hours more. If you need more broth, use it (or you can use warm water). The meat in the sauce should almost totally break down, making it almost like a meaty gravy. Add salt and pepper to taste.

Bring a large pot of salted water to a boil and add the pasta. Cook the pasta until it is al dente, about 12 minutes. Drain the pasta and transfer it to a serving bowl. Add the sauce and toss. Garnish the pasta with the cheese and serve immediately.

Elk Cannelloni

Serves 6 as a first course, 4 as a main course

I reserve this dish for special occasions because it's rather time-consuming. But it's worth the effort! Elk produces very little fat, so the pasta stays clean-tasting and greaseless.

You can use dried cannelloni tubes—preferably the kind you don't have to precook (I like Del Verde brand)—as an alternative to making crepes. Just stuff in the forcemeat, cover with the sauce, increase the oven temperature to 400°F, and cook for 30 minutes.

ELK FORCEMEAT

- 7 tablespoons olive oil
- 1 medium onion, finely chopped
- 2 tablespoons finely chopped fresh parsley
- 1 tablespoon finely chopped fresh basil
- 1 pound ground elk or very lean ground beef

  Salt and freshly ground black pepper
- 1/4 cup Vin Santo or other sweet wine
- 1/2 cup grated Parmesan cheese
- 1/2 teaspoon ground nutmeg
- 1 large egg, lightly beaten

SAUCE

- 1/4 cup olive oil
- 1 large onion, finely chopped
- 1 medium carrot, finely chopped
- 3 garlic cloves, finely chopped
- 1 tablespoon finely chopped fresh parsley
- 1 tablespoon finely chopped fresh basil
- 3 large tomatoes, peeled, seeded, and chopped, or 3 cups canned whole plum tomatoes, chopped

Salt and freshly ground black pepper

1/2 cup light cream

2 slices boiled potato or I cup cooked rigatoni or other large-cut pasta

1/4 teaspoon ground nutmeg

CREPES

3/4 cup all-purpose flour

I teaspoon baking powder

1/2 teaspoon salt

2 large eggs, lightly beaten

2/3 cup milk

1/3 cup water

3 tablespoons butter

I cup grated Parmesan cheese

To make the elk forcemeat: Heat 3 tablespoons of the olive oil in a medium skillet over medium heat. Add the onion, 1 tablespoon of the parsley, and the basil and sauté until the onion is translucent, about 5 minutes. Set aside.

Heat the remaining 4 tablespoons olive oil in a large nonstick skillet over high heat. Add the elk, salt and pepper to taste, and Vin Santo and sauté, stirring frequently, over high heat for about 10 minutes, or until the elk is cooked through. Let cool.

When the elk is cool, put it in a food processor with the onion mixture, Parmesan cheese, remaining 1 tablespoon parsley, nutmeg, and egg. Puree the mixture to a thick paste. Set aside.

To make the sauce: Heat the olive oil in a large skillet over medium heat. Add the onion, carrot, garlic, and herbs and sauté until the onion is translucent, about 5 minutes. Add the tomatoes and salt and pepper to taste. Cover the skillet, reduce the heat, and cook the tomatoes at a gentle boil for 20 minutes. Puree the sauce in a food processor, then return it to the skillet. Add the cream, potato or pasta, and nutmeg and simmer over low heat for 4 minutes. Discard the potato or pasta before using the sauce. (The reason you add the starch is to keep the cream from curdling.) Set aside.

To make the crepes: Combine the flour, baking powder, and salt in a large bowl. Combine the eggs, milk, and water in another bowl. Add the wet ingredients to the dry ingredients and mix them together with a few strokes. Don't worry about the lumps. Refrigerate the batter for 30 minutes.

Heat a small nonstick skillet over medium heat. Rub the skillet with the butter. Add 1 large cooking spoon of batter (less than 1/4 cup). Tip the skillet so that the batter evenly coats the bottom of the pan. Cook the crepe for 3 minutes, or until the edge looks dry. With a spatula, flip the crepe over and cook for 30 to 60 seconds. Lay the crepe on a piece of wax paper and cover with another piece of wax paper. Continue this process until all the batter is used.

To assemble: Preheat the oven to 350°F.

Lay 1 crepe on a work surface. Scoop up about 1/3 cup of the elk forcemeat and pinch it into a log shape on the bottom third of the crepe. Roll the crepe up and place it in a baking pan. You will probably need two 13-x-9-inch pans. Continue this process until all the crepes and forcemeat are used. Cover the crepes with the sauce and distribute the cheese over the top. Bake for 20 minutes, or until the cheese melts and the cannelloni are heated through. Serve immediately.

MAIN DISHES

Poached Trout with Horseradish Mayonnaise

Serves 4

This is one of our favorite ways to prepare freshly caught trout. It's a graceful dish that allows the delicate flavor of the trout to come through.

1 3-pound trout or two 1½-pound trout, gutted, with head(s) and tail(s) on
1 large bunch fresh mint
   Salt and freshly ground black pepper
2 cups dry white wine
2 cups water
4 large lettuce leaves, blanched
1 large egg yolk
1 teaspoon Dijon mustard
¾ cup vegetable oil (corn, safflower, or other oil—not olive oil)
1 tablespoon prepared white horseradish
   Lime wedges

Preheat the oven to 350°F.

Stuff the fish with the mint, using the hard stems to secure it inside. Season the fish with salt and pepper to taste.

Pour the wine and water into a flameproof baking pan. Bring to a boil over medium heat. Place the fish in the pan and drape the blanched lettuce leaves over the top of the fish. This will keep the fish moist while it poaches. Place the fish in the oven and poach until it is cooked through, about 25 minutes.

Meanwhile, make the mayonnaise. Place the egg yolk and mustard in a metal bowl. Whisk the egg yolk for a few seconds, then start pouring in the oil in a thin stream, whisking all the while. The mayonnaise should start thickening right away. Whisk constantly until you have used all the oil. Add the horseradish and salt and pepper to taste.

Remove the fish from the liquid and let it cool. Remove the mint and carefully fillet the fish. Transfer the fish to a platter and serve it with the mayonnaise and lime wedges.

Note: If you want to keep the mayonnaise in the fridge for a day or two, add about 1 teaspoon water to stabilize it.

Trout in Parchment

Serves 4

Cooking trout in parchment keeps in the moisture and fragile favors of the fish. It's a wonderful moment when you first open the paper and a waft of herb-scented river trout billows out. Should you have smaller trout, you can wrap them individually and let each diner open his or her own packet. We serve this dish with hot boiled potatoes dressed in olive oil and parsley.

In the rare instance when there is any leftover trout, we pull the fish off the bones and make a salad with sliced boiled potatoes, raw sweet onion, lemon juice, Dijon mustard, and parsley.

1 3-pound trout or two 1½-pound trout, gutted, with head(s) and tail(s) on
Salt and freshly ground black pepper
1 cup chopped fresh basil
¾ cup chopped fresh parsley
2 tablespoons minced fresh rosemary leaves
4 large garlic cloves, chopped, plus 8 large garlic cloves, minced
¼ cup olive oil
2 tablespoons extra-virgin olive oil
Juice of ½ lemon

Preheat the oven to 450°F.

Place a sheet of parchment paper on a rimmed baking sheet so that it drapes over the sides by a couple of inches. Place the fish on the paper and season the cavity with salt and pepper to taste. Stuff ¾ cup of the basil, the parsley, rosemary, and chopped garlic into the fish. Season the surface of the fish with salt and pepper to taste and pour the olive oil over the top. Place a second piece of parchment over the fish and crimp all along the edges of both sheets of paper to create a sort of envelope.

Bake the fish for 20 minutes (15 minutes if you are using two smaller fish). To be sure the fish is done, gently try to separate the flesh from the backbone with the tines of a fork. If it separates easily, it is done.

Combine the remaining ¼ cup basil, the minced garlic, extra-virgin olive oil, lemon juice, and salt to taste in a blender or small food processor. Puree the sauce until it is smooth. Drizzle the sauce over the cooked fish and serve immediately.

Note: You can substitute parsley, cilantro, or French tarragon for the basil in the pureed sauce.

Chicken with Peppers

Serves 4

This is a great dish to prepare in high summer, when the peppers come in. I make it half a dozen times in Colorado and then dream about its winy, herby taste all winter long. The chicken and vegetables are cooked separately, which preserves the individuality of the two very distinct flavors and ensures that the peppers do not become limp and mushy.

6 large, thick-skinned, mild chile peppers, such as Hungarian wax, Italian frying, or mild poblano, or a mixture
8 chicken thighs
1/4 cup minced fresh parsley
3 tablespoons minced fresh basil
3 tablespoons minced garlic
3 tablespoons olive oil
1 cup dry white wine

Preheat the oven to 500°F.

Place the peppers on a baking sheet and roast them for 25 minutes, or until they are blistered all over. Remove the peppers from the oven. When they are cool enough to handle, pull off the skin and remove the seedpods. Slice the peppers.

Wash and dry the chicken thighs. In a large cast-iron skillet, combine the chicken, basil, parsley, garlic, and olive oil. Bake for 30 minutes, or until the chicken is browned. Remove the skillet from the oven, turn the thighs over, add the wine, and return the skillet to the oven. Bake for 15 minutes. Combine the peppers and chicken in a large serving bowl and serve.

Chicken Shoemaker Style

Serves 4

My rosemary grows in great fat bushes along the porch, and there's plenty of the savory herb to decorate the plates and table. This dish, which showcases the clean taste of rosemary, is finger-licking savory, a hit with kids and adults alike.

I've enjoyed versions of it all my life, most notably those by my father's cousins in Offida, Italy, who prepare it with rabbit and chicken (cooked separately, then combined on the serving platter). In Sicily this dish is so named because the chicken is cut into small pieces with slivers of bone, which look like shoemaker's nails.

2 4-pound chickens, each cut into 16 pieces
Salt and freshly ground black pepper
¼ cup olive oil
8 garlic cloves, peeled and halved
4 tablespoons minced fresh rosemary leaves
1 cup dry white wine

Set aside the wingtips, backs, and gizzards of the chickens to use in another dish, such as soup. Wash and dry the remaining chicken parts and season them with salt and pepper to taste. In a very large nonstick skillet (I often use two), heat the oil over medium-high heat. Add the chicken parts and garlic cloves. Arrange the chicken so that the pieces are not sitting on top of one another. Brown the chicken on both sides, about 10 minutes per side. Don't turn the pieces over until they are thoroughly browned. The chicken must be well browned before you add the wine. Add 2 tablespoons of the rosemary and ½ cup of the wine. Cook, uncovered, until the wine cooks out, about 10 minutes. Add the remaining ½ cup wine and remaining 2 tablespoons rosemary and cook, uncovered, until the wine cooks out again, 10 minutes more. Serve.

Note: The savory oil from the pan is excellent drizzled on top of rice.

Chicken Croquettes with Cilantro

Makes 8 croquettes

I make this dish with leftover chicken or turkey. If you make these crunchy, tasty croquettes very small, they are terrific as appetizers. The recipe is adapted from *Craig Claiborne's The* New *New York Times Cookbook*.

CROQUETTES

- 1 tablespoon butter
- 1 small onion, minced
- 1 tablespoon all-purpose flour
- 1 cup low-sodium or homemade chicken broth, or more if needed
- 4 cups minced boiled chicken, bones removed (skin is okay)
- 1 large egg yolk
- 1 dried ancho chile, stem and seeds removed, then ground into a powder (about 2 teaspoons)
- Salt

COATING

- 1 cup all-purpose flour
- 3 large eggs, lightly beaten
- 2 cups bread crumbs
- Vegetable oil for frying (corn, safflower, or other oil—<u>not</u> olive oil)

PESTO

- 1 cup chopped fresh cilantro
- 3 garlic cloves
- ¼ cup pine nuts
- 3 tablespoons olive oil
- 2 tablespoons water
- Salt to taste

To make the croquettes: Heat the butter in a large nonstick skillet over medium heat. Add the onion and cook until it is translucent, about 5 minutes. Add the flour, mixing it in thoroughly so that all the onion is coated. Add the broth, lower the heat to medium-low, and stir until the mixture thickens. It should be the consistency of heavy cream. If the mixture thickens to a paste, add a little more broth to loosen it up. Add the chicken and cook until it begins to dry around the edges and becomes a mush, about 5 minutes.

Take the skillet off the heat and add the egg yolk, ancho chile, and salt to taste. Stir, return the skillet to the heat, and cook for about 3 minutes.

Transfer the chicken mixture to a loaf or similar pan. Cover it with wax paper, plastic wrap, or aluminum foil and refrigerate it for at least 3 hours.

To coat the croquettes: Place the flour, eggs, and bread crumbs on three separate plates. Heat about 3/4 inch vegetable oil in a large nonstick skillet over medium heat until a bread crumb thrown into the oil sizzles violently. Form the chicken mixture into oblong shapes about 4 inches long. Dredge the croquettes in the flour, dunk them in the eggs, and roll them in the bread crumbs. Fry the croquettes in batches, making sure they don't touch one another. Cook for about 3 minutes, or until they are golden. Drain the croquettes on paper towels. Continue until all of the chicken mixture is used, reheating the oil before frying each batch.

To make the pesto: In a small food processor or blender, puree all the ingredients to the consistency of heavy cream. Pour a puddle of the sauce on each plate, place 2 croquettes on top, and serve.

Chicken Legs Stuffed with Goat Cheese

Serves 4

One of my favorite chicken producers in the valley is Paul Chenault, who raises his birds on Closer to Heaven Farms. Paul feeds his chickens non–genetically altered organic feed and houses them in hay bale coops. All this is good, but I think the Grateful Dead music rolling in waves out of the house's open windows is what really makes his chickens so tender.

I use a creamy local goat cheese for this recipe, but you can use store-bought goat cheese. Just let it soften to room temperature before using.

4 whole chicken legs with thighs
3/4 cup fresh goat cheese, softened, or 3/4 cup ricotta cheese, drained in a sieve lined with cheesecloth for 30 minutes
1/4 cup minced fresh parsley
Salt and freshly ground black pepper
1/4 cup minced fresh rosemary leaves or 2 tablespoons dried
8 large garlic cloves, minced
4 medium white or red potatoes, quartered lengthwise and soaked in cold water until you are ready to use them
1/4 cup olive oil
1 cup dry white wine
1 teaspoon all-purpose flour

Preheat the oven to 400°F.

Wash and dry the chicken. With a small knife, cut the meat around the leg bone and push the meat down, like a sock. At the knuckle, remove the bone. If this proves too difficult, cut a deep, narrow gash along the bone, widening it as you cut deeper, to create a pocket.

Combine the cheese and parsley in a small bowl. Stuff about 3 tablespoons of the cheese mixture into each chicken leg cavity. Close the opening with a toothpick. Season the legs with salt and pepper to taste and place them in a flameproof baking pan. Sprinkle the legs with the rosemary and garlic and arrange the potatoes alongside them. Drizzle the oil over the chicken and add the wine to the pan.

Bake the chicken for 40 minutes, or until it is nicely browned. If the toothpicks look as if they are holding, you can turn the legs over, but if the cheese is beginning to spill out, it may not be worth flipping them. The potatoes will be cooked by then as well. Transfer the chicken and potatoes to a serving platter.

Add the flour to the pan drippings and place the pan over high heat on top of the stove. Let the sauce come to a boil, stirring to loosen the bits of skin clinging to the bottom of the pan, and cook until it is reduced by one half. Adjust the seasoning. Pour the sauce over the chicken and potatoes and serve.

Steak with
Charlie's Chimichurri Sauce

Serves 4

C harlie Gilman and his wife, Marilee, who own Four Directions Farm on Redlands Mesa, taught a cooking class on South American foods one summer. The class featured a variety of chimichurri sauces that the Gilmans had picked up on fishing trips throughout Argentina. This recipe is one of my favorites.

CHIMICHURRI SAUCE

- 2 cups boiling water
- 3 tablespoons red or white wine vinegar
- 2 tablespoons olive oil
- 6 garlic cloves, minced
- 10 fresh basil leaves, minced
- 2 tablespoons minced fresh oregano or 2 teaspoons dried
- 2 tablespoons minced fresh parsley
- 1 teaspoon freshly ground black pepper
- 4 bay leaves, broken into small pieces

STEAKS

- 4 8-ounce beef steaks, such as boneless sirloin, about 2 inches thick
- 1 tablespoon vegetable oil (optional)

To make the chimichurri sauce: Combine all the ingredients, except the bay leaves, in a blender and blend until well mixed. Add the bay leaves and refrigerate the sauce overnight.

To make the steaks: Butterfly the steaks by cutting them almost all the way through widthwise. Pound them with a meat tenderizer until they are no more than 1 inch thick.

You can grill or broil the steaks. If you grill, be sure the flames are high and hot. Grill for 3 to 4 minutes on one side, turn over, and grill for 3 to 4 minutes on the other side. Turn the meat over again and slather on the chimichurri sauce. Cook for 1 minute more. If you broil, preheat the broiler to very hot. Heat the oil in a skillet over high heat. Sear the steaks briefly in the skillet, 1 to 2 minutes per side, then transfer to a broiler pan. Broil for 4 minutes, turn the steaks over, slather on the chimichurri sauce, and broil for 1 minute more.

Serve the steaks whole or sliced.

Chili with Semolina Skillet Bread

Serves 4

I usually serve this chili with hot flour tortillas, chopped avocado, chopped red onion, minced cilantro, and sour cream on the table. Although I love controlling the meal, the truth is, my family prefers it when they can make their own garnish decisions, which is why I think this is such a favorite. The chili is cooked somewhat like a Bolognese sauce and distinguished by the addition of sun-dried tomatoes. I like it in a bowl with a squeeze of lime juice and a slice of semolina bread.

I don't care for beans in chili, but if you do, add semicooked pinto beans about 30 minutes before the dish is finished cooking.

1	tablespoon bacon grease or olive oil
1	onion, finely chopped
4	garlic cloves, finely chopped
2	large tomatoes, peeled, seeded, and chopped, or 2 cups chopped canned plum tomatoes
	Salt
1³/₄–2	pounds coarsely ground beef
³/₄	cup dry white wine
2	dried ancho chiles, stems and seeds removed, then ground in a spice grinder (about 1¹/₂ tablespoons)
2	teaspoons sweet paprika
1¹/₂	teaspoons dried oregano
1	teaspoon ground cumin
2	tablespoons sun-dried tomatoes, chopped
1¹/₂	cups water or low-sodium beef broth
1	tablespoon masa harina, mixed with 2 tablespoons water (optional)

1 small red onion, minced
½ cup chopped fresh cilantro
1 avocado, chopped
1 lime, cut into 4 wedges
Semolina Skillet Bread
(recipe follows)

Heat the bacon grease over medium heat in a small saucepan. Add the onion and garlic and sauté until they are soft, about 5 minutes. Add the tomatoes and salt to taste and continue to cook at a low boil for 5 minutes. Set aside.

Heat a Dutch oven or heavy-bottomed saucepan over medium-high heat until hot. Add the beef and salt to taste and sauté, breaking up the meat, until it begins to brown, about 10 minutes. Add the wine, ancho chile powder, paprika, oregano, and cumin. Cover and bring to a boil. Remove the cover and let the wine cook out, 2 to 3 minutes. The chili will be a rich brown color. Reduce the heat to medium-low and add the sun-dried tomatoes, mixing them in well. Add the tomato sauce and mix it in well. Add the water or broth, cover, and cook for 1 hour.

To thicken the chili, add the masa and water mixture, if using, and stir until it is thoroughly mixed in. Continue cooking for 10 minutes, or until thickened. Adjust the seasonings.

Serve the chili garnished with chopped red onions, cilantro, avocado, and lime wedges, with semolina skillet bread.

Semolina Skillet Bread

Serves 4

This is like a corn bread, but more elegant and delicate.

 2 tablespoons bacon grease or
    3 strips bacon
1½ cups semolina flour
 1 tablespoon sugar
 1 teaspoon baking powder
 1 cup milk
 1 large egg
 1 mild or hot green chile pepper,
    charred (see note, page 111),
    peeled, seeded, and chopped

Preheat the oven to 350°F.

Place the bacon grease in an 8-inch cast-iron skillet and put the skillet in the oven. If you are using bacon strips, cook them in the skillet over medium heat until the fat is rendered, about 4 minutes. Remove the bacon and drain it on paper towels. Crumble the bacon and set it aside. Use the fat to carry on with the recipe. Allow the skillet and bacon fat to heat in the oven while you prepare the batter.

Combine the flour, sugar, and baking powder in a medium bowl. Combine the milk and egg in another bowl. Remove the hot skillet from the oven and pour the bacon grease into the wet ingredients. Add the wet ingredients to the dry ingredients and combine with a few swift strokes. Add the chile pepper (and crumbled bacon, if you have it) and combine with a few swift strokes. Pour the batter into the hot skillet and return the skillet to the oven.

Bake the bread for 15 minutes, or until it is almost golden. If the bread doesn't seem to be turning color after 15 minutes, take it out and slip a thin knife into the middle to see if it is done. If the knife comes out wet, return the bread to the oven for another 2 to 5 minutes. Remove the bread from the oven and allow it to sit for a few minutes, then turn it out onto a rack and let it sit for a few minutes more before cutting.

Stewed Beef with Tortillas

Serves 4

There used to be a simple Mexican joint in Delta that served dark little mounds of stewed beef cheeks on top of a corn tortilla, garnished with a sprinkling of red onion and minced cilantro, and a lime wedge on the side. The dish was spectacular in its humility and zest.

This recipe is an Italianized version of that dish. The stewed beef is derived from a recipe of my grandmother's. After making a meat sauce for pasta, she'd set aside the savory cooked meat to serve as a second course. I also love to eat this beef with boiled potatoes.

- 2 strips bacon, chopped
- 1 medium onion, chopped
- 1 medium carrot, chopped
- 1 celery stalk, chopped
- 1 tablespoon olive oil (optional)
- 1½ pounds stew beef (3-inch chunks)
- 1 cup dry red wine
- 1 tablespoon chopped fresh basil
- ½ teaspoon dried oregano
- Salt and freshly ground black pepper
- 2 large tomatoes, chopped, or 2 cups chopped canned plum tomatoes
- Tortillas (recipe follows)
- 1 tablespoon mild powdered chile (optional)
- Chopped onion for garnish (optional)
- Chopped fresh cilantro for garnish (optional)

Place the bacon in a heavy 4-quart saucepan with a lid. Cook the bacon over medium heat until the fat is rendered, about 5 minutes. Add the onion, carrot, and celery and cook until the onion is wilted, about 5 minutes. If the vegetables have soaked up all the bacon fat, add the olive oil. Add the beef and brown it (don't stir, just turn over the pieces when browned on the bottom), about 8 minutes. Add the wine, basil, oregano, and salt and pepper to taste. Turn up the heat to high and boil until the wine is reduced by one half, about 5 minutes. Add the tomatoes, lower the heat to a simmer, and cover. Cook the stew for 2½ to 3 hours, or until the meat is so tender it is falling apart.

You can serve the stewed beef on top of the tortillas as is. Or you can stir the powdered chile into the beef, then place 1 to 2 heaping tablespoons of the stewed meat in the center of each tortilla and garnish with the onion and cilantro, if you like.

Tortillas

Makes 12 tortillas

Who told you tortillas are difficult to make? All you need is a tortilla press. This recipe is adapted from Diana Kennedy's *Cuisines of Mexico.*

2 cups masa harina
1¹/₃ cups water

Combine the masa harina and water in a medium bowl. The dough should be about the consistency of Play-Doh. Lay a piece of plastic wrap on a tortilla press. Place a 3-tablespoon lump of the dough just above the middle of the press. Place another piece of plastic wrap on top of the dough and press. Repeat with the remaining dough.

Cook the tortillas in a dry skillet until brown spots just begin to appear.

Beef Stew with Brussels Sprouts

Serves 4

My brother-in-law Paul Guilfoyle made this quintessential beef stew one night. The Brussels sprouts make for an unusual, toothsome garnish. Paul recommends that you drink it with Burgundy, Barolo, or Bud.

2 pounds beef chuck or triangle flank, whole if possible, otherwise cut into 2-inch chunks
   Salt and freshly ground black pepper
2 tablespoons vegetable oil
I large onion, finely chopped
4 large garlic cloves, finely chopped
I sprig fresh thyme
I bay leaf
I cup sweet or fruity white wine (but any white wine will do)
3 cups store-bought or homemade beef broth (chicken broth is okay, too)
2 tablespoons butter
I tablespoon all-purpose flour
2 large white or yellow potatoes, peeled and cut into I-inch cubes
3 medium carrots, sliced
I large parsnip, peeled and chopped into $1/2$-inch cubes
I pound Brussels sprouts
2 tablespoons olive oil
2 cups fresh peas or defrosted frozen peas
2–3 large pieces lemon peel
I cup cooked rice or couscous (optional)
$1/2$ cup finely chopped fresh parsley for garnish

Preheat the oven to 350°F.

Inspect the beef. Remove any silver skin on it by loosening the edge with a sharp knife and pulling it back with one hand while scraping it away from the meat with the knife. Wash and dry the meat well, then cut it into 2-inch chunks. Season with salt and pepper to taste.

Heat the vegetable oil in a heavy 6- to 8-quart Dutch oven over high heat. Sear the meat in small batches, about 5 minutes on one side and 3 minutes on the other. Transfer the meat to a platter. Turn the heat down to medium and add the onion, garlic, thyme, and bay leaf. Sauté until the onion is translucent, about 5 minutes. Add the wine, turn the heat back up to high, and deglaze the pan by bringing the wine to a boil and scraping the beef bits loose from the bottom of the pan. Return the meat to the pan and add 2 cups of the broth. Cover the pan, place it in the oven, and cook the stew for 1½ hours.

Remove from the oven and add the remaining 1 cup broth. Prepare a roux by melting the butter in a small saucepan over medium heat. Add the flour and stir until creamy. When it begins to color, add about ¼ cup of the stew juices. If the roux looks dry, add a little more of the juices. Spoon it into the stew and stir in well. Add the potatoes, carrots, and parsnip. Return to the oven and cook for 1¾ hours.

Meanwhile, bring a large pot of salted water to a boil over medium heat. Add the Brussels sprouts and cook for 6 minutes, or until al dente. Drain and cut in half. Arrange on a baking sheet, season with salt and pepper to taste, and drizzle with the olive oil.

If using fresh peas, bring a medium pot of salted water to a boil over medium heat. Add the peas and boil for 8 minutes, or until they are tender. Drain the peas and set aside.

Remove the stew from the oven. Preheat the broiler. Add the peas and lemon peel and adjust the seasoning. Let sit for 5 minutes.

Meanwhile, broil the Brussels sprouts until they are golden brown. This takes just a few minutes, so keep an eye on them.

Remove the lemon peel, thyme, and bay leaf from the stew. Serve the stew on top of the rice or couscous, if you like, garnished with the parsley and Brussels sprouts.

Meatballs with Peas
and Mushrooms

Serves 4

This is a fine dish to make in the early fall, when the mushrooms are in the woods and evenings are getting chilly. I tend to use a local ground beef, but ground beef, pork, and veal combinations work very well, too. You can add ½ cup of golden raisins to the meatball mixture to give the dish a lovely sweetness. We like to serve it with rice.

1 pound lean ground beef or a mix-
    ture of ground beef and veal
6 tablespoons fine cornmeal
1 medium onion, finely chopped,
    plus 1 medium onion, thinly
    sliced
2 large garlic cloves, finely chopped
1 tablespoon finely chopped fresh
    parsley
1 large egg white
    Salt
2 tablespoons olive oil
4 cups wild mushrooms, sliced
1 cup seeded and diced tomato
2 cups fresh peas or defrosted frozen
    peas
1 teaspoon dried basil
1 cup low-sodium or homemade
    chicken broth or beef broth

To make the meatballs, combine the beef, cornmeal, chopped onion, garlic, parsley, egg white, and salt to taste in a large bowl. Mash the ingredients together with your hands until they are thoroughly mixed. Form balls 1½ inches in diameter. You should get about 20 meatballs.

Preheat the broiler.

Heat the oil in a medium skillet or saucepan over medium heat. Add the sliced onion and mushrooms and cook, uncovered, until the onion is translucent, about 5 minutes. Add the tomato and salt to taste, cover the skillet, and cook over medium-low heat for 10 minutes, or until the tomato dissolves.

Meanwhile, grease a baking sheet with vegetable oil. Place the meatballs on the sheet and broil them close to the heat. Carefully turn the meatballs over with a spatula and brown them all over, about 6 minutes total.

Put the peas, basil, and broth in a large saucepan and boil for 1 minute. Add the meatballs and pea mixture to the mushroom mixture. Cover the pot and simmer for 30 minutes. Serve.

Pork Tinga

Serves 4

Guests like to cook at the ranch, and my friend Art Chandler made this dish when he and his wife, Lisa Krueger, came to visit our first summer in Colorado. An adaptation of a traditional pork stew from Puebla, Mexico, it's ravishing, wild, and a little dangerous. Prepare it in a well-ventilated place, because chile pepper fumes fill the air as the meat browns.

Serve this dish with tortillas, lime wedges, and sliced avocado. Art also made a tart little salad of sliced tomatillo, sliced onion, olive oil, and fresh lime juice.

4 tablespoons olive oil

8 garlic cloves

2 dried chile peppers, such as ancho, stems and seeds removed, then crumbled

2 pounds pork tenderloin

3/4 cup low-sodium or homemade chicken broth

1 small onion, peeled and stuck with 6 whole cloves, plus 1 medium onion, coarsely chopped

2 tablespoons chopped fresh oregano or 2 teaspoons dried

2 large tomatoes, coarsely chopped

2 chipotle peppers in adobo sauce

1/4 teaspoon ground cinnamon

3/4 pound bison sausages or chorizo, casings removed

1/2 cup water, or more if needed

1/4 cup rice vinegar

To make the marinade, combine 3 tablespoons of the olive oil, the garlic, and dried chile peppers in a blender and puree until smooth. Place the marinade in a ceramic or glass bowl large enough to hold the pork. Add the pork, cover, and let marinate for 2 hours in the refrigerator.

Preheat the oven to 425°F. Scrape off and discard most of the marinade from the pork, leaving some marinade on for flavor. Heat a heavy 6- to 8-quart Dutch oven over medium-high heat and add the pork. Sear until it is browned, about 7 minutes per side. Be sure you do this in a ventilated space, because the pepper fumes are intense.

Take the pan off the heat. Add the broth, enough water to cover the meat, the clove-studded onion, and the oregano. Cover the pan and braise the meat in the oven for 2 hours. Periodically check to be sure the water has not evaporated. If it has, add more.

Meanwhile, place the tomatoes, chipotle peppers, and cinnamon in a blender or small food processor and puree to a smooth consistency. Set aside.

Heat the remaining 1 tablespoon olive oil in a large nonstick skillet over medium heat. Add the chopped onion and sausage meat and sauté for 10 minutes, or until the sausage is browned and crumbled. Add the tomato mixture, water, and rice vinegar. Cook, uncovered, for 10 minutes, or until the mixture is reduced to a thick soup consistency.

Remove the pork from the oven. Reserve the cooking liquid. Let the pork cool, then cut it into thick slices and tease the meat apart into strips. Boil the cooking liquid until it is reduced to about 1½ cups, then add it and the pork to the sausage mixture. Cook over medium-low heat for 1 hour. If the stew seems dry, add more water. Serve.

Pork with Peanuts and Chocolate

Serves 4

S ince this dish is very rich, we often serve it with flour tortillas, diced avocado, and minced fresh cilantro and let everyone help themselves. I've also served it beside scrambled eggs for breakfast and stuffed it inside roasted poblanos that are then fried in a beer batter.

This is an adaptation of an adaptation via my sister-in-law's brother Bruce Valentino, and I think he found it on the Web. Anyway, the recipe is so durable it can take a lot of abuse.

1	dried ancho pepper
1	cup low-sodium or homemade chicken broth
1	cup shelled unsalted peanuts
2	cups chopped tomato
1	teaspoon salt
2	tablespoons olive oil
1	medium onion, chopped
2	large garlic cloves, minced
1½	teaspoons ground cumin
1	teaspoon mild powdered chile
1½	pounds pork tenderloin, cut into 2-inch pieces
3	tablespoons chopped fresh cilantro
	Salt
1	ounce unsweetened chocolate (1 square)
	Salt
2	avocados, cubed, for garnish
1	lime, cut into 4 wedges

Soak the ancho pepper in the broth. When it is soft, about 10 minutes, remove the seeds and stem. Place the broth, pepper, and peanuts in a blender and blend to a smooth puree.

Place the tomato and salt in a nonreactive bowl and allow the tomato to macerate for 1 to 2 hours. Drain the tomato and set aside.

Heat the oil in a large skillet with a lid over medium heat. Add the onion and garlic and sauté until the onion is translucent, about 5 minutes. Add the cumin and powdered chile. Stir, then add the pork. Continue stirring until the pork is coated with the spices and beginning to brown, about 5 minutes. Add the peanut puree, 2 tablespoons of the cilantro, and the tomato. Add salt to taste, cover the skillet, and cook for 35 minutes, or until the pork is cooked through.

Remove the pork from the skillet and shred it, using two forks to tear the meat into strips. Return the shredded pork to the sauce and add the remaining 1 tablespoon cilantro and the chocolate. Cook over medium-low heat, uncovered, until the chocolate melts, about 5 minutes. Garnish with the avocado and serve with the lime wedges.

Leg of Lamb

Serves 8 (with leftovers)

Many times, when I've had a large crowd coming for dinner, I've made this recipe. It produces a super-moist and tender lamb. It's also extremely low maintenance—it needs to be checked only every 20 minutes or so. And I get another meal out of it: Lamb Hash (page 230) with poached eggs on top, for breakfast the next day.

I use frozen leg of lamb because the best quality we can get—local, grass-finished lamb—is almost always sold frozen. This is the reality for small ranchers who lack the infrastructure to distribute their product fresh.

1	5½-pound frozen leg of lamb (see note)
1½	quarts water
2	large garlic cloves, each cut into 4 slivers
3–4	cups hot store-bought or homemade beef broth
	Salt and freshly ground black pepper
2	sprigs fresh rosemary
1	cup dry red wine
	Jalapeño Mint Jelly (page 297; optional)

Preheat the oven to 450°F.

Wrap the lamb loosely in aluminum foil, with the dull side out and the edges crimped at the top (so you will have access to the meat later on). Place the lamb in a roasting pan. Add the water and roast the lamb for 1 hour.

Open the foil and cut 8 slits in the meat. Shove the garlic slivers into the slits. Add 3 cups of the beef broth and salt and pepper to taste. Drape the rosemary sprigs over the roast and close up the foil. Lower the oven temperature to 350°F, return the roast to the oven, and cook for 2 hours. Check the roast after 1 hour to make sure the broth hasn't cooked out. If it has, add up to 1 cup more broth.

Remove the roast from the oven, open the foil, and add the wine. Close the foil and cook the roast for another hour or so, testing with a fork for doneness after the first 30 minutes. The meat should be easily pulled apart with the fork.

Remove the roast from the oven and let it sit for 15 to 20 minutes. Remove the meat from the foil and slice it. Lay the slices on a platter and cover them with foil to keep them warm.

Meanwhile, place the roasting pan on top of the stove over medium-high heat and reduce the cooking liquid by one half. Adjust the seasoning and pour the sauce over the sliced meat. Serve the lamb with Jalapeño Mint Jelly, if you like.

Note: If using fresh lamb, decrease the cooking time at 450°F to ½ hour, then roast at 350°F for 1 hour, checking after ½ hour to make sure the broth hasn't cooked out. Add the red wine, close the foil, and finish cooking for ½ hour more, testing for doneness after the first 15 minutes. Continue as directed.

Lamb Stew

Serves 4

In this recipe, the lamb is cooked much like osso buco, with gremo-lata—a mixture of chopped fresh herbs, lemon zest, and garlic—on top. This dish is sweet and piquant at the same time.

It's a shame we don't eat more lamb in this country. It's delicious, with fewer calories than pork, beef, or dark meat chicken.

1½ pounds lamb stew meat
(3-inch chunks)

½ cup all-purpose flour

2–4 tablespoons olive oil

1 medium onion, chopped

1 medium carrot, chopped

1 celery stalk, chopped

1 tablespoon chopped fresh rosemary leaves or 1 teaspoon dried

1 tablespoon chopped fresh thyme
or 1 teaspoon dried

½ cup dry sherry

1½ cups store-bought or homemade
beef broth

2 tablespoons minced fresh parsley

1 teaspoon minced fresh sage or
½ teaspoon dried

Zest of 1 lemon

1 garlic clove, minced

Wash and dry the lamb. Roll the meat in the flour. Heat 2 table-spoons of the oil in a heavy 4-quart saucepan or Dutch oven over medium heat. Cook the meat until it is browned, about 7 minutes, then transfer it to a warm plate. Add the remaining 2 tablespoons oil (unless the stew meat was fatty and there is fat remaining in the pan—then don't add more oil, since you don't need it), onion, carrot, and celery. Sauté the vegetables until they begin to soften, about 5 minutes. Add the rosemary, thyme, and sherry. Turn up the heat and cook the vegetables until the sherry cooks out, about 5 minutes. Add the broth and return the lamb to the pan. Bring to a boil, then lower the heat to medium-low. Cover the pan and cook the lamb for 30 minutes.

Meanwhile, make the gremolata. Mix the parsley, sage, lemon zest, and garlic in a small bowl. Scatter a little over each portion of stew and serve.

Lamb Hash

Serves 4

This hash is a very homey dish—real Colorado comfort food. One precaution: if you coarsely chop the vegetables and meat, the dish will be hard to serve once the eggs are on top. Mince them, and the dish will be mushy. You're looking for something in between.

1/4 cup olive oil

2 large onions, chopped

2 large red bell peppers, seeded and chopped

2 celery stalks, chopped

1 large mild chile pepper, such as Anaheim, charred (see note, page 111), peeled, seeded, and chopped

4 large garlic cloves, chopped

6 cups chopped roasted lamb

1/2 cup chopped fresh oregano or 1 tablespoon dried

2 tablespoons tomato paste

2 cups store-bought or homemade beef broth

8 large eggs (optional)

1/2 cup chopped fresh cilantro

Heat the oil in a large nonstick skillet over medium heat. Add the onions, bell peppers, celery, chile pepper, and garlic and sauté until they are tender, about 20 minutes. Don't let the vegetables brown. If they begin to, turn the heat down. Add the lamb, oregano, tomato paste, and broth. Mix the hash well and continue cooking it over slightly lower heat for 25 minutes, or until the broth is mostly cooked out. If you want to add the eggs, make eight indentations in the hash with the back of a spoon. Crack the eggs carefully into the indentations and cover the skillet. Poach the eggs for 6 to 8 minutes or until the whites have set or are done to your taste. Serve the hash with the cilantro sprinkled on top.

GAME

Chukar with Figs

Serves 4

Chukar are a type of partridge that live in the fields and canyons in our region. They taste a little less gamy than quail and are a bit larger. (You can substitute quail or other small game birds.)

Ever since I first made this recipe, which is derived from one served at D'Artagnan, a terrific restaurant in Manhattan, I've been pretty good about keeping around some kind of dried fruit macerating in alcohol. For pork and game dishes in general, it's nice to have on hand prunes, figs, apricots—really, any dried fruit—that have been resuscitated with cognac, Armagnac, grappa, or calvados. Just stuff the fruit in a jar, cover with booze, and wait 3 weeks.

> 4 chukar, 12–20 ounces each, or 8 quail, 6–10 ounces each
> Salt and freshly ground black pepper
> 8 figs that have been macerated in 2 cups cognac for 3 weeks
> 1 cup minced shallots
> 4 sprigs fresh sage or 1 teaspoon dried
> 1½ cups low-sodium or homemade chicken broth or game broth
> 2 tablespoons butter

Preheat the oven to 500°F.

Season the chukar inside and out with salt and pepper to taste. Stuff 2 figs into the cavity of each bird. Place the birds in a flameproof baking pan and pour the cognac from the macerated figs (about 1½ cups) over the birds. Cook the birds, basting them occasionally with the cognac, for about 12 minutes, or until they are golden brown.

Remove the birds from the oven and keep warm. Place the baking pan over medium-high heat. As soon as the juices begin to boil, add the shallots and sage. Loosen any bits of meat that are clinging to the bottom of the pan. Bring back to a boil and add the broth. Continue boiling until the sauce is reduced by half, about 20 minutes. Add the butter, stirring until it melts, and serve the sauce over the warm birds.

Chukar with Shallots

Serves 4

Chukar hop all over the cliffs along the Gunnison River. If other birds, such as quail, pheasants, guinea hens, or little chickens, are readily available, you can substitute any of them in this dish, which is adapted from Marie-Blanche de Broglie's wonderful book, *The Cuisine of Normandy*.

4 tablespoons (½ stick) butter
4 chukar, guinea hens, baby chickens, or pheasants, or 8 quail, 6–10 ounces each
Salt and freshly ground black pepper
1 pound shallots (about 32), peeled and sliced
1 tablespoon all-purpose flour
2 cups low-sodium or homemade chicken broth or game broth
4 sprigs fresh thyme, plus 4 sprigs for garnish

Heat 2 tablespoons of the butter in a heavy 6- to 8-quart Dutch oven over high heat. Season the birds with salt and pepper to taste. Place them in the pot and brown them, about 5 minutes per side. Remove the birds and set aside.

Add the shallots to the pot, turn down the heat to medium, and cook for 5 minutes, or until they are soft. Remove the shallots and set aside.

In the same pot, melt the remaining 2 tablespoons butter over medium heat. Add the flour and stir for 2 minutes. Add the broth and stir. Return the birds and shallots to the pot and lower the heat to medium-low. Add the thyme, cover, and cook for 15 to 20 minutes, or until the birds are tender. Serve each bird garnished with a sprig of fresh thyme.

Pheasant Burritos

Serves 4

This stew is savory, spicy, and very flavorful. It's better served rolled in a tortilla than in a bowl: it's a little too intense to eat straight. We use pheasants from Charlie and Marilee Gilman's Four Directions Farm (see Sources), but fine-quality pheasants also can be found at specialty butcher shops. This is a great dish to make when you have only one bird. It is adapted from a recipe by Mary Evely.

2 pheasants (about 3 pounds),
    cut into quarters
4 cups low-sodium or homemade
    chicken broth
1 cup fig, plum, or apricot jam (the
    less sweet, the better), or dried
    figs pureed with a little warm
    chicken broth
1/4 cup sun-dried tomatoes, soaked in
    warm water until soft, then
    minced
1/4 cup soy sauce
1/4 cup dry red wine
2 dried ancho chiles, stems and
    seeds removed, then ground in a
    spice grinder (about 1 1/2 table-
    spoons)
2 garlic cloves, minced
2 sprigs fresh rosemary
2 sprigs fresh thyme
    Salt to taste
8 large flour tortillas
4 sprigs fresh thyme for garnish

Preheat the broiler.

Place the pheasant pieces on a broiler pan and broil until browned, about 7 minutes. Turn the pieces over and brown the other side, about 5 minutes. You can also brown the pheasant pieces in a hot skillet.

Meanwhile, place the remaining ingredients, except the tortillas, in a heavy 4-quart saucepan. Cover and bring to a boil over medium heat. Add the pheasant pieces, cover, and cook at a low boil for 30 minutes, or until the meat is tender. Allow the pheasant pieces to cool in the sauce, then remove them. Strain the sauce and return it to the pot. Cut the pheasant meat off the bones and chop it into bite-size pieces. Place the meat in the sauce, add salt to taste, and cook over medium heat until the sauce is reduced by one third, about 15 minutes.

Warm the tortillas by placing them on a hot griddle or in a skillet over medium-low heat. Watch them carefully, because the line between warm and burned is very fine. Place about ½ cup of the pheasant meat on the bottom third of a warm tortilla and roll it up. Drizzle some of the sauce over the top. Repeat with the remaining tortillas. Serve 2 burritos on each plate, garnished with a sprig of fresh thyme.

Pheasants in Cream

Serves 4

I made this simple, elegant dish for friends in the North Fork Valley one evening. The next day, we threw the carcasses and drippings into a pot of water with an onion, a carrot, a few sprigs of thyme, and some black peppercorns and boiled it down for a couple of hours. After straining, we boiled spaghettini in the broth until it was al dente and served the pasta with minced parsley and Parmesan cheese. This recipe is adapted from *The Memphis Cookbook*.

4   strips bacon
2   pheasants (about 3 pounds each)
4   tablespoons ($^1/_2$ stick) butter
12 shallots, peeled and sliced
$^1/_4$ cup cognac
    Salt and freshly ground black pepper
2   cups low-sodium or homemade
    chicken broth or game broth
$^1/_2$ cup heavy cream
$^1/_2$ teaspoon prepared white
    horseradish
    Fresh marjoram, oregano, or thyme
    sprigs for garnish

Preheat the oven to 350°F.

Wrap 2 strips of the bacon around each bird and tie them securely with cooking twine.

Melt the butter in a heavy 6- to 8-quart Dutch oven over medium heat. Add the shallots and birds. Brown the birds on both sides, about 5 minutes per side. Add the cognac and turn up the heat to medium-high. Cook the birds until the cognac evaporates, about 2 minutes. Season the birds with salt and pepper to taste and add the broth to the pan.

Cover the pan and place it in the oven. Cook the birds for 30 minutes, basting periodically. Add the cream and horseradish and cook for 20 minutes more.

Transfer the birds to a platter and pour the sauce over them. Garnish with the herb sprigs and serve.

Elk Tenderloin with Wild Mushrooms

Serves 6

A whole or half elk tenderloin is a magnificent, kingly meat. The first time we ate it was at Kathryn and Michael McCarthy's Sunshine Mesa Ranch. A huge herd of elk winters in their hay fields, and by law the McCarthys are entitled to cull a couple of animals.

When we order the tenderloin, which is about 6 pounds whole, we ask the elk rancher to freeze it in two pieces. I learned how to cook chanterelles from reading *A Cook's Book of Mushrooms* by Jack Czarnecki.

1 medium onion, coarsely chopped, plus ¹⁄₂ cup minced onion

2 garlic cloves, coarsely chopped

3 cups dry red wine

²⁄₃ cup water

3 pounds elk or beef tenderloin

4 tablespoons (¹⁄₂ stick) butter

2 cups sliced chanterelles or other wild mushrooms

¹⁄₂ teaspoon soy sauce

¹⁄₂ teaspoon sugar

Salt

1 teaspoon cornstarch, dissolved in 2 tablespoons cold water

Freshly ground black pepper

Preheat the grill, or preheat the oven to 500°F.

Make the marinade by combining the chopped onion, garlic, red wine, and ¹⁄₃ cup of the water in a large nonreactive bowl. Add the elk and refrigerate for about 1 hour. Don't let it marinate too long. The elk has a delicate taste that too much marinating will kill. (Sometimes we don't marinate it at all, so it's okay to skip this stage altogether.)

Melt the butter in a medium saucepan over medium heat. Add the minced onion and sauté until it is soft, about 5 minutes. Add the mushrooms and the remaining ⅓ cup water, cover, and cook until the mushrooms release their liquid, about 15 minutes. Remove the cover and add the soy sauce, sugar, and salt to taste. Stir until the sugar dissolves, about 1 minute. Add the cornstarch mixture and continue cooking over low heat until the sauce thickens, about 2 minutes. Set aside and keep warm.

If you are grilling, remove the elk from the marinade. Season it with salt and pepper to taste. Place the elk on the grill and cook until it is just medium rare, about 15 minutes.

If you are using the oven, heat a large skillet over medium-high heat. Remove the elk from the marinade and sear it in the hot skillet, 3 to 4 minutes per side. Place the elk on a rack in a roasting pan and cook for 15 to 20 minutes. The internal temperature should be 125°F to 130°F for medium rare.

Let the elk rest for 5 minutes, then slice. Transfer the mushrooms to a platter and place the sliced elk on top. Serve.

Elk Stroganoff

Serves 4

We usually buy elk from Mendicant Ridge Elk, a beautiful ranch owned by Ed and Pam Bliss, who are good friends. Even so, when Pam leaves a message on my answering machine, she identifies herself as "Pam. With the elk."

This is adapted from *The Memphis Cookbook,* produced by the Junior League of Memphis. You can substitute beef for the elk.

1½ pounds elk tenderloin or beef round steak, cut into 1-x-2-inch strips
3 tablespoons Dijon mustard
4 tablespoons (½ stick) butter
1 medium onion, sliced
2 tablespoons tomato paste
1½ cups water, plus more if needed
1 tablespoon Worcestershire sauce
1 tablespoon sweet paprika
1½ cups sliced porcini (boletus) or mixed wild mushrooms
Salt and freshly ground black pepper
½ cup sour cream
½ pound 2-inch-wide egg noodles
¼ cup chopped fresh parsley for garnish

Combine the elk and mustard in a large bowl and refrigerate for 1 hour. Heat 2 tablespoons of the butter in a large skillet with a lid over medium heat. Add the onion and cook until it is translucent, about 5 minutes. Increase the heat to high, add the elk, and sear it until it starts to brown, about 3 minutes. Add the tomato paste, water, Worcestershire sauce, and paprika and stir. Lower the heat to medium and simmer for 30 minutes, or until the meat is tender when pierced with a fork. If you are using round steak, it will take up to 1 hour. If the sauce seems a little dry before the meat is tender, add a few more tablespoons of water.

Heat the remaining 2 tablespoons butter in a medium skillet over medium heat. Add the mushrooms and sauté until they release their liquid and the liquid dries out, about 10 minutes. Add salt and pepper to taste. Add the mushrooms and sour cream to the meat. Continue cooking for a few minutes more, until all the ingredients are hot.

Meanwhile, bring a large pot of salted water to a boil. Add the egg noodles and cook until they are al dente, about 6 minutes. (Egg noodles take less time to cook than regular pasta, and taste worse when overcooked, so watch out.) Drain the noodles and transfer them to a platter. Pour the stroganoff on top, garnish with the parsley, and serve.

BREAKFAST AND BRUNCH

Amaretto French Toast

Serves 4

I love having a big breakfast ready for my family and company in the morning. But since the early part of the day is always spent outside, when it is still cool, sometimes rushing in to make breakfast before 10:00 A.M. is difficult. That's when this toothsome dish comes in handy.

It's an adaptation of a breakfast dish served at the Leroux Creek Inn. The proprietor, Yvon Gros, makes the bread and cream cheese loaf the night before, wraps it in plastic, and sticks it in the fridge. Doing this doesn't make any difference tastewise, but it is wonderfully convenient to have the thing ready to go in the morning. One note: my kids don't like the taste of liquor, so if you are cooking for children, you may want to omit the amaretto.

I   large loaf soft Italian bread (don't
    use a crusty bread), about 14
    inches long
I   cup cream cheese, softened, or half
    an 8-ounce package
I   cup fruit preserves (not jelly)
4   large eggs
¼   cup heavy cream
2   tablespoons amaretto or sweet
    wine such as Marsala
4   tablespoons (½ stick) butter
    Confectioners' sugar and/or pure
    maple syrup (optional)

Slice the bread lengthwise, as you would for a hero sandwich. Smear the cream cheese on one side of the bread and the preserves on the other. Press the two sides together. At this point, you can wrap the loaf in plastic and refrigerate it overnight. Or you can carry on and slice the loaf into 1- to 2-inch-wide slices.

Whisk together the eggs, cream, and amaretto in a wide bowl. Heat 2 tablespoons of the butter in a large nonstick skillet over medium-low heat. Dunk the bread slices in the egg mixture and place the bread in the skillet — I usually cook 4 slices at a time. Cook the bread until it turns golden brown, then flip it over and continue cooking until the other side is golden brown, about 3 minutes per side. Heat the remaining 2 tablespoons butter and cook the remaining bread slices the same way.

Serve with confectioners' sugar and/or maple syrup, if you like.

Apricot Coffee Cake

Serves 8

I grew up with this moist coffee cake, but once I came to the valley, I started making it with apricot puree, which I think makes it even better. I've also made it with plum puree and with raspberries, which you just drop into the pan after pouring in the batter. The cake is best when it first comes out of the oven. This recipe is adapted from an old, tattered *Woman's Exchange of Memphis Cookbook,* which my mom has baked from for forty years.

1 large egg
³/₄ cup sugar
1 tablespoon unsalted butter,
    melted, plus 2 tablespoons
    unsalted butter, softened
1 cup sour cream
1 teaspoon vanilla extract
1¹/₂ cups all-purpose flour, sifted, plus
    2 tablespoons all-purpose flour
2 teaspoons baking powder
¹/₄ teaspoon baking soda
³/₄ teaspoon salt
¹/₂ cup light brown sugar
¹/₂ teaspoon ground cinnamon
²/₃ cup Apricot Honey (page 296)

Preheat the oven to 375°F. Butter an 8-inch square baking pan.

In a large bowl, beat the egg until it is frothy. Add the sugar and melted butter and continue beating until the mixture is light and fluffy. Add the sour cream and vanilla and blend well. Sift the 1¹/₂ cups flour, baking powder, baking soda, and salt together into a medium bowl. Add the flour mixture to the sour cream mixture and blend well.

Make the topping by combining the brown sugar, 2 tablespoons flour, cinnamon, and softened butter together in a small bowl. I find it is easiest just to mash it with my fingers. It should be crumbly. If it is very wet and greasy, add another teaspoon of flour.

Pour the batter into the prepared pan and sprinkle the topping over it. Drizzle the Apricot Honey in swirls on top. The fruit will penetrate the batter; this is good.

Bake the cake for 25 to 30 minutes, or until a knife inserted in the center comes out clean. Do not overcook; this should be a moist cake. Serve warm.

Note: Instead of making Apricot Honey, you can buy apricot jam and beat it with a little warm water until it is pourable.

Zucchini Flower Omelets

Serves 4

F ried zucchini flowers are one of our staple hors d'oeuvres at the ranch, and sometimes (rarely) we have leftover flowers. We make this omelet with them the next morning. If you use previously made flowers, just crisp them in a 400°F oven for about 5 minutes.

You can also make this dish as a frittata. Just pour the egg mixture into a large nonstick skillet, push in the fried flowers, cover, and cook over low heat for about 20 minutes, or until a knife slipped into the center comes out clean. Let the frittata rest for 10 minutes, then flip it over onto a board and cut it like a pie.

16	zucchini flowers
1	cup lager beer
1	cup all-purpose flour
1	teaspoon baking powder
$1/2$	teaspoon salt
	Vegetable oil for frying (corn, safflower, or other oil—<u>not</u> olive oil)
8	large eggs
$1/3$	cup grated Parmesan cheese
$1/4$	cup chopped fresh tarragon
	Zest of 1 lemon (about 1 tablespoon)
	Salt and freshly ground black pepper
4	tablespoons ($1/2$ stick) butter

Check the insides of the zucchini flowers for insects and shake them out. Brush any dirt off the flowers, but do not wash them, or they won't be crisp when you fry them.

Combine the beer, flour, baking powder, and salt in a medium bowl and refrigerate for 1 hour.

Heat about ¾ inch vegetable oil in a large nonstick skillet over high heat. It must be very hot. (You can test it by flicking a drop of the batter into the oil. If it boils violently, the oil is ready.) Dip the flowers in the batter and lay them in the hot oil. Do not let the flowers touch. Fry in small batches, about 6 flowers at a time. Do not flip the flowers over until the lower edges have turned golden brown, about 2 minutes. If you are using a cast-iron skillet and the flowers stick, let them cook for 30 seconds more. Turn the flowers over with tongs and fry for 1 minute. Remove them from the skillet and drain on paper towels. Do not add more battered flowers until you are sure the oil has come up in temperature again. When the flowers have drained, cut them on the diagonal into ½-inch-thick slices and set aside.

Combine the eggs, Parmesan, tarragon, lemon zest, and salt and pepper to taste in a medium bowl. Melt 1 tablespoon of the butter in a small nonstick skillet over medium heat. Pour one quarter of the egg mixture into the skillet and stir with the flat of a fork until the eggs begin to set, about 2 minutes. Allow the omelet to cook for 3 minutes, or until the edge is firm. Press one quarter of the fried zucchini flowers onto half of the omelet. Flip the opposing half over the flowers and close the edges of the omelet by gently pressing with the tines of the fork. Continue cooking for 3 minutes more. Serve immediately. Repeat to make the remaining 3 omelets.

Note: You can make one large omelet, using all the ingredients at once. To serve, just cut it into quarters.

Stewed Onion and Jack Cheese Omelets

Serves 4

This recipe calls for a lot of onions, but they cook way down and become very sweet. If you use store-bought beef broth, don't salt the onions, only the eggs. You can make one large omelet, using all the ingredients at once, and cut it into quarters.

$1/4$ cup olive oil

4 medium-large onions, thinly sliced

2 cups store-bought or homemade beef broth

2 tablespoons minced fresh marjoram or $1^1/2$ teaspoons dried

Salt and freshly ground black pepper

8 large eggs

2 tablespoons butter

1 cup grated Monterey Jack cheese (use the large holes of the grater)

Heat the oil in a medium heavy-bottomed pot over medium heat. Add the onions and sauté for about 20 minutes, stirring frequently until they are translucent, tattered, and beginning to dry out. Add the broth and marjoram. Boil gently over medium heat, uncovered, for 45 minutes, or until the broth evaporates and the onions are reduced to about 2 cups. Add salt and pepper to taste.

Beat 2 of the eggs in a bowl and add salt and pepper to taste. Heat a small nonstick skillet over medium-low heat. Melt $1/2$ tablespoon butter in the skillet, add the eggs, and stir with the flat of a fork until they begin to set, about 2 minutes. Allow the omelet to cook for about 3 minutes, or until the edge is firm and the eggs seem wet but no longer soupy. Place one fourth of the cheese and one fourth of the onions on one half of the omelet. Gently flip the other half over the filling. Continue cooking the omelet for about 3 minutes more, or until firm. Serve immediately. Repeat to make the remaining 3 omelets.

Eggs and Vegetables

Serves 4

This recipe really sings, due in part to the incredibly fresh eggs we get. The vegetable stew can be made countless ways. Be sure to cook the vegetables until they are soft and chop them small enough to create a nice nest for the eggs. At the ranch, we eat this with hot sauce and warm tortillas.

> ¼ cup olive oil
> 2 red bell peppers, seeded and chopped
> 2 medium onions, chopped
> 2 large tomatoes, peeled, seeded, and chopped
> 1 medium zucchini, sliced into rounds and chopped
> 2 tablespoons chopped fresh basil or 1 tablespoon dried
> Salt
> 8 large eggs
> Grated Parmesan cheese
> Freshly ground black pepper

Heat the olive oil in a large skillet with a cover over medium heat. Add the peppers and onions and cook for 8 minutes, or until the peppers are almost soft. Add the tomatoes, zucchini, and basil and cook for 10 minutes, or until all the vegetables are soft. Add salt to taste.

With the back of a spoon, create eight indentations in the vegetables. Carefully crack the eggs into the indentations. Don't let the eggs touch the bare bottom or sides of the pan, or they will burn or stick. Turn the heat down to medium-low, cover, and cook until the whites of the eggs are set, 6 to 8 minutes. Sprinkle cheese and salt and pepper to taste over the eggs and serve immediately.

Scrambled Egg Enchiladas

Serves 4

We use our own ancho peppers in this dish, but store-bought ones work perfectly well. You almost need another pair of hands to make these excellent enchiladas, but the result is worth the effort. This recipe is adapted from one by Joe Gracey, originally published in his wife, Kimmie Rhodes's, book, *The Amazing Afterlife of Zimmerman Fees,* a wild, out-of-body travelogue with recipes.

2 cups store-bought or homemade chicken broth

2 dried ancho peppers, stems and seeds removed

4 tablespoons olive oil

2 cups chopped onion, plus ½ cup chopped onion for garnish (optional)

I tablespoon minced fresh oregano or I teaspoon dried

I teaspoon ground cumin, or more to taste

Salt

6 large eggs

1½ cups minced fresh cilantro

Vegetable oil for frying (corn, safflower, or other oil—<u>not</u> olive oil)

8 corn tortillas

1½ cups grated Monterey Jack or mild cheddar cheese (use the large holes of the grater)

Preheat the oven to 400°F.

In a small saucepan, heat the chicken broth over medium heat. Add the peppers and cook until they are soft, about 10 minutes.

In a small skillet, heat 2 tablespoons of the olive oil over medium heat. Add 1 cup of the onion and sauté until it is soft, about 5 minutes.

In a blender, combine the peppers, 1 cup of the broth (be sure to reserve the remaining broth), and the sautéed onion. Puree until the mixture is a loose paste.

In a large skillet, combine the pepper paste, the remaining 1 cup broth, the oregano, cumin, and salt to taste. Cook over medium-low heat until the mixture is reduced by about one quarter and the sauce thickens, about 10 minutes.

In a medium bowl, whisk together the eggs and 1 cup of the cilantro.

In a medium skillet, heat the remaining 2 tablespoons olive oil. Add the remaining 1 cup onion and sauté over medium heat until it is soft, about 5 minutes. Add the egg mixture and scramble the eggs until they are done but soft, about 5 minutes. Set aside.

In a small skillet, heat about 1 inch vegetable oil over medium heat until the oil is hot enough to pop when you throw in a pinch of flour.

Now have everything ready (and be ready to get a little messy). Smear a couple of tablespoons of the pepper sauce in the bottom of a 12-x-6-x-2-inch baking dish. Fry the tortillas one at a time in the vegetable oil. Fry only a couple of seconds on each side so that the tortillas are soft and pliable. Dredge the tortillas in the sauce and place them on a big plate.

Starting with the top tortilla, spoon about ¼ cup of the scrambled eggs onto the bottom third of the tortilla. Roll it up and place it in the baking dish. Continue with all the remaining tortillas. Pour the remaining sauce over the tortillas and sprinkle them with the cheese. If the sauce has gotten too thick to pour, add a little warm water or warm chicken broth to loosen it up.

Bake the enchiladas for 15 to 20 minutes, or until the cheese is melted. Serve garnished with the remaining ½ cup cilantro and ½ cup chopped onion, if using.

Chanterelle Crepes

Makes about 12 crepes

After spending an afternoon visiting the vineyards around Grand Junction, my brother, Cham Giobbi, his wife, Laine, and I headed over the Grand Mesa toward home. We stopped midway across the mesa, at about nine thousand feet, and there found a colony of orange chanterelles growing in a grove of soaring blue spruces. We made this delicate dish for dinner that night.

Queso anejo is an aged, salty, crumbly cheese from Mexico. The best substitute I know for it is dried ricotta, also called *ricotta salata.*

FILLING

- 5 tablespoons butter
- 1 medium onion, chopped
- 2 pounds chanterelles or other wild mushrooms, cut into 2-inch pieces
- 1/2 teaspoon sugar
- 1/2 teaspoon salt
- 1/2 teaspoon soy sauce
- 2 cups crumbled queso anejo or dried ricotta cheese (ricotta salata)

CREPES

- 3/4 cup all-purpose flour
- 1 teaspoon baking powder
- 1/2 teaspoon salt
- 2/3 cup milk
- 2 large eggs, lightly beaten
- 1/3 cup water

To make the filling: Heat 2 tablespoons of the butter in a large non-stick skillet over medium heat. Add the onion and cook until it is translucent, about 5 minutes. Add the mushrooms and cook until the liquid cooks out, about 15 minutes. Add the sugar, salt, and soy sauce and stir well. Transfer the mushrooms to a bowl. Add 1 cup of the cheese and carefully mix it in.

To make the crepes: Combine the flour, baking powder, and salt in a bowl. In a separate bowl, combine the milk, eggs, and water. Add the wet ingredients to the dry ingredients and mix them together with a few swift strokes. Don't worry about the lumps. Refrigerate the batter for 30 minutes.

Heat a small nonstick skillet over medium heat. Rub the interior of the skillet with some of the remaining 3 tablespoons butter. Add 1 large cooking spoon of batter (less than ¼ cup). Tip the skillet so that the batter evenly coats the bottom of the pan. Cook the crepe for 3 minutes, or until the edge looks dry. With a spatula, flip the crepe over and cook for 30 to 60 seconds. Lay the crepe on a piece of wax paper and cover with another piece of wax paper. Continue this process until all the batter is used up.

To assemble: Preheat the oven to 400°F. Place 1 crepe on a clean counter or other surface. Place about 3 tablespoons of the mushroom mixture on the lower third of the crepe, roll it up, and place it in a 13-x-9-inch baking dish. Continue doing this until all the crepes are filled (you may need a second dish). Distribute the remaining 1 cup cheese evenly over the crepes. Bake the crepes until the cheese is melted and the mushrooms are heated through, about 10 minutes. Serve.

Broiled Pepper Tart

Makes one 9-inch tart

There are always lots of peppers hanging around our kitchen in Colorado, and often I just roast and peel them and serve them with garlic, olive oil, and salt. Any and all leftover roasted peppers — green, yellow, or red peppers — go into this neat little tart — the more colors the better. This savory dish is tasty as a first course and terrific as a light main course, served with a green salad and a glass of white wine.

You can use any combination of broiled mild peppers. You can add cooked sliced onions as well.

I red bell pepper
I green bell pepper
2 poblano peppers
2 mild Hungarian wax peppers (or hot, if you like)
I Anaheim pepper
4 tablespoons (1/2 stick) cold butter
I cup all-purpose flour
1/2 teaspoon salt
I large egg
1/2–I teaspoon cold water, as needed
I cup fresh goat cheese
3 large egg yolks
Salt (optional)
Freshly ground black pepper

Preheat the broiler.

Place the peppers on a baking sheet and broil on all sides until they blister. Remove the peppers from the oven. When they are cool enough to handle, remove the skin, stems, seeds, and veins. Cut the peppers into thin matchsticks. (There should be about 2 cups.) Place the peppers in a colander and allow them to drain.

Preheat the oven to 350°F. Butter a 9-inch tart pan.

To make the pastry, cut the butter into pieces and place it in a food processor with the flour, salt, and egg. Pulse the processor to blend the dough until it forms a ball, or a lot of tiny soft balls, about 1 minute. Add the water if the dough is not coming together. Wrap the dough in wax paper and refrigerate it for about 30 minutes.

On a lightly floured surface, roll out the dough by pressing in the center of the ball with your rolling pin and slowly pressing outward in all directions. Place the dough in the prepared tart pan. Spread the peppers evenly in the crust.

Combine the goat cheese and egg yolks in a blender and puree until the mixture is smooth. If the goat cheese is salty, do not add salt. If it is not salty, add salt to taste. Add black pepper to taste. Pour the cheese mixture over the peppers.

Place the tart on a baking sheet and bake for 30 minutes, or until the top is just beginning to brown and looks puffy and a knife inserted in the middle comes out dry. Allow the tart to sit for 5 minutes before cutting and serving.

Leek and Cilantro Pesto Tart

Makes one 9-inch tart

I took this tasty tart to a potluck winetasting at Ela Family Farms on Rogers Mesa. We drank Chilean wine and watched a big orange moon rise between the peach trees.

4 large leeks, washed well and sliced
   into thin rounds (6 cups)
1 tablespoon unsalted butter, plus
   4 tablespoons (1/2 stick) butter,
   cut into large pieces
1 large egg
1 cup all-purpose flour
1/2–1 teaspoon cold water, as needed
3 large egg yolks
1 cup heavy cream
   Salt and freshly ground black pepper
1 cup fresh cilantro leaves
1/4 cup pine nuts
1/4 cup olive oil
1 large garlic clove

Preheat the oven to 350°F. Butter a 9-inch tart pan.

Heat 1 tablespoon of the butter in a large nonstick skillet over medium heat. Add the leeks and cook until they are soft, about 15 minutes, stirring frequently to be sure they do not burn.

To make the pastry, cut the remaining 4 tablespoons butter into pieces and place in a food processor with the egg and flour. Pulse to blend until the dough forms a ball, or a lot of tiny soft balls, about 1 minute. Add the water if the dough is not coming together. Wrap the dough in wax paper and refrigerate it for about 30 minutes.

In a large bowl, whisk together the egg yolks and cream. Add the cooked leeks and salt and pepper to taste and combine.

In a food processor or blender, combine the cilantro, pine nuts, olive oil, and garlic until the mixture is a nubbly puree. Add salt to taste.

On a lightly floured surface, roll out the dough by pressing in the center of the ball with your rolling pin and slowly pressing outward in all directions. Place the dough in the tart pan. Pour in the leek mixture. Spread the cilantro pesto over the top as best you can (it doesn't have to cover the entire top).

Place the tart on a baking sheet and bake for 30 minutes, or until the top is just beginning to brown and looks puffy and a knife inserted in the middle comes out dry. Allow the tart to sit for 5 minutes before cutting and serving.

Ricotta Pie

Serves 8 as a first course, 4 as a main course

A wonderful dish for brunch or supper, ricotta pie is a favorite at our house (which means the children will eat it). The ricotta holds up marvelously, and the pie is substantial enough to satisfy the men who help Kevin with various ranch projects and who always seem to be around for meals. My aunt Ada from Italy makes this dish with ricotta and artichoke hearts. My dad and I developed this version.

FILLING

- 1½ pounds spinach (two 10-ounce bags), washed and picked over
- 2 pounds ricotta cheese (two 15-ounce containers)
- 1 cup chopped boiled ham (optional)
- 2 large egg whites
- 3 tablespoons chopped fresh parsley
- ½ teaspoon ground nutmeg
- Salt and freshly ground black pepper

CRUST

- 2 cups all-purpose flour
- 8 tablespoons (1 stick) unsalted butter, cut into large pieces
- 2 large eggs
- Pinch of salt
- Pinch of yeast, dissolved in 1 teaspoon water
- ½–1 teaspoon cold water, as needed

Preheat the oven to 350°F. Butter a deep 9-inch pie plate.

To make the filling: Steam the spinach for 5 to 7 minutes, or until wilted. Drain and allow it to cool. Squeeze out all the water you can and chop it coarsely. You should have about 2 cups. In a large bowl, combine the spinach, ricotta, ham (if using), egg whites, parsley, nutmeg, and salt and pepper to taste.

To make the crust: Make the crust by combining all the ingredients in a food processor and pulsing for about 60 seconds, or until the dough forms a ball. If the dough does not come together in a ball, or many small balls, add the cold water and pulse again.

Separate the dough into 2 balls, one a little larger than the other. Wrap the dough in wax paper and refrigerate it for 30 minutes.

On a lightly floured surface, roll out the larger dough ball by pressing in the center with your rolling pin and slowly pressing outward in all directions. Place the dough in the prepared pie plate. Place the spinach and ricotta mixture in the crust.

On a lightly floured surface, roll out the remaining dough ball by pressing in the center with your rolling pin and slowly pressing outward in all directions. Place the dough on top of the pie. Crimp the edges and cut a few slashes in the top. Brush the top with a little water or beaten egg and bake for 1 hour, or until the top is nicely browned and a toothpick inserted in the center comes clean. Cool slightly, cut into wedges, and serve.

DESSERTS

Cantaloupe Freeze

Serves 4

M rs. Burritt's cantaloupes, which she grows on Redlands Mesa, are known to everyone in the valley. Ripened on the vine, they are small and sweet. Only after we have finished gorging ourselves on fresh cantaloupe do we freeze what's left into a no-egg gelato and serve it with whipped cream. I learned the technique for this dish from an excellent New York–based home cook named Hisachika Takahashi. He makes it with mangoes, lemon juice, and crème fraîche. This is the Colorado version, which I usually prepare the night before I plan to serve it. You can substitute fresh peaches for the cantaloupe.

2 tablespoons sugar
2 tablespoons fresh lime juice
2 tablespoons tequila
1 ripe cantaloupe
 Whipped cream for garnish
  (optional)

Combine the sugar, lime juice, and tequila in a small bowl and mix until the sugar dissolves. Cut the cantaloupe in half, remove the seeds and rind, and cut the flesh into bite-size cubes. Place the cantaloupe in a glass bowl. Add the lime mixture and toss it with the cantaloupe. Cover the bowl with plastic wrap and place it in the freezer.

Allow the cantaloupe to freeze hard, about 6 hours. An hour before serving, remove the bowl from the freezer and let the cantaloupe come up in temperature until it is icy but not rock hard. You should be able to spoon out the cantaloupe with an ice cream scoop. Serve the cantaloupe garnished with whipped cream, if you like.

Ricotta Salad with Cantaloupe and Walnuts

Serves 4

In blistering weather—and it can be ninety-plus degrees in the North Fork Valley during the summer—everyone wants something cool and delightful. I often serve this sweet salad as a dessert, but sometimes I eat it as a snack. I may substitute blueberries for the cantaloupe and feta for the ricotta cheese.

> 1/2 ripe cantaloupe, cubed
> 1 cup ricotta cheese
> 1/2 cup walnut pieces
>   Freshly ground black pepper
>   Honey

Gently toss the cantaloupe, ricotta, and walnuts in a medium bowl. Divide the mixture among four serving dishes, sprinkle with pepper to taste, and drizzle with honey. Serve.

Poached Pears with Basil Syrup

Serves 4

This is a delicate dessert, perfect after a big dinner. The pears are very tender, tasty, and light—lovely on the plate. I usually use Bosc, but Anjou and Bartlett are good, too. Choose pears that are slightly underripe; overly ripe pears may become mushy when poached. This recipe is durable: I've even substituted Orangina (a French orange soda) and Gatorade for the cider.

I learned the basil sauce recipe in one of Kathryn and Michael McCarthy's cooking classes, conducted by Chef Andrade and Chef Hedenäs of the 14th Street Grill in Boulder.

- 2 large, slightly underripe pears (see headnote)
- 1 cup port or red wine
- 1 cup apple cider
- 1 2-inch cinnamon stick
- 3 whole cloves
- 2 cups water, plus more if needed
- 2 cups fresh basil leaves
- 1¼ cups sugar
- 2 large amaretto cookies, ground to crumbs

Halve, peel, and core the pears. Place the pear halves in a wide saucepan. Add the port and cider and place the pan over medium heat. When the liquid comes to a boil, lower the heat and add the cinnamon stick and cloves. Cover the pan and cook the pears at a low boil until they are cooked through, 12 to 15 minutes. Stick a fork into a pear to judge its doneness: it should be soft and yielding, but not mushy. Remove the pan from the heat and let the pears cool in the liquid.

Meanwhile, bring the water to a boil in a medium saucepan. Using a sieve, blanch the basil leaves in the boiling water. Remove the basil and set it aside. Add the sugar to the boiling water and allow the mixture to reduce by one half, about 20 minutes. Set the syrup aside to cool. (If it gets stiff, just add a few tablespoons of water and warm it over medium heat.) When the syrup is cool, puree the blanched basil and syrup in a blender until it is smooth. Strain the mixture through a sieve and refrigerate it until you are ready to use it.

To serve the pears, pour a puddle of the basil sauce on each plate. Place a poached pear half in the middle and sprinkle it with cookie crumbs.

Note: Some good substitutions are to replace the amaretto cookie crumbs with crumbled blue cheese. Or add a few sprigs of fresh thyme to the boiling port and cider mixture. Or instead of basil sauce, whip 1 cup heavy cream with ¼ teaspoon almond extract, put a dollop of cream on the pears, and sprinkle with sliced almonds. Or use a fruit puree as a sauce.

Sweet Potato Soufflé

Serves 6

This delightful soufflé goes well with many of the meals I like to prepare: elk, chukar, pheasant, lamb, beef. You can freeze the soufflé before baking. Just let it sit for a few minutes at room temperature before you put it in the oven. (It won't rise quite as high, though.)

Heavy ramekins with thick ceramic walls make the best soufflés. You can also make this in one large soufflé dish, baking it a little longer.

- 1 medium sweet potato
- 4 tablespoons ($^{1}/_{2}$ stick) unsalted butter, plus more for the ramekins
- $^{1}/_{2}$ cup sugar, plus more for the ramekins
- $^{3}/_{4}$ cup milk
- 3 tablespoons all-purpose flour
- 3 large egg yolks
- 4 tablespoons amaretto
- $^{1}/_{2}$ teaspoon grated fresh ginger or $^{1}/_{4}$ teaspoon ground
- $^{1}/_{4}$ teaspoon ground nutmeg
- 6 large egg whites
  Confectioners' sugar for garnish

Preheat the oven to 425°F.

Bake the sweet potato until it is soft, about 25 minutes. Remove it from the oven and peel off the skin. Allow the potato to cool, then mash it with a fork. You should have about $^{1}/_{2}$ cup mashed sweet potato.

Butter six $3^{1}/_{2}$-inch ramekins, then coat them with sugar.

Place the milk in a small saucepan and bring it to a gentle boil over medium heat. Keep warm.

Melt the butter in a medium saucepan over medium-low heat. Add the flour and whisk until the butter and flour are well blended, a few seconds. Slowly pour in the boiling milk, whisking all the while, until well blended. It's okay if the mixture is very thick, as long as it is smooth. Cook the mixture for 1 to 2 minutes, or until it is hot enough to boil, then remove the pan from the heat. Add the egg yolks, one at a time, whisking them in well. Add the mashed sweet potato, amaretto, ginger, and nutmeg and whisk together well.

The soufflé can be made up to this point and refrigerated for up to 6 hours.

In a large bowl, whisk the egg whites until they form soft peaks, 1 to 2 minutes. Add the sugar in a stream, whisking all the while. Add about one third of the egg whites to the sweet potato mixture and fold them in to soften the batter. Add the remaining egg whites and fold them in carefully with a few swift strokes. Pour the mixture into the ramekins, filling them about four-fifths full.

Bake the soufflés for about 15 minutes, or until they are tall and golden brown. Remove the soufflés from the oven, garnish with a sprinkling of confectioners' sugar, and serve immediately. The soufflés will be very hot to eat, but you should serve them promptly, because they will collapse quickly.

Ricotta Balls with Plum Puree

Makes about 30 balls

The best, lightest ricotta comes from the whey of sheep's milk, but this recipe works fine with supermarket cow's milk ricotta as well. If you don't have the plum puree, just thin whatever preserves you do have with a little orange juice, puree until smooth, and warm in a small saucepan over medium heat. You can also serve ricotta balls with confectioners' sugar, hot chocolate sauce, or *dulce de leche*.

3 large eggs, lightly beaten
2 tablespoons sugar
1 pound ricotta cheese
1 cup all-purpose flour
4 teaspoons baking powder
5 tablespoons amaretto or brandy
2 teaspoons grated lemon zest
  Pinch of salt
  Vegetable oil for frying (corn, safflower, or other oil—<u>not</u> olive oil)
1/2 pint Blood Plum Puree (page 298)

Combine all the ingredients except the oil and puree in a medium bowl. Mix well, cover the bowl, and refrigerate for 1 hour.

Heat 1½ to 2 inches oil in a large nonstick skillet over medium-high heat. Test the oil to make sure it is hot by dropping a bit of the batter in the oil. If the oil boils violently, it's ready. Drop rounded teaspoonfuls of the batter into the hot oil and fry, a few at a time, until golden, about 5 minutes. Ricotta balls brown quickly, but that doesn't mean they are done inside. Let them cook for 1 minute after they have turned golden, and they will be dry and fluffy inside. Drain the ricotta balls on paper towels.

Heat the plum puree in a small saucepan over medium-low heat until it is warm and loose. Serve the puree alongside the ricotta balls.

Russian Teacakes with Mint

Makes 24 cookies

K athryn McCarthy's herb garden on Sunshine Mesa Ranch is one of the grandest I've seen in the valley. Kathryn adds dried mint from her garden and homemade mint jelly to these cookies, which gives them a sophisticated, after-dinner taste. Her mother-in-law, Mary Louise McCarthy, has made these cookies for sixty years.

16 tablespoons (2 sticks) unsalted butter, softened
1½ cups confectioners' sugar
2 tablespoons dried mint
½ teaspoon salt
1 teaspoon vanilla extract
2¼ cups all-purpose flour
¾ cup finely chopped walnuts
1 cup mint jelly

Place the rack in the middle of the oven. Preheat the oven to 400°F.

Cream together the butter, ½ cup of the confectioners' sugar, the mint, salt, and vanilla. Add the flour and blend it in well. Add the walnuts and blend them in well. Roll 1 tablespoon of the dough at a time between your palms to make walnut-size balls. Place the balls on an ungreased baking sheet. Use the back of a teaspoon to press down on the balls, flattening them slightly (they should still be pillowy), then make an indentation in the center of each cookie with your fingertip. Bake the cookies for 14 to 17 minutes, or until they start to turn golden. Do not let them brown.

Place the remaining 1 cup confectioners' sugar in a paper bag. Drop the hot cookies into the bag and shake them well until they are covered with sugar. Remove the cookies, place them on a platter, and allow them to come to room temperature. Drop about ½ teaspoon of the mint jelly into the indentation of each cookie. Eat the cookies immediately, or cover them with plastic wrap and refrigerate them.

Note: You can freeze these cookies without the jelly in plastic bags or containers for up to 2 months. Defrost them at room temperature.

Cherry Brownies

Makes 16 brownies

C herry Days in Paonia is the start of the cherry season. Throughout the month of July, cherries make their way into all kinds of desserts: rolled in sweet crepes, dipped in chocolate, studding vanilla ice cream. I like to drop pitted Bings into brownies, where they add both moisture and flavor.

This recipe is adapted from one of Maida Heatter's recipes that I'm particularly fond of, because the brownies are fudgy but not sticky, cakelike but not dry.

8 tablespoons (1 stick) unsalted butter, cut into large pieces, plus 1 tablespoon butter

3 tablespoons fine bread crumbs or ground amaretto cookies

4 ounces semisweet chocolate (4 squares)

3 large eggs

1¼ cups sugar

1 teaspoon orange extract

¼ teaspoon salt

¾ cup all-purpose flour

1 cup pitted Bing cherries

1 cup chopped dried apricots

Place the rack in the bottom third of the oven. Preheat the oven to 350°F. Butter a 9-inch square baking pan with the 1 tablespoon butter. Dust the bottom with the bread crumbs, shaking out any excess crumbs.

Place the chocolate and remaining 8 tablespoons butter in the top of a double boiler over medium heat. Cover the pan and cook until the chocolate and butter are melted. Remove the cover and stir until the mixture is smooth. Set aside.

In a small bowl, beat the eggs until they are foamy. As you are beating (with an electric mixer or by hand), add the sugar, then the orange extract, salt, and chocolate mixture. Beat the batter only to combine the ingredients well. Do not overbeat, or the brownies will be too cakey and dry. Add the flour, mixing it in with a rubber spatula.

Pour the batter into the prepared pan and drop in the cherries and apricot bits. Bake the brownies for 35 minutes, or until a thin knife inserted in the center comes out clean. Allow the brownies to cool in the pan, then flip them over and allow them to cool for 25 minutes on a wire rack. Slice the brownies when they are cool, or refrigerate them and slice them when they are cold.

Chocolate Zucchini Cake

Serves 8

The grated zucchini keeps the cake moist and light. You can ice this cake with a chocolate butter icing, but I prefer a sprinkling of powdered sugar, as the cake is rich. This recipe is adapted from one given to me by our former neighbor in Crawford, Nola Hicks.

9 tablespoons unsalted butter

2 cups grated zucchini (2 small zucchini; use the large holes of the grater)

2³/₄ cups all-purpose flour

¹/₄ cup unsweetened cocoa powder

1¹/₄ teaspoons baking soda

1 teaspoon salt

1¹/₂ cups sugar

¹/₂ cup vegetable oil (<u>not</u> olive oil)

2 large eggs

1 teaspoon vanilla extract

¹/₂ cup buttermilk

¹/₄ cup confectioners' sugar

Preheat the oven to 325°F. Butter a 9-inch cake pan with 1 tablespoon of the butter.

Wrap the zucchini in a double layer of cheesecloth and squeeze out as much water as possible. Place the zucchini in a bowl and set aside.

Sift the flour, cocoa powder, baking soda, and salt together into a medium bowl and set aside.

Cream the remaining 8 tablespoons butter and the sugar in a large bowl, beating with an electric mixer until the mixture is fluffy, about 4 minutes. Add the oil and beat it in well. Beat in the eggs, one at a time. Add the vanilla and reduce the mixer speed to low. Add the dry ingredients and the buttermilk in three alternate batches. Stir in the zucchini.

Pour the batter into the prepared pan and bake until a knife inserted in the center comes out clean, about 1 hour and 20 minutes. Remove the cake from the oven and let it cool. Invert the cake onto a plate, dust it with confectioners' sugar, and serve.

Peach Cake with Maple Icing

Serves 8

I started making this cake, and variations of it, when I began to accumulate canned fruits. It's an adaptation of an applesauce cake from *Joy of Cooking*. You can use just about any pale-colored pureed fruit, such as apricots and pears, but I like pureed peaches best.

9 tablespoons unsalted butter, softened
3 tablespoons fine bread crumbs or ground amaretto cookies
1 cup sugar
1 large egg
1³/₄ cups all-purpose flour
1 teaspoon baking soda
1 teaspoon ground ginger
¹/₂ teaspoon salt
¹/₄ teaspoon ground cloves
1 cup drained and pureed canned peaches in syrup
1¹/₂ cups confectioners' sugar
About ¹/₄ cup pure maple syrup
¹/₂ teaspoon vanilla extract

Place the rack in the center of the oven. Preheat the oven to 350°F. Butter a 9-inch tube pan with 1 tablespoon of the butter and sprinkle the pan with the bread crumbs. Shake the pan until the bread crumbs have coated the sides. Discard any excess by tapping the pan over the garbage.

Using an electric mixer, cream the remaining 8 tablespoons butter and add the sugar slowly, beating all the while. Beat the butter and sugar until they are light. Add the egg and continue beating until the egg is thoroughly incorporated.

In a separate bowl, combine the flour, baking soda, ginger, salt, and cloves. Add the dry ingredients to the butter mixture in three batches, beating in the dry ingredients on the mixer's low setting. Add the peach puree and mix until it is incorporated. The batter will be heavier than average cake batter, more like a fruit bread batter.

Pour the batter into the prepared pan and bake for 40 minutes, at which point you should smell the fruit cooking. Test the cake for doneness by inserting a thin knife in the center. If the knife comes out clean, the cake is done.

Allow the cake to cool in the pan, then flip it over onto a plate and remove the pan.

To make the icing, combine the confectioners' sugar and 2 tablespoons of the maple syrup in a small bowl, mixing well. Continue adding maple syrup, 1 teaspoon at a time, until the icing is smooth yet firm enough to spread. It is very easy to add too much maple syrup and end up with runny icing (you can always add more confectioners' sugar, but then you'll end up with too much icing). Add the vanilla and mix well. Ice the cake, slice, and serve.

Note: If the cake batter is very thick or you didn't have quite enough peach puree, you can thin it with 1 to 2 tablespoons apple cider or sweet fruit juice.

Almond Shortbread Cake in Honey Syrup

Serves 12

I first tasted this dessert, which is sweet and soft and crunchy and sticky all at once, at the Leroux Creek Inn, where we spent Easter week one year. Eleni Stelter brought it, and it's one of her most elegant desserts. The recipe comes from her maternal grandmother.

3½ cups sugar

1½ cups plus 2 tablespoons water

2 6-inch cinnamon sticks

Peel from 1 lemon

½ cup honey

8 tablespoons (1 stick) unsalted butter, softened, plus 4 tablespoons (½ stick) unsalted butter, melted

½ cup confectioners' sugar

2¼ cups all-purpose flour

6 large eggs, separated

½ teaspoon almond extract

½ teaspoon baking powder

2 cups ground almonds, with or without skins

Pinch of salt

8 sheets phyllo dough

Place the rack in the center of the oven. Preheat the oven to 350°F.

To make the syrup, place 3 cups of the sugar and 1½ cups of the water in a medium saucepan and dissolve the sugar over medium heat. Add the cinnamon sticks and lemon peel. Bring to a boil and let boil for 10 minutes. Add the honey and bring to a boil again. Remove the syrup from the heat, strain, and set aside to cool. The syrup must be completely cool before you use it.

In a medium bowl, cream the softened butter until it is smooth. Add the confectioners' sugar and mix well. Add 2 cups of the flour, a little at a time, until it is blended. Add the remaining 2 tablespoons water and mix. The pastry will be crumbly. Press the pastry evenly into the bottom of a 9-inch springform pan. Bake the pastry for 15 to 20 minutes, or until it is lightly browned. Remove the pan from the oven and allow the pastry to cool. Leave the oven on.

In a large bowl, beat the egg yolks, remaining ½ cup sugar, and almond extract until the mixture is thick and light. Set aside. In a medium bowl, sift the remaining ¼ cup flour with the baking powder and stir in the almonds. Fold this mixture into the beaten egg yolks.

In a large bowl, beat the egg whites with the salt until they are stiff but not dry. Fold the whites carefully into the almond mixture. Pour the batter onto the cooled shortbread.

Place 2 sheets of phyllo on a flat surface and brush the top sheet generously with the melted butter. Repeat this process with the remaining 6 sheets of phyllo. Place the phyllo on top of the almond batter and trim the edges to fit the pan. Brush the top generously with butter. Score the phyllo into 12 slices.

Bake the cake for 45 minutes, or until the top is golden brown and the filling is set. Remove the cake from the oven.

Where the top is scored, cut all the way through the cake to the bottom of the pan. Pour the cooled syrup over the hot cake. It will seem as if the cake is flooding; it's okay. Allow the cake to rest until it absorbs all of the syrup and cools to room temperature. Serve.

Note: This cake can be made 2 days or more in advance. It freezes well for 1 month. Let it defrost at room temperature.

Sour Cherry Pie

Makes one 9-inch pie

Leaving the pits inside the cherries is supposed to enhance their flavor, but because the pits also can crack a tooth, I always opt to pit cherries. The job seems to take years: pie cherries are small and tend to slip through my pitting machine, get caught up on the pit puncher, or just get crushed to a pulp. Recently, I've taken to buying prepitted, fresh-frozen pie cherries from Stahl Orchards.

I like a hard, slightly sweet crust with fruit pies, but if you prefer a tender crust, use the recipe from Golden Delicious Apple Pie (page 285). Just roll the bottom crust out a little thicker than an average pie crust.

FILLING

- 4 cups pitted sour cherries (fresh or canned unsweetened)
- 2½ cups sugar, plus 2 tablespoons for the top
- 3 tablespoons all-purpose flour
- 1 teaspoon almond extract

PASTRY

- 2½ cups all-purpose flour
- ½ cup confectioners' sugar
- ½ teaspoon salt
- 8 tablespoons (1 stick) unsalted butter, cut into large pieces
- 2 large egg yolks
- 1 teaspoon vanilla extract
- 1½ teaspoons cold water as needed, plus 2 tablespoons for the top

To make the filling: Drain off the juice from the cherries (about 1 cup) and save it to make cherry sodas. Combine the cherries, sugar, flour, and almond extract in a large bowl. Set aside.

To make the crust: Put the flour, confectioners' sugar, and salt in a food processor. Add the butter and pulse until the dough is crumbly. Beat the egg yolks in a small bowl with the vanilla. Pour the wet ingredients into the dry ingredients while the machine is running. If necessary, add cold water, a little at a time, until the dough begins to form a ball. It takes about 3 minutes for the dough to come together. Remove the dough and separate it into 2 balls, one slightly larger than the other. Shape each ball into a thick patty, wrap in wax paper, and refrigerate for 30 minutes.

Bake the pie: Place the rack in the bottom third of the oven. Preheat the oven to 350°F.

Place the larger ball of dough on a lightly floured surface and pat it in all directions with a floured rolling pin. Beginning in the center, roll the dough out in all directions. Loosen the dough from the surface and reflour the rolling pin and surface as necessary.

Fold the dough gently into quarters, place it in a deep 9-inch pie plate, and unfold it. Fit the dough into the plate loosely and press it against the plate without stretching it.

If the cherry filling has leached more than a couple of tablespoons of cherry juice while resting, pour off the juice. Put the cherry filling into the crust.

Roll out the other ball of dough a little thinner and a little larger than the first one and place it on top of the pie filling. Crimp the edges of the pastry to seal the bottom crust with the top crust. Brush the top crust with the 2 tablespoons cold water, then sprinkle with the 2 tablespoons sugar. Cut a few slits in the top crust. Place the pie on a baking sheet and bake for 20 minutes, or until the crust is golden brown and the cherry juice is bubbling through the slits. Allow the pie to cool before slicing and serving.

Wine Grape Tart

Makes one 10-inch tart

This tart is intense and a little like mincemeat. It's a fall or winter dessert, with dark tastes of wine, semisweet chocolate, and nuts. For some, it's the ultimate elixir. I love the way the fresh globe grapes taste next to the earthy-sweet mustiness of the grape concentrate. Globe grapes are so large that peeling is justified, but you can use any grape big enough to cut in half. Getting wine grapes for the concentrate is easy in the North Fork Valley, but if you don't live near a vineyard, you can replace the concentrate with prune or fig preserves.

PASTRY

- 1¼ cups all-purpose flour
- ¼ cup confectioners' sugar
- 4 tablespoons (½ stick) unsalted butter, cut into large pieces
- 1 large egg yolk
- 1 teaspoon grated lemon zest
- ¼ teaspoon salt

FILLING

- 2 cups Wine Grape Concentrate (recipe follows)
- 1 cup finely chopped pecans or walnuts
- ⅓ cup grated semisweet chocolate (use the large holes of the grater)

  About 20 globe or other large grapes, peeled, halved, and seeded
- 1 cup heavy cream
- 3 tablespoons sugar
- 3 tablespoons Marsala

Place the rack in the lower third of the oven. Preheat the oven to 350°F.

To make the pastry: Place all the ingredients in a food processor and pulse until the dough comes together. Form the dough into a ball, cover it with wax paper, and refrigerate for 1 hour.

Place the dough on a lightly floured surface and pat it in all directions with a floured rolling pin. Roll the dough out, beginning in the center and rolling in all directions. Loosen the dough from the surface and reflour the rolling pin and surface as necessary. Fold the dough gently into quarters, or roll it up on the rolling pin. Place the pastry in a buttered 9-inch tart pan and unfold it. Fit the dough into the pan loosely and press it against the pan without stretching it.

To make the filling: Combine the Wine Grape Concentrate, nuts, and chocolate in a medium bowl. Spread the mixture evenly over the pastry. Arrange the grapes in concentric circles on top.

To bake and finish the tart: Place the tart on a baking sheet and bake for 20 minutes, or until the crust turns light brown. Let the tart sit for about 20 minutes before serving so that the filling can firm up.

Meanwhile, whip the heavy cream in a cold metal bowl until it holds peaks, about 2 minutes with an electric mixer, more if you are beating by hand. Slowly add the sugar in a steady stream as you continue whipping. Gently fold in the Marsala.

Serve the tart with dollops of the Marsala cream.

Wine Grape Concentrate

Makes 4 half pints

Occasionally, my father makes this thick, dark concentrate to use in an Italian Christmas pastry called *calgionetti,* a fried turnover with chocolate and almonds. He makes it in the fall, when the wine grapes come in. It is best to make it with sweet red wine grapes, such as Zinfandel.

7 pounds whole sweet red wine grapes, crushed (about 20 cups)

Place the grapes in a very large, shallow, heavy-bottomed saucepan. Bring to a low boil over medium-low heat. Cook for 1 hour, or until they have released their liquid.

Arrange a jelly bag or a sieve lined with two layers of cheesecloth over a deep pot. Wet the bag or cheesecloth so it doesn't absorb any of the juice. Ladle the grapes and their juice into the jelly bag and let the juice drip through into the pot. You will need to do this in a few batches. Go ahead and press the jelly bag: this is not a clear jelly. You should have about 10 cups of juice.

Return the juice to the saucepan and cook the concentrate over medium-low heat for 40 minutes, or until the concentrate is reduced by more than one half.

Pour the concentrate into sterilized jars, wipe the rims, screw on the lids and bands, and process them in a water bath for 5 minutes. Allow the jars to cool. Check the seals, label the jars, and store them in a cool, dark place for up to 1 year.

Golden Delicious Apple Pie

Makes one 9-inch pie

Lois Wiancko, who lives in Paonia, thought I might be surprised at how good this simple recipe is—and she was right! The trick, she says, is using Golden Delicious apples, which have lots of pectin. If you don't use Golden Delicious, she suggests adding a tablespoon of flour to the apple mixture. In the fall when the apples come in, Lois adds a tablespoon of lemon juice to each pie mixture, pours it into an 8-inch aluminum pie plate, and bags the plates in resealable plastic bags. Then, she says, "I stack them in the freezer like cord wood." When she wants a pie, she inserts the frozen pie filling into a fresh 9-inch crust and bakes it for about an hour.

> 5 Golden Delicious apples, peeled, cored, and cut as you would for hash browns (I use a mandoline; about 5½ cups)
>
> 1 cup sugar
>
> 1 teaspoon ground cinnamon
>
> ½ teaspoon ground nutmeg
>
> Pie Crust (recipe follows)
>
> 2 tablespoons butter, cut into pieces (optional)

Preheat the oven to 450°F.

Combine the apples, sugar, cinnamon, and nutmeg in a bowl. Pour into the bottom crust. Distribute the butter pieces on top of the apple filling, then place the top crust over the filling and crimp the edges of the top and bottom crusts together. Cut a few slashes in the top crust. Bake the pie for 10 minutes, then reduce the heat to 350°F and bake for 40 to 45 minutes more, or until the crust is golden brown. Let the pie sit for about 15 minutes before serving.

Pie Crust

Makes two 9-inch pie crusts (top and bottom)

Lois prefers to use this crust with her apple pie. The recipe is from her neighbor, Josie.

$2^1/_2$ cups all-purpose flour
1 tablespoon sugar
$^1/_2$ teaspoon salt
14 tablespoons shortening
    (such as Crisco)
1 large egg, lightly beaten
$^1/_4$ cup cold water
1 teaspoon white vinegar

Combine the flour, sugar, and salt in a large bowl. Using two table knives, cut in the shortening until the mixture resembles oatmeal.

Place half of the beaten egg in a small bowl. Discard the remaining egg. Add the water and vinegar to the egg and beat. Mix the egg mixture with the flour mixture. Press the dough together and form 2 balls. Wrap the dough in wax paper and refrigerate for about 30 minutes. (This crust is fine waiting in the fridge overnight.)

Place 1 dough ball on a lightly floured surface and pat it in all directions with a floured rolling pin. Roll the dough from the center out in all directions. Loosen the pastry from the surface and reflour the rolling pin and surface as necessary.

Fold the pastry gently into quarters, or roll it up on the rolling pin. Place it in a deep 9-inch pie plate and unfold it. Fit the dough into the plate loosely and press it against the plate without stretching it.

Roll out the other dough ball similarly and place it on top of the filling. Crimp the edges of the top and bottom crusts together. Cut a few slashes in the top crust and bake as directed.

Ellie's Raspberry Empanadas

Serves 4

We buy our raspberries from a beautifully situated Mennonite farm in Hotchkiss. These empanadas, which my mother makes, are wonderful when the raspberries are in season and bountiful, as the pastries are best frozen for a while before being fried. You can replace the raspberries with any kind of berry or with Wine Grape Concentrate (page 284). You can also make them ravioli-size.

FILLING

- 1 cup raspberries
- 4 tablespoons sugar
- 4 teaspoons chopped walnuts

PASTRY

- 1¼ cups all-purpose flour
- ¼ cup confectioners' sugar
- ¼ teaspoon salt
- 4 tablespoons (½ stick) unsalted butter, cut into large pieces
- 1 large egg yolk
- 1 teaspoon vanilla extract

  Vegetable oil for frying (corn, safflower, or other oil—<u>not</u> olive oil)
- 2 teaspoons sugar

To make the filling: Combine all the ingredients in a small bowl.

To make the pastry: Combine all the ingredients in a food processor and pulse until the dough comes together. Form the dough into 4 balls, cover them with wax paper, and refrigerate for 30 minutes.

Place 1 dough ball on a lightly floured surface and pat it in all directions with a floured rolling pin. Roll the dough from the center out in all directions. Loosen the pastry from the surface and reflour the rolling pin and surface as necessary. Roll the dough into a circle about the size of a saucer. Place one quarter of the filling in the lower third of the pastry circle and turn the upper half of the pastry over to create a half-moon–shaped empanada. Seal the edges of the pastry with a fork. Continue with the 3 remaining dough balls and the remaining filling.

Wrap the empanadas in aluminum foil and freeze overnight or for up to 1 week.

Heat about 2 inches oil in a small skillet over medium heat until it is very hot—to the point of just smoking. Add 1 frozen empanada carefully, as the pastry may be brittle, and fry until golden brown on both sides, about 15 seconds per side. Drain on paper towels and sprinkle with ½ teaspoon sugar. Repeat with the remaining empanadas.

Sherry Bread Pudding

Serves 8

We always have stale bread around the ranch kitchen. I make this dish, or a small variation of it, probably once a week. The ginger-and-sherry-flavored custard is best served warm. My children love bread pudding for breakfast, and I've busted company eating it as a midnight snack.

4 tablespoons ($\frac{1}{2}$ stick) unsalted
    butter, softened
12 1-inch-thick slices day-old French
    or Italian bread
3 large eggs, lightly beaten
3 large egg yolks, lightly beaten
2 cups whole milk
$\frac{1}{2}$ cup sweet sherry
1 cup sugar
1 tablespoon grated fresh ginger or
    1 teaspoon ground
Confectioners' sugar for garnish

Place the rack in the lower third of the oven. Preheat the oven to 350°F. Butter a loaf pan.

Butter the bread on one side, then lay the bread buttered side up in the prepared pan. Arrange the bread so that it fits together snugly. Combine the eggs, egg yolks, milk, sherry, sugar, and ginger in a medium bowl and mix well. Pour this mixture over the bread, making sure the bread is well saturated.

Place the loaf pan in a deep baking pan. Pour boiling water into the baking pan until the water reaches halfway up the loaf pan, then place both pans in the oven. Bake for 1 hour, or until the custard has set. Remove from the water bath and let cool to room temperature. Flip the pudding onto a serving platter and remove the loaf pan. Sprinkle with confectioners' sugar and serve.

Note: You can sprinkle the bottom of the loaf pan with raisins before adding the bread, if you like.

CANNING AND
PRESERVING

A Note on Canning

Canning is not a complicated science, but it is a science, and there are a few rules that can make the difference between perfection and a god-awful mess.

I use glass Ball or Kerr jars, with screw-on bands and lids. You can reuse the glass jars if they have no chips on the rims, and the metal bands as well if they aren't rusty, but you must buy new lids (the flat disks that the bands screw down on the jars) for every new sealing. I prefer wide-mouthed jars because they're easier to pack. Most bacteria can be killed in the heat of a water bath (about 220°F). Botulism, however, needs 240°F to be killed. Botulism does not live in acidic products such as fruits and tomatoes, or in pickled goods, which get their acid from the vinegar you use. But it can grow in foods with low acidity. To avoid any risk of botulism, can low-acid foods in a pressure canner, where the heat can come up high enough to kill the bacteria.

Avoid canning overripe fruits, as they lose some of their natural acid content. Canning should be done when you first pick or buy your fruit, not after you have eaten all you can hold and *then* decide to preserve the leftovers. For the first-time canner, it's a good idea to start out canning high-acid foods that are appropriate for water-bath processing.

To sterilize jars, bands, and lids, bring them to boil in a deep pot of water. The optimum setup is a large pot with a fitted rack in the bottom, so the jars don't touch the bottom of the pot. But canning can be done without a rack (in fact, I don't have one). Don't put a cold jar, empty or filled, into boiling water, or it could crack. Let the jars come up in heat with the water. Remove the jars and drain. You should pack the foods into the jars while the jars are still hot. Once they are filled, wipe the rims of the jars of any food drips and screw on the sterilized lids and bands. Be sure you leave ½ to ¾ inch of headroom in the jars after putting in the fruit. If the water in the pot left over from sterilizing the jars is still hot, pour most of it out and add enough cold water to bring down the temperature. (Otherwise, start over with a pot of cool water.) Return the full jars to the pot. Be sure there is 2 to 4 inches of water covering the jars. Bring the water to a boil. Be sure to boil the jars for the prescribed amount of time.

Remove the jars and check the seals. If liquid is dribbling out, the seal didn't take. If you hear a hissing sound at first, don't be alarmed; it will probably stop after a few minutes. If the hissing continues after the jar is cool, you have a poor seal and should open the jar, put aside the fruit, discard the lid, resterilize the jar and band with a new lid, and reprocess. (You can reprocess the same fruit.) Store the jars in a cool, dark place, as sunshine will eventually bleach out many fruits. Once sealed, the jars can be stored for a year or more. You don't need to put them in the fridge until after they have been opened. Discard any canned food that looks or smells funky or has mold growing in the jar.

Candy Cane Jelly

Makes 4 half pints

I won a blue ribbon at the Delta County Fair for this jelly, made from the lone crab apple tree on our place that wasn't murdered by our neighbor Clair's cows. It has a very old-fashioned taste, sweet and tart, perfect with white toast or scones.

1 quart crab apples (about 2½ pounds), quartered, with stems and blossom ends removed
4 cups sugar
1 large bunch fresh spearmint on the stem (about 10 sprigs)

Place the crab apples in a heavy 6- to 8-quart Dutch oven. Add water to just cover the crab apples. If the fruit floats, you've added too much water. Cook the crab apples, uncovered, until they are soft, 10 to 15 minutes. The crab apples will look as if they have exploded.

Arrange a jelly bag or a sieve lined with two layers of cheesecloth over a deep pot. Wet the bag or cheesecloth so it doesn't absorb any of the juice. Ladle the crab apples and their juice into the jelly bag and let the juice drip through into the pot. You aren't supposed to squeeze the jelly bag because it can make the jelly cloudy, but I do a little pressing anyway to speed up the process and have never had a problem. Measure 4 cups of juice. Save any extra juice to make another batch of jelly later on.

Place the juice and sugar in the clean Dutch oven and boil until a candy thermometer reaches 220°F. If the jelly doesn't get hot enough, it won't gel. Watch the foam. When the jelly foam seems to be losing some of its volume and the foam darkens in color, the jelly is usually ready. Check the temperature, or you can test the jelly by letting a spoonful cool slightly. If the jelly drips off the spoon in dribbles, it's not ready. If it shears off the spoon in a single drop, you're fine. As soon as you are close to having jelly, swish in the spearmint for 1 minute. The longer the spearmint is in the hot jelly, the stronger the flavor. Remove the spearmint before ladling the jelly into the jars.

Spoon the hot jelly into sterilized jars, wipe the rims, screw on the lids and bands, and process the jelly in a water bath for 5 minutes. Allow the jars to cool. Check the seals, label the jars, and store them in a cool, dark place for up to 1 year.

Apricot Honey

Makes 10 half pints

B eulah Martin Fletcher, who is ninety-eight and still cooking in Paonia, has been making a version of this recipe for seventy-seven years (she adds crushed pineapple). She doesn't know why it's called a honey, but maybe it's because the consistency is loose and the taste is sweet. Anyway, I spread it on pancakes in lieu of maple syrup and use it in Apricot Coffee Cake (page 246). Beulah says apricot honey makes a delicious flavoring for homemade ice cream. This recipe is adapted from one she published in *Fruit Fixins of the North Fork.*

3 quarts apricots (about 36 small apricots, or 2 pounds), unpeeled, pitted, and ground in a food processor

10 cups sugar

$\frac{1}{2}$ cup fresh lemon juice

Combine the ground apricots, sugar, and lemon juice in a heavy 6- to 8-quart Dutch oven. Cover the pan and cook the apricots at a low boil over medium-low to low heat for 20 minutes, stirring frequently. After the first 10 minutes or so, the puree will get thinner; it's okay. Uncover the pan and continue cooking. The puree will darken and thicken. Pour the puree into sterilized jars, wipe the rims, screw on the lids and bands, and process the apricot honey in a water bath for 10 minutes. Allow the jars to cool. Check the seals, label the jars, and store them in a cool, dark place for up to 1 year.

Note: If you boil the apricots too fast, they will produce a lot of foam, so keep the heat low. You can, if you prefer, cook the apricots in a 300°F oven for about 30 minutes, stirring occasionally, until thickened.

Jalapeño Mint Jelly

Makes 2 half pints

We often buy lamb chops from the Deutsch Ranch, a beautiful family-owned spread in the Missouri Flats region of Crawford. We grill the chops and serve them with this easy jelly. The only trick to making it is to have all the ingredients ready, because it boils, then gels, fast. This recipe is adapted from the mint jelly in *Putting Food By* by Janet Greene, Ruth Hertzberg, and Beatrice Vaughan.

- 1 cup fresh mint on the stem (1 small bunch)
- 3½ cups sugar
- 1 cup water
- ½ cup cider vinegar
- 2 small hot (<u>not</u> mild) jalapeño peppers, seeded and minced (about 2 teaspoons)
- 1 3-ounce pouch liquid pectin (I like Certo), poured into a glass
- 2 drops green food coloring

Bruise the mint by rubbing it with a wooden spoon in the bottom of a heavy 4-quart saucepan. Add the sugar, water, and vinegar to the pan. Bring to a boil over high heat and cook at a hard boil until the sugar dissolves, about 2 minutes. Add the jalapeños and boil for 1 to 2 minutes more. Add the liquid pectin and food coloring. Be careful about dropping food coloring straight from the bottle into your jelly—too much color is ghastly. I put 2 drops in an espresso spoon, then swirl the spoon in the jelly. Boil the jelly hard for about 30 seconds.

Take the pan off the heat, strain the hot jelly through a sieve to remove the mint and jalapeño, and pour it into sterilized jars. The jelly has to be liquid in order to strain, so don't let it sit; have your strainer ready. Wipe the rims, screw on the lids and bands, and process the jelly in a water bath for 5 minutes. Allow the jars to cool. Check the seals, label the jars, and store in a cool, dark place for up to 1 year.

Blood Plum Puree

Makes 10 half pints

You can make this recipe with any sweet plum, but blood plums are especially glorious, if you can find them. They are plentiful in August in the valley. I love serving this sweet puree with ricotta balls (see page 270) or drizzled over poached pears (see page 266). You can also add this puree to deglazed game or pork drippings. This recipe was adapted from one created by Venus Ewing of Paonia, who made it a conserve by adding walnut meats. She published it in the community cookbook *Fruit Fixins of the North Fork*.

6 pounds plums, pitted and pureed
  (6–8 cups)
8 cups sugar (or the same number of
  cups as fruit)
⅓ cup grated orange zest
⅓ cup fresh orange juice
⅓ cup fresh lemon juice

Combine the plum puree and sugar in a heavy 6- to 8-quart Dutch oven. Cover the pan and bring the puree to a low boil over medium-low heat. Cook the puree for about 40 minutes, then add the orange zest, orange juice, and lemon juice. Continue cooking for 10 to 15 minutes, or until the puree has thickened to the consistency of applesauce. After the first 10 minutes or so, the puree will get thinner. It's okay; it will darken and thicken. Pour the puree into sterilized jars, wipe the rims, screw on the lids and bands, and process the puree in a water bath for 10 minutes. Allow the jars to cool. Check the seals, label the jars, and store them in a cool, dark place for up to 1 year.

Rainier Cherries with Basil

Makes 8 half pints

Rainiers are large yellow cherries with a red blush, a tender taste, and a strong perfume. They ripen in the North Fork Valley in July, and I make this recipe religiously every year. Rainiers aren't as crisp and robust as Bings and so are perfect canned in their sweet syrup and rolled into crepes or dumped on top of vanilla ice cream. You can substitute any sweet cherry, although yellow ones are prettier with the basil leaves.

12 cups Rainier or other sweet
cherries (about 4 pounds)
12 cups sugar
Juice of 2 lemons (about 6
tablespoons)
16 fresh basil leaves

Place the cherries and sugar in a heavy 6- to 8-quart Dutch oven. Using a large spoon, gently combine. Add the lemon juice. Bring the cherries to a low boil over medium heat and cook for about 10 minutes. Reduce the heat to medium-low, ensuring that the cherries do not boil too rapidly. Cook the cherries for 20 minutes, checking periodically to make sure the fruit doesn't look wrinkled or exploded. If you start to see wrinkled cherries, take the pot off the heat. Add the basil leaves and cook, uncovered, for 2 to 4 minutes. The cherries should be whole and floating in the sugar syrup.

With a slotted spoon, fill eight sterilized half-pint jars with cherries and 2 basil leaves each, leaving 1 inch of headroom. Add the syrup, leaving ½ inch of headroom. Wipe the rims, screw on the lids and bands, and process the cherries in a water bath for 15 minutes. Allow the jars to cool. Check the seals, label the jars, and store them in a cool, dark place for up to 1 year.

Kathryn's Hot Peppers

Makes 6 half pints

O ur friend Kathryn McCarthy makes dozens of half pints of these peppers every summer. They are in high demand. Like a lot of people in the valley, I'd choose this as my favorite pepper condiment, hands down. I combine these peppers with cheese to spread on crackers (see page 110), add them to chili, and scramble them into eggs. Once I even made a pasta sauce with them. You will need a gallon-size crock with straight sides and a plate or round piece of wood that fits snugly inside the crock to weight them. We vacuum-pack our wood top to make sure no water gets in, or it will swell and stick.

This recipe is an adaptation of one called Aunt Lena's Peppers, which was given to Kathryn by her friend Bobby Orlando.

8   cups hot Hungarian wax peppers,
      cored and thinly sliced
3   cups mixed jalapeño and Anaheim
      peppers, cored and thinly sliced
6   tablespoons kosher salt
      Olive oil to cover (about 2 cups)
1   cup minced garlic
1   tablespoon dried oregano

Combine the peppers in a large bowl. Place 1 to 2 cups of the peppers in the bottom of a crock. Add 1 tablespoon of the salt. Place another 1 to 2 cups of peppers in the crock and another tablespoon of salt. Keep layering the peppers and salt until the peppers are all used up.

Place a plate or wooden lid on the peppers and add weights (I use canned goods or bricks). Within the first hour, water will start to come out of the peppers. Pour the water off and add more weights. Continue pouring off the water as it accumulates and increasing the weight, if possible, for 3 to 5 days, or until no more water comes out of the peppers. The volume of peppers will be reduced by three quarters or more.

After no more water can be poured off, remove the weights and add enough olive oil to cover the peppers. Add the garlic and oregano and mix well. Let the peppers sit for another day, then ladle them into sterilized half-pint jars. You do not have to process the peppers.

Store in the refrigerator and return to room temperature before using. The peppers will keep indefinitely.

Note: The quickest way to slice the peppers is to use a food processor.

Canned Tomatoes

Makes 5 pints

There is no more rewarding canning project than tomatoes. They improve any dish they are in. Tomatoes are incredibly easy to can, and you don't need a professional-size kitchen to do so. Indeed, I often can small batches of four half pints at a time and process them in a pasta pot. Tomatoes are the item I can most—about seventy-five pints a year.

Too many people have become victims of a culture of fear about canning tomatoes. I believe this has been perpetrated by those who benefit when you buy store-bought canned tomatoes. Forget them. There is simply no substitute for home canning and the culinary independence it brings.

There are two ways to go about this: you can pack tomatoes with the skin and seeds, which is what I do when I'm rushed, or you can peel and seed them before packing. The second is the better method, because the skin and seeds can emit a slight bitterness when you cook them and it is difficult to remove the skin and seeds after the tomatoes have been canned.

2	pounds nearly ripe tomatoes
10	fresh basil leaves
5	tablespoons fresh lemon juice
5	teaspoons kosher salt

Cut off the stems and remove any black blemishes from the tomatoes. To remove the skin and seeds, drop the tomatoes in a pot of boiling water and quickly scoop them out again. When the tomatoes are cool enough to handle, remove the skin—you can practically rub it off—and cut the tomatoes in half. Press out the seeds with your thumbs. If the tomatoes are very watery, you can give them a squeeze, too. (Save the juice! It makes great Bloody Marys and tomato aspic.) Otherwise, just wash the tomatoes and cut them into quarters (or in half if they are plum tomatoes).

Stuff the tomatoes into sterilized pint jars, adding 2 basil leaves and 1 tablespoon lemon juice per jar. Tomato juice will accumulate in all or part of the jar. With a butter knife, press aside the tomatoes to fill any air pockets in the jar with juice. (You don't have to get crazy about this—just fill in the biggest gaps.) When the jar is full, put 1 teaspoon salt on top. Wipe the rims, screw on the lids and bands, and process the tomatoes in a water bath for 25 minutes. Allow the jars to cool. Check the seals, label the jars, and store them in a cool, dark place for up to 1 year.

Note: Adding the lemon juice is a USDA-recommended precaution. The USDA also recommends processing for 1 hour and 25 minutes.

Note: If you want to put up cherry tomatoes, boil them until they are slightly cooked, about 4 minutes, then pass them through a sieve to remove the skin and seeds. Can the resulting puree in sterilized jars as for whole tomatoes.

Tomatillo Sauce

Makes 2 half pints

I use tomatillo sauce as a condiment for a wide range of Mexican-inspired dishes, such as scrambled egg enchiladas, chili con carne, and pheasant burritos. You don't need a lot, as the sauce is quite pungent, so I make only a couple of half pints for winter use. During the summer at the ranch, I make it fresh as needed. I got this recipe from my daughter's godfather, Sean Sullivan.

10–12 tomatillos, husked and rinsed
2 tablespoons chopped fresh cilantro
1 jalapeño pepper, stem and seeds removed
2 garlic cloves
1 tablespoon fresh lemon juice
Salt

Bring a medium pot of water to a boil over medium heat. Blanch the tomatillos until they fade to a pale green. Drain.

Place the tomatillos, cilantro, jalapeño, garlic, lemon juice, and salt to taste in a food processor and process to a loose and slightly lumpy sauce. Transfer the tomatillo sauce to a medium heavy-bottomed saucepan and bring to a boil over medium heat. Boil the sauce for 20 minutes. Take the sauce off the heat and allow it to cool.

You can eat the sauce right away, or, if you plan to put it up, pour the sauce into sterilized jars, wipe the rims, screw on the lids and bands, and process the sauce in a water bath for 20 minutes. Allow the jars to cool. Check the seals, label the jars, and store them in a cool, dark place for up to 1 year.

Smoked Jalapeños

Our jalapeño pepper plants are very prolific. We tried various methods of preservation before our friend Ross Brazil, a great outdoorsman from Denver, pointed out the obvious: smoking. These peppers add a wonderful flavor to stews and soups.

Prepare your smoker according to the manufacturer's instructions. Place the jalapeño peppers on a rack and smoke them for 40 minutes, or until they are black and wrinkled.

Remove the jalapeños and allow them to dry in a basket in the sun for about 8 hours or in a 250°F oven for about 2 hours. When they are done, they should be leathery. Pack the jalapeños in plastic bags and freeze them for up to 1 year.

HIGH-ALTITUDE CONVERSIONS

❖

SOURCES

❖

INDEX

HIGH-ALTITUDE CONVERSIONS

Crawford's elevation is 6,400 feet, and that makes for problematic baking. I've used a variety of standards, tips, and recommendations, but nothing seems to work for every recipe. Unfortunately, high-altitude cooking is a matter of trial and error. Ultimately, the best authority is your local Department of Agriculture Cooperative Extension Office, a marvelous resource. Here are a few adjustments I've made.

For Baking

For every 1,000 feet above an elevation of 1,000 feet:
- Decrease sugar by ½ tablespoon per cup. Full sugar measurements can cause cakes to fall in the center.
- Decrease leavening (baking powder, baking soda) by ⅛ teaspoon. However, cakes that use a *combination* of baking soda and an acidic ingredient such as sour cream need no adjustments.
- Increase flour by 1 teaspoon per cup.
- Decrease shortening or butter by ½ teaspoon.
- If the batter seems dry, increase liquid by 1 tablespoon per cup.

For every 1,000 feet above an elevation of 5,000 feet:
- When baking at oven temperatures between 360°F and 375°F, increase the temperature 5 degrees and increase the cooking time slightly.

For Water-Bath Canning

I use the tables in *Putting Food By* by Janet Greene, Ruth Hertzberg, and Beatrice Vaughan, a great book and one that every home canner should have.

For every 1,000 feet above an elevation of 1,000 feet:

- In recipes calling for a processing time of 20 minutes or less, add 1 minute of boiling time.
- For recipes calling for a processing time of more than 20 minutes, add 2 minutes boiling time.

Jelly is especially problematic because the juice evaporates faster as the altitude increases, which can lead to a very stiff, sticky jelly. If you are using a candy thermometer, don't wait for the jelly to reach 220°F. Decrease your goal temperature by 2 degrees for every 1,000 feet above an elevation of 1,000 feet. If you are using the sheeting test (dribbling the jelly off the spoon), use your eye and boil the juice according to the recipe.

Increase the headroom (the space between your preserves and the lid) by ¾ of an inch for pints processed above 3,000 feet.

In general, please be smart about canning low-acid foods. High-altitude water baths boil at a lower temperature than water baths at sea level (water at sea level boils at 212°F, but water at 5,000 feet boils at just 203°F). The higher temperature is necessary to kill bacteria. The *Putting Food By* folks say the only certain way to kill microorganisms above 2,500 feet is to pressure-can. Tomatillos and tomatoes are the exception, as they are high in acid. They can be canned using the water-bath method with the addition of lemon juice. I pressure-cook all other vegetables. Fruits are high in acid, so you can safely can them in a water bath, but pressure-cooking is an excellent and safe alternative.

Use the instructions on your pressure canner for times, but *Putting Food By*'s table suggests adding ½ pound of pressure for every 1,000 feet above an elevation of 1,000 feet for fruits, which usually call for about 5 pounds of pressure.

For Deep-Frying

Lower the temperature of the oil by 3°F for every 1,000 feet above an elevation of 3,000 feet. I never take the temperature of my oil, because it is easy to test its heat manually, and most of my recipes will give you instructions on how.

For Boiling

Be sure you have lots of water in the pot, as it will evaporate faster than at sea level. To cook dried pasta, add 1 minute for every 2,000 feet above an elevation of 2,000 feet to the recommended cooking time. The same is generally true for vegetables, but this varies from vegetable to vegetable, so prod a piece with a fork to make sure you are not overcooking. In general, add ¼ cup of water for each cup used over 6,000 feet, and expect everything to take longer to cook than at sea level.

Similarly, you may want to keep extra broth on hand for stew and soup recipes. Broth evaporates more quickly at higher altitudes, and you may need to add more liquid in order to maintain the volume. Checking by eye is the best way to avoid this problem.

SOURCES:

A SELECTION OF LOCAL PRODUCERS

Vegetables and Fruits

Orchards and Farms to Visit

Big B Fruit Stand
769 2075 Road (at Highway 92)
Reed, CO 81416
(970) 874-8136
Roasted green chiles and a
variety of dried beans and other
vegetables.

Burritt Produce
12335 Burritt Road
Hotchkiss, CO 81419
(970) 835-3252
Cantaloupes, lemon cucumbers,
and a variety of other vegetables.

Caja's Veggies
Kathy English
Highway 92 at 1800 Road
Delta, CO 81416
(970) 258-1718
Olathe sweet corn, fresh dried
pinto beans, and a variety of other
vegetables.

Stahl Orchards
4006 O-90 Drive
Paonia, CO 81428
(970) 527-3100
www.stahlorchards.com
Cherries, apricots, plums, peaches,
pears, and apples.

Orchards That Ship

Ela Family Farms
30753 L Road
Hotchkiss, CO 81419
(970) 872-3488
www.elafamilyfarms.com
Peaches, pears, apples, jams, fruit
butters, fruit nectars, and apple-
sauces.

Mesacrest Farm
Hotchkiss, CO 81419
(970) 872-3911
Peaches, apricots, and apples. Call
for information on seasonal avail-
ability. Shipping is handled by
Rogers Mesa Fruit Company,
(970) 872-2155.

Palisade Pride
P.O. Box 447
Palisade, CO 81526
(970) 464-0719
(800) 777-4330
www.palisadepride.com
Peaches, apples, and chocolate-
dipped dried fruits.
(For more information on fruit in
the Palisade area, visit the Palisade
Chamber of Commerce Web site,
www.palisadecoc.com.)

Meat

*Except where noted, all producers
ship.*

Closer to Heaven Farms
1212 2550 Road
Hotchkiss, CO 81419
(970) 835-4050
Chickens and eggs. (Eggs are not
shipped.)

DeVries Buffalo Ranch
8688 6025 Road
Olathe, CO 81425
(970) 323-6559
Buffalo meat and hides. Products
are not shipped.

Four Directions Farm
2690 O Road
Hotchkiss, CO 81419
(970) 835-3658
(800) 653-0096
www.fourdmarketing.com
Pheasants.

Haugen's Mountain Grown Lamb
  & Pelts
45995 County Road J
Center, CO 81125
(719) 754-2176
www.haugenslamb.netfirms.com
Lamb meat, pelts, and wool
products.

High Wire Ranch
2749 M50 Road
Hotchkiss, CO 81419
(970) 835-7600
www.highwireranch.com
Buffalo meat and hides, elk meat,
hides, and velvet antler capsules
(reputed to be good for arthritis).

Homestead Market (a producers'
  co-op)
P.O. Box 743
101 Grand Avenue
Paonia, CO 81428
(970) 527-5655
Beef, lamb, elk, and buffalo.

Mendicant Ridge Elk Ranch
3131 Clear Fork Road
Crawford, CO 81415
(970) 921-7477
www.mrelk.com
Elk meat.

Scenic Mesa Ranch
P.O. Box 370
727 3300 Drive
Hotchkiss, CO 81419
(877) 770-6372

www.scenicmesa.com
Buffalo meat and hides; hand-crafted furniture with buffalo leather upholstery.

Storm King Elk Ranch
35679 Highway 550
Montrose, CO 81401
(970) 249-3873
Elk meat.

Tabeguache Beef
Hansen Ranch
1322 Clear Fork Road
Crawford, CO 81415
(970) 921-4444
Beef by the quarter.

Theos Lamb
6909 RVC 49
Meeker, CO 81641
(970) 878-4485
Whole fresh lamb or half carcasses.

Cheese and Pantry Items

Bingham Hill Cheese Company
1716 Heath Parkway
Fort Collins, CO 80524
(970) 472-0702
www.binghamhill.com
Artisanal cheeses.

Enstrom's Almond Toffee
P.O. Box 1088
Grand Junction, CO 81502
www.enstrom.com
(800) 367-8766

Almond toffee.
Fire Mountain Fruit
1058 3200 Road
Hotchkiss, CO 81419
(970) 872-2260
www.alidasfruits.com
www.coloradocherrycompany.com
Jams, jellies, and syrups.

Hubbard Creek Company
P.O. Box 573
Paonia, CO 81428
(970) 872-3532
Pestos, caramel sauce, mustards, and savory fruit sauces.

Wine

Colorado Wine Industry
    Development Board
4550 Sioux Drive
Boulder, CO 80303
(720) 304-3406
www.coloradowine.com

Terror Creek Winery
1750 4175 Drive
Paonia, CO 81428
(970) 527-3484
Pinot Noir, Chardonnay, and Gewürztraminer.

Lodging and Adventure

Anasazi Heritage Center and
    Canyons of the Ancients
    National Monument:
www.co.blm.gov/ahc and
www.co.blm.gov/canm/index.html

Black Canyon Guest Ranch
P.O. Box 3
Crawford, CO 81415
(970) 921-4252
Hunting, hiking, and horseback riding.

Casa Encantada
Four Directions Farm
2690 O Road
Hotchkiss, CO 81419
(970) 835-3658
(800) 653-0096
www.fourdmarketing.com
Pheasant and chukar hunting; fishing.

Elk Mountain Lodge
P.O. Box 148
Second and Gothic Avenue
Crested Butte, CO 81224
(970) 349-7533
(800) 374-6521
www.elkmountainlodge.net
Skiing and dining.

Gunnison Gorge National
  Conservation Area:
www.co.blm.gov/ggnca

Gunnison River Pleasure Park
P.O. Box 32
Lazear, CO 81420
(970) 872-2525
(888) 782-7542
www.troutfisherman.net
Fishing and rafting.

Hotel Colorado
526 Pine Street
Glenwood Springs, CO 81601
(970) 945-6511
(800) 544-3998
www.hotelcolorado.com
Glenwood Hot Springs.

Leroux Creek Inn
P.O. Box 910
1220 3100 Road
Hotchkiss, CO 81419
(970) 872-4746
www.lerouxcreekinn.com
Hunting, horseback riding, fishing, hiking, and fine dining.

Powderhorn Resort
P.O. Box 370
48338 Powderhorn Road
Mesa, CO 81643
(970) 268-5700
www.powderhorn.com
Skiing.

Redstone Inn
82 Redstone Boulevard
Redstone, CO 81623
(970) 963-2526
(800) 748-2524
www.redstoneinn.com

Scenic Mesa Ranch
P.O. Box 370
727 3300 Drive
Hotchkiss, CO 81419
(877) 770-6372
www.scenicmesa.com
Hunting and fishing.

Smith Fork Ranch
P.O. Box 401
4536 East 50 Drive
Crawford, CO 81415
(970) 921-3454
www.smithforkranch.com
Hunting, horseback riding, fishing, hiking, and fine dining.

St. Elmo Hotel
P.O. Box 667
426 Main Street
Ouray, CO 81427
(970) 325-4951
(866) 243-1502
www.stelmohotel.com

Telluride Mushroom Festival
Fungophile
P.O. Box 480503
Denver, CO 80248
(303) 296-9359
www.shroomfestival.com

Wiesbaden Hot Springs Spa &
    Lodgings
P.O. Box 349
625 Fifth Street
Ouray, CO 81427
(970) 325-4347
www.wiesbadenhotsprings.com
Vaporcave.

Shopping

Colorado Wool Growers
    Association
Arvada, CO 80005
(303) 431-8310
Wool blankets.

Davis Clothing Company
401 Main Street
Delta, CO 81416
(970) 874-4370
Cowboy hats.

Farmer Frank's
36310 Highway 133
Hotchkiss, CO 81419
(970) 527-4223
Ranch clothes and boots.

Gene Taylor's Sporting Goods
445 West Gunnison Avenue
Grand Junction, CO 81505
(970) 242-8165
www.genetaylors.com
"Largest sporting goods store between Salt Lake City and Denver."
Fishing, hunting, and hiking gear.

INDEX

Marilee's Tortilla Soup, 134–36
mayonnaise
    Cilantro Mayonnaise, 119
    Lime-Flavored Mayonnaise,
       124
meat. *See also specific types of meat*
    sources for, 314–15
Meatballs with Peas and
    Mushrooms, 220–21
mint
    Candy Cane Jelly, 294–95
    Green Bean and Mint Salad,
       155
    Jalapeño Mint Jelly, 297
    Peas with Mint Butter, 154
Monterey Jack cheese
    Chiles Stuffed with Corn
      and Jack Cheese,
      168–69
    Macaroni with Cheese,
      184–85
    Scrambled Egg Enchiladas,
      252–53
    Stewed Onion and Jack Cheese
      Omelets, 250
mushrooms
    Chanterelle Crepes, 254–55
    Eggplant and Porcini
      Mushroom Dip, 112–13
    Elk Stroganoff, 240–41
    Elk Tenderloin with Wild
      Mushrooms, 238–39
    Fettucine with Wild
      Mushrooms, 188
    Meatballs with Peas and
      Mushrooms, 220–21
    Oxtail Soup with Porcini
      Mushrooms, 146–47
    Warm Mushroom Watercress
      Salad, 163

    Whole Porcini in Parchment,
      173
    Wild Mushroom Soup, 137

navy beans
    Vegetable Soup with Pesto,
      132–33
nuts
    Almond Shortbread Cake in
      Honey Syrup, 278–79
    Pasta with Tomatoes and
      Almonds, 192
    Wine Grape Tart, 282–84

omelets
    Stewed Onion and Jack Cheese
      Omelets, 250
    Zucchini Flower Omelets,
      248–49
onions
    Eggs and Vegetables, 251
    Scrambled Egg Enchiladas,
      252–53
    Stewed Onion and Jack Cheese
      Omelets, 250
Oxtail Soup with Porcini
    Mushrooms, 146–47

pantry items, sources for, 315
Parmesan cheese
    Fettucine with Wild
      Mushrooms, 188
    Macaroni with Cheese, 184–85
    Pasta with Beet Sauce, 186
pasta
    Egg Pasta with Elk Bolognese,
      194–95
    Elk Cannelloni, 196–98
    Elk Stroganoff, 240–41
    Farfalle with Ricotta, 183

porcini mushrooms
  Eggplant and Porcini
    Mushroom Dip, 112–13
  Elk Stroganoff, 240–41
  Oxtail Soup with Porcini
    Mushrooms, 146–47
  Whole Porcini in Parchment,
    173
pork. *See also* ham
  Beef Soup with Sausage
    Omelet, 144–45
  Pork Tinga, 222–23
  Pork with Peanuts and
    Chocolate, 224–25
potatoes
  Chicken Legs Stuffed with
    Goat Cheese, 208–9
  Chile Potatoes, 178
  Rigatoni Salad, 180–81
  Summer Vegetable Mélange,
    164–65
pudding
  Sherry Bread Pudding, 289
purslane
  Summer Vegetable Mélange,
    164–65

quail
  Chukar with Figs, 232
  Chukar with Shallots, 233
  Game Bird Broth with Cilantro
    Crespelle, 148–49
queso anejo
  Chanterelle Crepes, 254–55

Ranch Carbonara, 182
Rainier Cherries with Basil, 299
raspberries
  Ellie's Raspberry Empanadas,
    287–88

refried beans
  Fried Zucchini Flowers Stuffed
    with Refried Beans, 166–67
  Refried Bean Crostini, 114–15
rice
  Italian Rice and Beans, 176–77
ricotta cheese
  Chanterelle Crepes, 254–55
  Farfalle with Ricotta, 183
  Hubbard Creek Company
    Pesto Torta, 120–21
  Ricotta Balls with Plum Puree,
    270
  Ricotta Pie, 260–61
  Ricotta Salad with Cantaloupe
    and Walnuts, 265
  Yvon's Vegetable Terrine,
    174–75
Rigatoni Salad, 180–81
Russian Teacakes with Mint, 271

salads
  Avocado Salad, 158
  Fennel and Red Pepper Salad,
    157
  Green Bean and Mint Salad,
    155
  Ricotta Salad with Cantaloupe
    and Walnuts, 265
  Rigatoni Salad, 180–81
  Warm Mushroom Watercress
    Salad, 163
sauces
  Charlie's Chimichurri Sauce,
    210
  Marilee's Hot Sauce, 136
  Tomatillo Sauce, 304
sausage
  Beef Soup with Sausage
    Omelet, 144–45

Scrambled Egg Enchiladas, 252–53
Semolina Skillet Bread, 212–14
shallots
    Chukar with Shallots, 233
shellfish
    Bean Soup with Shrimp, 142–43
Sherry Bread Pudding, 289
shopping, 317
shrimp
    Bean Soup with Shrimp, 142–43
Smoked Jalapeños, 305
smoked trout
    Farfalle with Smoked Trout,
        193
    Smoked Trout Crostini,
        116–17
    Zucchini Flowers Stuffed with
        Smoked Trout, 122–23
sorrel
    Sunshine Mesa Ranch Sorrel
        Soup, 131
    Vegetable Soup with Pesto,
        132–33
soufflé
    Sweet Potato Soufflé, 268–69
soup. *See also* stew
    All-Purpose Beef Broth, 152
    All-Purpose Chicken Broth,
        150–51
    Bean, Corn, and Chile Soup,
        138–39
    Bean Soup with Cooking
        Greens, 140–41
    Bean Soup with Shrimp, 142–43
    Beef Soup with Sausage
        Omelet, 144–45
    Cold Zucchini Soup, 126–27
    Game Bird Broth with Cilantro
        Crespelle, 148–49
    Green Chile Soup, 128–29

Marilee's Tortilla Soup, 134–36
Oxtail Soup with Porcini
    Mushrooms, 146–47
Sunshine Mesa Ranch Sorrel
    Soup, 131
Sweet Pea Soup, 130
Vegetable Soup with Pesto,
    132–33
Wild Mushroom Soup, 137
Sour Cherry Pie, 280–81
Spaghettini with Anchovies, 190
spinach
    Ricotta Pie, 260–61
squash flowers. *See also* zucchini
    flowers
    Poblanos Stuffed with Grated
        Zucchini, 170–71
Steak with Charlie's Chimichurri
    Sauce, 210–11
sterilizing canning jars, 292
stew
    Beef Stew with Brussels
        Sprouts, 218–19
    Lamb Stew, 228–29
    Pheasant Burritos, 234–35
    Pork Tinga, 222–23
Stewed Beef with Tortillas, 215–17
Stewed Onion and Jack Cheese
    Omelets, 250
storing canned foods, 293
Stuffed Eggs with Chile, 111
Summer Vegetable Mélange,
    164–65
Sunshine Mesa Ranch Sorrel
    Soup, 131
Sweet Pea Soup, 130
Sweet Potato Soufflé, 268–69
Swiss chard
    Summer Vegetable Mélange,
        164–65